MONSTROUS REGIMENT
Women Rulers in Men's Worlds

BETTY MILLAN

THE KENSAL PRESS

British Library Cataloguing in Publication Data.

Millan, Betty

Monstrous Regiment

1.   Women in politics — History

I.   Title

305.4'3351   HQ1236

ISBN 0-946041-01-6

Published by The Kensal Press,
Shooters Lodge, Windsor Forest, Berks.

Printed in Great Britain by
Butler & Tanner Ltd, Frome and London

Contents

Illustrations

'To promote a woman to beare rule, superioritie, dominion or empire above any realme, nation, or citie, is repugnant to nature, contumelie to God, a thing most contrarious to his reveled will and approved ordinance, and finalie it is the subversion of good order, of all equitie and iustice.'

— John KNOX, *The First Blast of the Trumpet Against the Monstruous Regiment of Women* (1558, reprinted Amsterdam 1972), p.9

PREFACE

There has never been a state habitually ruled by women, but in every society outstanding women have gained supreme power in defiance of patriarchal conventions. This book aims to explore that intriguing paradox by studying some of the most conspicuous 'power-women', as I call them, who have ruled men's worlds from the time of Cleopatra to that of Mrs. Gandhi and Mrs. Thatcher. The examples are intended to illuminate some fundamental questions: how have women got to the top? How have they used supreme power once they have acquired it? Is there a chracteristic syndrome — psychological or behavioural — of the power-woman?

This subject has been neglected, even in the era of 'women's studies' and in a time when women have assumed power in many states of the world: Sri Lanka, India, Israel, Argentina, the United Kingdom, Norway and Iceland have all had female chief executives or elected heads of state in the recent past, or have them today. Over the next few years, other countries will certainly join this select sorority. The subject is, by any standards, engrossing. But most exponents of women's studies are feminists and feminists are more interested in the fate of female masses than in the altogether exceptional — even freakish — women who have occasionally dominated national political arenas. The topic may have deterred investigtors because it is so unwieldy: numerous ill-assorted prosopographies have to be strung together; divers cultures and period have to be traversed. I have had to be selective: one could have said more about power-women in Islamic states, about queenship in 'primitive' societies, and about the singular, if largely unexploited opportunities for power-women in some parts of west Africa. I have steered in the mainstream tradition of western power-women from antiquity to the present day, making only occasional side-trips into the exotic. Even so, I have not made very deep wakes in some of the waters I have cleft: I hope there will be few experts who will be offended and some — at least — who will be interested or entertained. I have not tried to address any particular class of reader as the subject is of such very wide appeal. I have concentrated on women who have exerted power in connexion with nominal sovereignty or as chief executives of their states. Regencies and instances of informal influence are only included to illustrate particular points.

I start with two assumptions, both of which extreme feminists will reject: first, that gynecocracy is a myth. No convincing evidence of a thoroughly matriarchal society has ever been found; in the absence of such evidence it seems sensible to assume patriarchy as a norm against which the careers of power-women must be judged. Secondly, I assume that there exists a distinctive female identity: that is, that the terms 'male' and 'female' imply useful classifications, corresponding to genuine and deep-seated differences of anatomy, mentality and behaviour between the sexes. Consistently with what I hope is feminine common sense, I assume that this distinctive female identity is determined by or at least closely connected with women's special sexual and psychological needs and reproductive and nutritive functions. This may seem an obvious declaration to most readers but, as there are others to dispute it, it has to be made. On the other hand, I accept that environmental factors and social prejudies are largely responsible for the historic subjection of women. Indeed, in the pages which follow, evidence will be found to support such a view.

The pleasure of writing this book has been increased by the help and generosity of many friends, most of whom would be embarrassed to be mentioned by name.

CHAPTER ONE

Cleopatra and the Ancient World

Women in power have been a fascinating subject for tragedians, for tragedy nearly always has a dilemma at its heart: hovering between the mutually exclusive demands of public and private life — so that whatever choice they make is fatal either to their personal happiness or to their responsibilities in the state — women rulers seem condemned to a poignant end.

That is why tragic heroines tend to seem all alike, whereas men can be treated by dramatists with infinite variety. Heroines are presented in play after play or poem after poem, struggling in the narrow cleft between emotional demands of one sort or another and the painful exigencies of political duty. They may be amorous demands — like those to which Shakespeare's Cleopatra succumbs or Schiller's *Maria Stuart*: these are excellent epitypes of women who sacrifice the state to their amorous appetites. They may be the demands of feminine sensibility or clemency, like Kingsley's St. Elizabeth, or of devotion to one's children. But in every case, the kind of flaw peculiar to women in authority is seen by dramatists and poets as essentially the same: women are creatures of passion; their passions cannot be regulated by the rational means that political life requires. And thereby they are incapacitated for the discharge of power.

Such deficiencies of feminine rulers were fully apparent to the tragedians of antiquity. But to understand the classical image of the woman of power, it is necessary to re-express the same idea in other terms — terms more readily translatable into the language of the primitive worlds of savagery and magic, power and terror, pre-history and myth to which classical writers were remarkably close and on which they drew for themes and notions. The sort of passions of which women were prisoners — at least, in the poetic imagination — were very close to instinct. The sex urge, pity, maternal affection: these things are as nearly instinctive as any human characteristics. They are distinct from reason, if not altogether incompatible with it. They belong to a sub-rational or supra-rational world which is not fully or characteristically human, or, at least, not fully or characteristically civilised. This was the world of which women were thought to be part. Classical

Cleopatra, Queen of Egypt, before Caesar.

antiquity relegated them to the overlapping fringes of the civilised and barbarian ways of life on the one hand, the real and mythical universe on the other, just as in the Middle Ages they would be banished to the nether links of the chain of being, along with vaguely anthropoid monsters, like cyclops and sciapods, and pygmies and apes.

Two examples from antiquity should be enough to make this clear: the Amazon myth and the Attic dramatists' image of *Medea*. The Bassae frieze in the British Museum, with its startling evocation of the Amazons, expresses all the fear and loathing of women — and of female power in particular — of which ancient Greek men were capable. Here the Amazons are chosen to symbolise barbarity, locked in precarious and open-ended conflict with civilisation, represented by Hellenic males. The conflict of male and female is made to stand for that of reason and passion as well as of civility and savagery. In general, in all its manifestations, the Amazon myth represented for the Greeks the monstrousness of a female polity.

The Amazons emblemised a fourfold monstrousness: their society was monstrous in excluding men — except occasionally for the strict purposes of procreation. Their nature was monstrous in that it was both feminine and warlike — this was as prodigious as the nature of the centaurs, who combined the human and the equine in a single cloud-born contradiction. Their morality was monstrous in sanctioning the killing of their own children if these happened to be male. And in some versions of the myth, their appearance was monstrous because they mutilated their right breasts to facilitate archery. It is not surprising that Herodotus locates them in that strange geo-political penumbra, beyond the familiar world of Hellas and the neighbouring barbarians, where only monsters and the more bizarre barbarians dwelt. Yet they remain essentially feminine. The legend of

Mural tablet showing the Amazons in a trial of strength with men.

9

Hippolyta, the Amazon queen, demonstrates that — and there can be no more representative example of a woman ruler than a ruler of women. In a typical act of feminine submission to a man, she surrendered her girdle to Heracles who had been ordered to obtain it as one of his twelve labours. In some versions of the story, she falls victim to the usual consummation of feminine hubris by dying at Heracles' hand. In others, she ransoms her favourite general, Melanippe, with the precious girdle: here, we see again an example of the tragic elaboration of clemency in a woman ruler. The sequel to her encounter with Heracles, in these versions, rounds off Hippolyta's story. She leads an Amazon army against Athens but is defeated and taken to wife by Theseus: thus the political survival of the Amazon state is endangered by the weaknesses of women and the susceptibilities of a queen.

It was the role of poets in antiquity to mediate to classical civilisation the images transmitted by myth. In the *Medea* of Euripides, the horror and fear inspired by the idea of women in power are brilliantly dramatised. Medea was a barbarian and a witch: she was therefore beyond civilisation and beyond reason, a creature of the twilight to which the very notion of a power-woman belonged. She echoed the Amazons, preferring 'to fight three battles than bear one child'. Although she was not a queen-regnant, but rather a consort, and although she immersed her own political ambitions in those of her husband Jason, it was her involvement in the politics of Greek cities that provided the mise-en-scène for the tragedy that was wrought around her. And again it was feminine flaws — sexual passion and unreasoning vindictiveness — that triggered disaster. In the traditional myth, she began her destructive career when she fell in love with Jason. For the sake of that love she betrayed her family and homeland by helping him steal the Golden Fleece and murder her brother. The curse of this horrible parricide clung to her despite the ritual purification to which her sorceress aunt, Circe, submitted her. Parricide could always be calculated to send a frisson of horror down an Athenian audience's spines. She advanced her husband's interests by tricking an enemy's daughters into hacking their own father to pieces — corrupting Greek maidens with her hideous alien vices. Finally, at the point where Euripides takes up the tale, she avenges herself on the faithless Jason by murdering the children she bore him. As if the point of her story were not already apparent enough, the traditional myth goes on to implicate her in an attempt to poison Theseus, the stepson of her next marriage. Appropriately, it is Theseus who later tames the Amazon Hippolyta.

Euripides presents the Medea story at a safe remove from reality, curtained by a veil of magic and the supernatural, as when, at the climax of the drama, Medea escapes certain justice for her crimes by fleeing in her enchanted chariot. None of these fantastic trappings, however, surrounds the similar but more realistic figure of Clytemnestra, queen-consort and regent of Mycenae, who was the Attic dramatists' favourite image of queenship. As the wife of Agamemnon, Clytemnestra was a proto-historical or historical personage to the Greeks. All the tragedians — even the richly fanciful Euripides — depict her with cold realism as an example of the political menace which feminine passions present. Her regency is ended by her husband's return from the Trojan war. When she murders him in his bath — a spot peculiarly vulnerable, in western literature and history, to female assassins — it is in collusion with her lover, who is also her husband's step-brother. As well as of lust and political ambition, her crime is a product of revenge, for she blames on Agamemnon the sacrifice of their daughter, Iphigenia, demanded by the gods in return for a favourable wind for the homecoming Greek fleet.

The real queens of post-classical times were therefore burdened, as they approached their task as rulers, with a mythical and poetic reputation that must adversely have influenced their subjects' expectations and, indeed, their own self-image.

Their predicament was intensified by the prevailing misogyny that informed much political and pathological thought. The source of this was Athens, where women were encumbered with enough civil disabilities to make the strictly classical civilisation of the fifth and early fourth centuries B.C. one of the most hostile to women there has ever been. Unluckily for the female sex, Athenian thought was *par excellence* the leading influence in the Hellenistic world, even after the political collapse of Athens. In Athens, not only were women rulers unthinkable, women were forbidden any responsibility and excluded from citizenship, which was open to all men except slaves. Aristotle explained that women's powers of reason were defective — 'without authority'. To women he ascribed the ruin of Sparta, the decrepitude of oligarchies, the decay of democracies. To allow them any political influence was always fatal. 'What does it matter if women rule or are ruled? The result is always the same.' Athenian society carried this discrimination against women into practice in an extreme manner. Women were not even accorded a legal personality in the sense of being able to make contracts in their own right. As a result, they were bereft of all economic power. Apart from their clothes and their jewels they owned nothing in their own right, but everything belonged to their menfolk. Economically dependent on male guardians, they were assumed also to be the legal dependants of men. That this subordinate female role was deeply ingrained in Athenian society is shown by the attitudes of the poets. It is commonly thought that the Attic tragedians created masterful women of action — but Medea and Andromache are exceptional. And, significantly, they are also foreigners. More typical (if equally foreign) are the *Trojan Women* of Euripides, who wait and wail, passive and submissive, with no source of power over men except their sex appeal. When we do encounter a woman who acts decisively, she has to call in a man to do her dirty work — like Electra calling on her brother to avenge Agamemnon. Or else, like Hecuba, she acts herself but is punished by literal translation into the sub-human world to which, conceptually, women belonged. Hecuba blinds the murderer of her son but is herself turned into a bitch. In almost every poem or play about a woman, her story ends with marriage or childbirth if she escapes early death: for women, therefore, fulfilment was equivalent to the extinction of personality.

Where did the Athenians get their collective misogyny from? It is unlikely to have been imposed by a single lawgiver — even the homosexual Solon, to whom the laws of Athens were traditionally ascribed, probably with more piety than accuracy. It is unlikely to have been borrowed from elsewhere: even by the standards of ancient Greece, Athens was peculiarly inimical to women. Rather, it arose within Athens itself, where its origins were twofold: political and psychological. Politically, it was the fruit of democracy. Psychologically, it was the product of fear. Athenian democracy was an alliance of vested interests; such alliances need enemies or, at least, excluded groups. Women and slaves were the only groups in Athens whom aristocrats and hoi polloi could unite in despising. But it is hardly credible that women should have been so heavily victimised had they not also been feared: feared as witches, like the 190 women once slaughtered for witchcraft in Athens at a single judicial immolation; feared as potential rebels like the mythical women of Lemnos, who, in the tale of the Argonauts, rose up and massacred their menfolk. They were feared for the esoteric power they wielded as initiates of ancient, numinous mysteries, mostly imported into Athens from the dubious frontiers of the Greek world: these sacred cults of secret sororities remained important in later Hellenistic history and, as we shall see, many women of power — including political power — belonged to them. Perhaps women were feared because of the religious power proper to them in connection with rites for whose efficacy their participation was indispensable: Athens was heir to many survivals of primitive fertility religions in which women played an important part. But ultimately, they were feared because they were not understood. Their baffling moods and secret physiology defied the Athenian men, who liked to have an explanation for everything. In most societies there is an element of sheer bewilderment in male fear of women of power. Arguably in Athens it was particularly pronounced.

Thus the Athenians made bogies of women. They took seriously, for instance, a seventh-century poem on women by one Semonides of Amorgos, of whose work this single fragment has survived solely because of the comfort it offered to misogynists. Semonides probably intended his satire playfully, but like all satire it became a victim of its readers' literal minds. It presents women's minds as created by Zeus separately from those of men. Most women were created from the baser quadrupeds, others from monkeys and mud. All share the characteristics of their protean substances. Thus there are pig-women, ass-women, cow-women and so on. The irony was crude, but it spoke to Athenian depths. The separate creation of women, their kinship to beasts, their inferiority to men, their destructiveness and — another quality Semonides emphasised — their sexual depravity were all aspects of womankind with which the Athenians thought themselves familiar. Here was a recipe for contempt, which is a safe outlet for fear. Fear *tout court* comes through an Athenian treatise *About Virgins* ascribed to Hippocrates. And here again it is fear arising, almost explicitly, from imperfect understanding. Ancient physicians were well aware that certain pathological syndromes were peculiar to women. Popular medical conceptions also identified particular psychological disorders as properly feminine. Aeschylus depicts these for us in the ravings of Io in *Prometheus Bound:* she rants madly, proclaims a death wish, longs for immolation, burning or drowning and believes herself committed to an assignation with Zeus whom she fancies consumed with lust for her. Euripides makes the chorus of *Hippolytus* describe a less obviously insane form of hysteria — somewhere between menstrual tension and madness. Symptoms in the same range are discussed with scientific niceness by the author of the *Virgins* treatise. He knows women's susceptibility to visions, delusions, passing numbness or paralysis, loss of reason and self-control — in a word 'hysteria', literally 'that which is of the womb'. The physiology of these aberrations resists analysis. It is all part of the dark, obnubilated workings — as esoteric as the mysteries of any 'orphic' sisterhood — of women's deeply concealed inner organs, to which men may penetrate with their bodies but not their minds. The author identifies sexual disorders as the cause of the trouble. By way of cure, he recommends marriage, sex and childbirth. It is the same consummation as poets and playwrights generally offered as the climax of a woman's life-story.

Outside Athens, and generally in the Hellenistic world after the eclipse of Athenian power, women had more opportunities to exercise authority. In states where the laws allowed them to accumulate wealth they could perhaps buy their way into minor magistracies. In states where power descended by hereditary right, they could rule at the apex of government, as consorts or regents or even in their own right. The state which produced some of the most conspicuous power-women, in a political sense, was also that which, after Athens, had the greatest influence in the Hellenistic world — an influence mediated through no intellectual legacy but through conquest and the seeding of ruling dynasties throughout the conquered lands. This state was Macedon. The conquests were Alexander's and it was Alexander's mother, Olympias, who founded a tradition of dynamic queenship that was transmitted to later queens of Macedonian provenance and ultimately found its greatest expression in the last of them, Cleopatra. Olympias fitted the Athenian stereotype of womankind in at least one respect: she inspired fear. She was reputed to be an initiate of the secret women's rites and to have the power to command — and even sleep with — serpents. It was said to be fear of a predatory bedfellow and perhaps of magic that put her husband off her. The court of Philip of Macedon was like a seraglio. He was amorous and philoprogenitive. Olympias had to be tough to get the throne for her son. The possibility that she murdered her husband cannot be discounted. Certainly, amid the constant intrigue and political manoeuvring to which her roles, first as a precarious then as a discarded consort, committed her, she had no time to practise the characteristically womanly virtues of homemaking, sewing and passivity as the writers of Athens conceived them. A hundred years after her time, among the Macedonian dynasties which Alexander's conquests had distributed around the world, some of her qualities were reincarnated in Arsinoë II of Egypt, who ruled jointly with her brother, Ptolemy II and showed, by universal assent, the greater political sagacity. It was traditional for Egyptian queens to be the consorts of their brothers and this, like many other Egyptian national traditions, was appropriated by the Macedonian Ptolemies in their efforts to reconcile themselves to the conquered race they ruled. But Arsinoë's place as consort far exceeded the role tradition assigned. She was portrayed on coins and hymned by poets as co-equal with or superior to her sibling-husband. She showed a political ruthlessness worthy of Olympias in procuring the deaths by judicial murder or assassination of all who opposed her.

This is the background against which the phenomenon of Cleopatra must be understood. Her story is too often abstracted from its historical context and given the timeless, universal setting of literature and art. There is a kind of irony in the fact that Cleopatra, who was a political victim of the ancient tragedians' stereotype of women, should have become in her turn a subject of tragedies. Through the pages of Shakespeare, Dryden and Shaw, for instance, Cleopatra has reinforced the ancient stereotype in the minds of modern English readers and playgoers. She has come to symbolise the perils of female frailty in a position of political importance. She has become a universal symbol of female sexual potency whom neither age can wither nor custom stale. She is thought to have captivated the captains of the Roman world by her beauty alone, without any strictly political allure, so that if her nose had been a fraction shorter, as the saying goes, the whole course of history would have been different. The title of Dryden's play about her, *All For Love,* summarises the popular conception admirably: the collapse of the Egyptian state and the deaths of two potential world-rulers were the result of amorous excesses induced by this royal succubus. Political interests, military exigencies and practical concerns were flung aside for love, with fatal consequences for Caesar, Antony, Cleopatra and Egypt. The image of the *femme fatale* is so indelibly associated with Cleopatra that it is hard to reach beyond it to the historical reality of a woman ruler in a man's world who handled her predicament with considerable skill and flair.

Cleopatra was born in 69 B.C. into a large, complex, indulgent and introspective family and court. The introspection was a result partly of the pharaonic tradition of sibling marriage, which the Ptolemies continued, partly of the divine aloofness which the Hellenistic kings affected, again in imitation of the Pharaohs. The indulgence was a result of Egypt's vast surplus of ill managed wealth and of the inclinations of the feckless ruler, Cleopatra's father, Ptolemy XII.

The common people of Egypt had hardly been Hellenised by Macedonian rule. Their concept of kingship, expressed in their changeless popular iconography, remained unaltered since pharaonic times. Their king

OLIMPIA E ALESSANDRO   *In Cameo*

Tesoro di S. Alt. il Duca Odescalchi

Olympias. Macedonian Queen. Wife of Philip II of Macedonia 382-336 B.C. Mother of Alexander the Great.

was a god — 'god and lord', petitions in surviving papyri call him. Gods were above mortal morality. Ptolemy and his companions amused themselves best with drunkenness and buggery: even the divine majesty of a Pharaoh was compromised in the dirty jokes that abounded in the court, in which the king was represented as a catamite or a blue comedian.

He loved music — often a sign of carelessness of state for ancient observers — but no more than every other form of sensual pleasure. His household was a den of licence and intrigue. If he upheld few of the good traditions of his dynasty, he preserved their reputation for incest and parricide. In 59 B.C. when Cleopatra was ten, he was driven or fled from the kingdom by a court coalition manipulated by his elder daughters, one of whom, Berenice, took effective control of the state. Used to the political companionship of eunuchs, Berenice murdered the first of the husbands she took to bolster her rule, and discarded another, thus achieving an autocracy that was cut short in its turn by her father's return in 55 B.C. Repossessing the kingdom with Roman help, he had his daughter decapitated. The young Cleopatra, who was by now Ptolemy's eldest surviving child, had thus been brought up on practical if unsavoury examples of statecraft.

Politically, in the interludes permitted by the demands of pleasure and parricide, Ptolemy's energies were absorbed by the problem of preserving Egyptian independence in the face of Roman expansion. Egypt was the only one still to survive of the kingdoms founded by the companions of Alexander the Great. Most of the others had fallen to Persia or Rome and it was Rome in particular that arrogated to herself the heritage of the Hellenistic world. She threatened to turn the Mediterranean into a Roman lake, stretching tentacles to every shore of that 'frog-pond', around which classical civilisation had developed. In 65 B.C. the Senate discussed the conquest of Egypt. This project not only suited the Romans' conception of their role, and the cultural and geographical modalities that determined the shape of their growing empire, but was also alluring in its own right because of the fabulous riches the country commanded — the fruits of the fertile silts of the Nile, the commerce of the great entrepôt at the overlapping edges of the east and the west. Caesar went to Gaul instead, but the idea of absorbing Egypt remained in Roman minds. Ptolemy was obliged to buy off Roman generals with vast ladlings of payola. His lavish personal gifts to Caesar and Pompey were supplemented with subsidies to the Roman state. These disbursements bought him time, but only made Egypt's ultimate fate more certain. It was like trying to repel flies with honey. In 59 B.C. the Senate declared him an ally of the Roman people. This sounded well but was a common prelude to subjection.

Cleopatra's inauguration into active politics probably coincided with the Roman expedition that reinstated her father, after his exile, in 55 B.C. The arrival of the Romans gave her a chance to see how political fortunes are made by big battalions — and incidentally to meet Marc Antony, at that time a dashing young subordinate commander. The execution of her sister, moreover, gave her political prominence for the first time. She was not the heir apparent, for a younger brother, the future Ptolemy XIII, although a child, enjoyed that role. But the royal custom of sibling marriage ensured that she would reign at his side, if Roman power allowed. Her father, moreover, was bound to support her for the succession. He was so firmly in the hands of the Romans, to whom he owed his throne and his life and a heavy debt of further subsidies for many years ahead, that he had to back the eldest of his children as the only chance of preserving some shred of independence for this kingdom. By his explicit legacy, therefore, the claims of his younger daughter, Arsinoë, and youngest son were overlooked at his death in favour of Cleopatra and Ptolemy XIII, who together ascended the throne, after the traditional formalities of a marriage, in 51 B.C. Cleopatra was nearly eighteen. Her brother-consort was about ten.

The two tasks that immediately confronted the queen remained the keynotes of her reign throughout its duration: first, how to keep power in that emulous court, in competition with men; secondly, how to fend off the tentacles of Rome. Her first rival was her brother-husband. He represented a threat that grew as he grew up. He had to be bundled into the background and obliterated or, if necessary, eliminated. No fraternal compunction was likely to impede the daughter of Ptolemy XII from serving her own ends ruthlessly. The power-struggle is discernible only in glimpses through the few surviving sources. Cleopatra suppressed her brother's name in her coins and papyri, which proclaimed Queen Cleopatra alone. The king was reduced to the status of a non-person, unacknowledged in the most solemn records of the royal house. At some point, apprehensive of the fact that he was growing up, Cleopatra seems formally to have dethroned him. She probably married the youngest brother, who acceded as Ptolemy XIV in his place: this child would make a more easily manageable consort.

Ptolemy XIII, however, had his partisans. Cleopatra made a dangerous error in not killing him while she could, for another palace revolution in 48 B.C. turned the tables on her, reinstated the king and forced her to flee to the eastern frontier of the kingdom. While he, too, contracted an incestuous remarriage with his remaining sister, Arsinoë, Cleopatra began to gather an invasion force. He marched to confront his ex-wife, but was prevented from trying conclusions by the sudden inruption into Egyptian politics of the civil war between Caesar and Pompey, by which the Roman state was then convulsed.

As a brilliant populist of unimpeachable antecedents, Caesar had gradually built up a network of personal power in Rome that threatened to over-trump the Senate and eclipse the traditional power of the patrician class. To forestall him, the conservatives adopted the successful professional general, Pompey. Both men were so gigantic in political stature and military power that the traditional republican constitution would probably have been incapable of withstanding either's victory. In the event, the fortunes of war favoured Caesar. His rival, defeated in the field, fled to the only part of the classical world which the victor did not directly control, to Egypt. Caesar was bound to pursue him there. The Egyptian king dealt with the embarrassment, and sought to curry favour with the ascendant party in a style traditional to the Ptolemies. Suspending his forthcoming campaign against Cleopatra, he had Pompey murdered unceremoniously and sent his severed head to Caesar.

Caesar, however, was unmoved by the grisly bribe. He did not feel beholden to Ptolemy for the cowardly killing of a respected foe. His only aim was to impose on Egypt, before he left, a political solution favourable to Rome. Although Cleopatra had formerly been in correspondence with Pompey, her restoration might be advantageous in this respect. It would keep the fountainhead of power in Egypt divided and would prevent the kingdom from acting independently. It would preserve rival power-factions in an equilibrium that would keep them reliant on Rome. It would offset the growing power of the dangerously successful Ptolemy XIII, whose head had been turned by his successive coups in expelling Cleopatra and slaughtering Pompey. If Caesar himself was in any doubt of Cleopatra's utility, the queen in person soon disabused him.

With breathtaking audacity, she left her own army and smuggled herself, almost alone, through the lines of both Ptolemy's and Caesar's troops into the presence of the Roman general. According to tradition, she arrived wrapped in the coils of a carpet and was revealed in a dramatic discovery as the rich offering was unfurled before him. This was just the sort of impact she wished to contrive. Her usefulness to Caesar was political. But the grounds on which she chose to appeal to him were simply, un-sentimentally sexual. It was a role for which she was admirably equipped. Caesar could and did have his pick of women, but Cleopatra was offering him in addition the unique relish of enjoying a queen and a goddess. All ancient authorities confirm what her clumsy coin-portraits suggest: that she was not beautiful by the strictest canons of taste. Her nose was too long and a trifle too imperious, her mouth too wide, her lips too thick. But her figure, her presence, her style and her feminine power of enchantment were universally acknowledged. She made the best of herself. First, she knew how to contrive the right setting for sex. When she entertained him Caesar was primed by exposure to all the exotic luxury habitual in the Egyptian court, but as yet unknown in Rome, with a splendour, according to the poet Lucan 'too costly even for an age corrupted with spendthrift pleasure'. The wealth of the kingdom, no longer adequate to equip efficient armies, could still enable the ruling dynasty to put on a lavish show. The ambiance was completed by parades of choice slaves, pruriently selected to incite to lust — blonde boys who could titillate by their rarity, caponised negroes, calculated to appeal to a classical gentleman's taste. Cleopatra, surrounded by these stimuli, spared no pains to make her own person alluring. The diaphanous silks in which she dressed accentuated more than they concealed. Lucan describes her breasts, perfectly displayed beneath the smooth and insubstantial tissue. The promise of her body was implicit in the pearls, round, pale and gleaming, that bedecked her. The riches of her dynasty hung in clusters from her breasts and limbs to be plucked like fruit. She was encased, as it were, in a rich husk of silks and jewels to be peeled off and savoured as an apéritif before devouring the luscious morsel within. And if this shimmering sexuality needed any further enhancement, the famous perfumes and aphrodisiacs of Egypt were no doubt present to provide it. Tradition ascribed to her authorship antiquity's most authoritative treatise on cosmetics, as well as another on alchemy. Finally, Cleopatra had a geisha's gift for making sex seem civilised by surrounding it with a subtle kind of ceremonious intimacy spun from cultured conversation — at which she was adept in several languages — and music, in which she was a skilled performer.

By becoming his paramour, Cleopatra gained unrivalled access to Caesar's counsels. She was surely too shrewd to be motivated by lust. The part of Caesar's anatomy in which she was most interested was his ear. For once he became the arbiter of Egypt's political future, a vantage point, from which he could be influenced, was the prize to which she bent her amorous arts. In accepting her favours, Caesar did not commit himself to her politically. He was no *ingénu*, to be enthralled by a mistress. Still, she had better cause than her rivals to be satisfied with the settlement Caesar dictated. He re-scrambled the bizarre matrimonial lives of the Ptolemies, insisting that Cleopatra and Ptolemy XIII resume joint rule of mainland Egypt, while Arsinoë and Ptolemy XIV should go off to reign in Cyprus. It was a deliciously malevolent and wholly unworkable compromise. Ptolemy XIII rejected Caesar's arbitration and resorted to arms. The war was a near-run thing which almost ended Caesar's career, but its results were wholly satisfactory to Cleopatra. Her recalcitrant ex-husband paid for his temerity in challenging Caesar by forfeiting his life on campaign. Arsinoë was exiled. Cleopatra was restored to the throne as the senior partner of Ptolemy XIV. She had triumphed by femininity supplemented by luck. But 'skill loves luck and luck skill,' as Agathon said, and Cleopatra had unquestionably worked wonders with her chances. From a defeated renegade she had turned herself into the autocrat of a great country and the closest associate of the world's most powerful man.

Obscurity surrounds the next phase of her life, because the successors of Caesar distorted the historical record to minimise her role and excise her hated memory. But she must have been well contented with her own performance as Egypt's ruler, confident that her authority was firmly imposed, for within two years she departed for Rome, in Caesar's footsteps, to remain there continuously — except perhaps for one brief return visit to Egypt — until her lover's death. This was not a sentimental journey. A personal motive may have been involved, for at some stage it is certain that Cleopatra conceived Caesar's child. If this was during their first spell of dalliance, she may have taken the infant — a boy whom she called Caesarion in allusion to his illustrious paternity — to Rome to display to Caesar. As the only man-child of his body, the boy, though a bastard in Roman law, had some claim to Caesar's legacy and might be expected to command a special place in the dictator's affections. But whether or not in the company of Caesarion, Cleopatra still had every reason to retain her influence with Caesar, even at the cost of neglecting Egypt. In the first place, Egypt's vital interests remained in Caesar's palm even when he was far from the country. Moreover, a greater prize than Egypt was now at stake. Caesar was the ruler of the Roman world. He turned his dictatorship into multiple dictatorships, into life dictatorship and into perpetual dictatorship. He was on the threshhold of enthronement as a king. Already the popular and orientalised elements in Rome were worshipping him as a god — something which Cleopatra, coming from a land of divine kingship with her own self-conception as a goddess, was equipped to understand. Caesar had a lawful wife in Rome, but Roman senators in those days divorced their wives as readily as they doffed their togas. If Cleopatra could cement her relationship with Caesar she could rule not only Egypt, but, through him, the entire known world.

She had not brought these plans to maturity when they were wrecked by Caesar's assassination in 45 B.C. But though she had attracted odium as an alien meddler in Rome's affairs, and infected Caesar with her unpopularity, she had not wasted the years spent in her well-gardened villa across the Tiber. She had gained a thorough knowledge of Roman politics. *Le tout Rome* had come to court her, partly out of deference to Caesar, partly out of fascination with the romantic and the exotic, which she so ideally represented. Even sententious old senators like Cicero, who was loudest in his condemnation — from a safe distance — of her loose morals and foreign ways, visited her ingratiatingly and to some extent succumbed to her spell. She could take the measure of the two men who would dominate the next phase of Roman history — Antony, Caesar's henchmen, and Octavian, Caesar's nephew. While Caesar lived, she influenced his policy, weaning him gradually from his stern loyalty to the republican constitution, inveigling him with dreams of kingship and deification. He fuelled her own cult in a dramatic way that scandalised Rome. Cleopatra saw herself — daringly even by Egyptian standards — as the incarnation of the supreme goddess, mother of the gods, Isis. By one of the subtle metamorphoses that influenced the exchange of gods and goddesses between the various pantheons of antique societies, Isis was identified not only with earth-mother goddesses of Greece and Rome but also with Venus-Aphrodite, the goddess of love. In Egypt, therefore, Cleopatra chose the iconography of Isis for her public image, and in Rome that of Venus — an appropriate guise for this queen of love. In the mythical genealogy of Caesar's house, Venus was his ancestress. When, therefore, Caesar erected in the temple of Venus a golden statue of Cleopatra, the gesture was replete with significance.

Cleopatra even extracted one small gain from the debacle of Caesar's death. She took the opportunity to murder her brother-husband, Ptolemy XIV, who had been quietly growing up, under Caesar's protection, in her Tiberside household. The boy was now old enough to act independently and threaten her power. So he was ruthlessly despatched with poison. In general, however, Caesar was an irremediable loss. She could count on no other protector in Rome and was obliged to return precipitately to Egypt, where her ambitions were now to be temporarily confined once again.

In her homeland, she was a benevolent despot. From the few sources that have survived, she appears as an efficient ruler, who fed her people despite two terrible famines, when the Nile floods failed, and subsequent plagues. Without provoking rebellion — a rare record in Egypt in those days — she extracted enough wealth from the country to supply all Antony's armies. She left at her death a treasury so full and rich that its capture caused inflation in Rome. She ruled nominally in conjunction with Caesarion, her son by Caesar, called Ptolemy XV, but actually — of course — in untrammelled autocracy, without exciting any criticism of her sex. To judge from the iconography of her divine image, her cult as a goddess was embraced by her people with peculiar devotion.

In Egypt, she had every problem under control. There were still potential foci of disloyalty to trouble her outside the kingdom — her sister Arsinoë, nourishing her meagre pretensions to the crown at Ephesus, and a bogus pretender, claiming to be Ptolemy XIII, who drifted from court to court around the eastern Mediterranean in search of succour. She soon persuaded Antony to have these sources of embarrassment extinguished for her by judicial murder. It was thus from a home base in a relatively stable and secure kingdom that she was able to launch her next bid, when the chance came, for a world role. After sparring for a while following Caesar's death, Antony and Octavian had destroyed Caesar's assassins, virtually suspended the Roman constitution and divided the Roman world between them. Antony as the senior partner with the biggest military force, got the lion's share — almost literally, as he was fond of applying leonine imagery to himself — including the entire eastern Mediterranean, where his activities in government renewed his old acquaintance with Cleopatra and gave her a chance to contract an alliance that would renew her own assault on universal dominion.

Their mutual attraction was based — like Caesar's and Cleopatra's — on political interest and sex. But there was an additional element here that made this later alliance closer. Their images of themselves and of each other, refracted through the opaque lens of antique mystery-religion, exactly corresponded. In this sense, Antony and Cleopatra were made for each other.

Cleopatra, like Olympias and Arsinoë before her, was an initiate of mystery-cults. In some sense, the forms of devotion they favoured originated in Phrygia or Thrace before the sixth century B.C. Taught, according to legend, by Orpheus, they included music and dancing and a ritual meal, in which animals, usually fawns, were torn apart and devoured. This act, sacrificial and terrible, referred to the myth of Zagreus, whose heart Zeus devoured, with characteristic theophagy, prior to his reincarnation as Dionysius. But at the heart of the mystery lay more than a mere act of remembrance. The initiates may have believed that their rites preserved within their soul the balance of good and evil which Zagreus was thought, in some versions of the myth, to have introduced to human nature. Like all secret rites, those of Dionysius were detested by excluded parties. Their devotees believed that detractors would be maddened or destroyed, yet the detractors persisted — especially male detractors of the particular cults which confined participation to women, or gave women a central role in the rites. All these derived in some measure from the mysteries celebrated at Eleusis in Attica, which spread to Athens and thence throughout the Hellenistic and Roman worlds albeit with a myriad of prismatic variations from place to place and time to time. These forms of the cult, although faithful to the Dionysius myth, focussed on the part of Persephone, mother of Zagreus. Among the Romans, they were often exclusively for women and were associated with the worship of an earth-mother goddess, Ceres or Bona Dea. It was in rites belonging to this tradition that the Macedonian queens engaged.

What actually happened at the initiates' meetings is not known for sure. Their secrets were well kept. And women's events attracted little literary attention, save for the occasional scurrilous satire or pornographic poem. Probably there was a dramatic re-enactment of the myth, climaxing in the ritual meal. Certainly there was drinking — for Dionysius was the inventor of wine — and orgiastic possession. But less important than what happened is what was thought to happen. And certainly, by Cleopatra's day, the Dionysian and Eleusinian and related mysteries had acquired a lamentable reputation for decadence and sexual turpitude.

Male moral repugnance at feminine mysteries had begun as early as fourth century Athens. In the *Bacchae* of Euripides, the censorious old moralist King Pentheus of Thebes suspects the god's female followers of promiscuous orgies. He is punished for his hostility to Dionysius by suffering, at his mother's hands, the horrible fate of a Bacchanalian sacrifice:

he is torn apart, alive. In this play, the dramatist addresses a rebuke to the sententious hypocrisy of the foes of innocent — even religious — revels, much as the Jacobean playwrights might lampoon the Puritans. In Cleopatra's time, however, criticism was more widespread and its substance perhaps more sound. 'Mixed' mysteries — those in which both sexes took part — were evidently thoroughly decadent. There is hardly a vase painting in which Dionysian rites are depicted without whores running amok and displaying all the tools and artifices of their trade. This degenerate reputation overspilled to besmirch the matronly rites of the women's cults. Caesar's first wife, for instance, who should have been 'above suspicion', fell from favour as a result of her involvement in a scandal in 63 B.C., when the rites were profaned by the infiltration of a man. Ptolemy XII incurred his obscene reputation in celebration of Dionysius with coarse transvestism. Cleopatra's enemies did not scruple to cite her devotion to the mysteries as evidence of her sexual insatiability. Their accusations were commonplace by the end of the first century A.D., when the satirist Juvenal, with evident relish and feigned disgust, professed to deplore the Roman version of the Eleusinian mysteries as covens of depravity, in which drunken dance-crazed whores and nymphomaniacs vied in Lesbianism, brandishing dildos, before raising the cry, 'Bring on the men!' By then, if Juvenal's joke could be taken seriously, the mystique of the rites had been lost along with their secrecy and decorum. But Cleopatra's participation in them a century and a half earlier still evoked the two great weapons of the Macedonian queens: mystery and sex.

It also brought her into natural alliance with Antony. He had already been a devotee of Dionysius while still a relatively staid soldier in Rome. In the east, he came to see himself *as* Dionysius, a divine incarnation. He crowned himself with ivy, the god's own symbol, and wreathed himself, in his coin-portraits, with the god's serpents. The alcoholic orgies in which he delighted thus became self-referential acts of worship. He had himself proclaimed as Dionysius throughout the Greek east, and topped the Acropolis in his capital at Athens with a shrine to himself as a setting for his revels. When he met Cleopatra for a political summit in 42 B.C., it was rumoured that Dionysius had come to woo Aphrodite. They met not only as old friends and potential allies, but fellow-initiates and fellow-divinities.

Antony had none of Caesar's power to resist the force of events and the influence of others. He came of patrician stock, but his house had fallen on hard times. He had none of the confidence that comes from vast wealth and a top-drawer upbringing, such as Caesar enjoyed. His head was more easily turned. In the eastern Mediterranean he was rapidly seduced by the exotic culture and the easy pace of life. He 'went native' like a nineteenth-century colonial governor, escaping from the conventions of home, into a self-indulgent world where all was luxury and relaxation and where his Dionysian fantasies could become real. He ruled his eastern dominions like a satrap, milking them for what he could get, neglecting their government but extorting their wealth. He also neglected his own political fortunes. His rivalry with Octavian was like the hare's race against the tortoise. Secure in his enjoyment of the greater share of the booty of the civil war, he allowed Octavian to catch up unobserved. And he took no care of Italy, which by the terms of their agreement was meant to be held in common, but which gradually passed into Octavian's control: as the heartland of the empire, it was a vital possession which might tip the scale.

Antony's enchantment by Cleopatra was all part of the same syndrome of submission to the lure of the east. She used the same arts to ensnare him as she had practised on Caesar, but he was a relatively easy catch. The image which Shakespeare's genius has associated inseparably with her name, of the sybaritic queen floating to meet her lover in her gilded barge with silver oars, purple sails and crew of nymphs and cherubs, is well authenticated. The playwright took it from Plutarch who was repeating respectable tradition. Cleopatra, in short, was treating Antony to one of her cleverly contrived erotic displays. When he feebly tried to outdo the lustre of her hospitality in entertaining her to a banquet in his camp, he took refuge in laughter at the rusticity of his efforts. Outclassed in sophistication, he was also outstripped in ambition. Cleopatra intended him to use the wealth of Egypt to conquer Octavian's portion of the Roman world, but Antony was too dazzled to act. He wasted wealth in ostentation and time in play. Cleopatra had continually to recall him to himself. On one occasion, she lost patience with his inordinate love of fishing. '*Autocrator*,' she exclaimed, calling him by a royal title detested in Rome, 'hand over your rod to the fishers of Pharos and Kanopos. Your sport is to catch cities, kingdoms and empires.'

Antony did show some resistance to Cleopatra that was not the result merely of indecision. He did not attempt to have their union legalised in Rome, where he had still not abjured his own wife. Nor would he break definitively with Octavian, but continued to hope for a rapprochement, even while his rival was betraying him by gobbling up Antony's western provinces and insinuating his authority into Italy (which was supposed to be neutral ground). Nor did he do anything to vindicate the rights of the son Cleopatra had borne to Caesar. On the other hand, he probably gave some formal guarantee of Egyptian independence: when Cleopatra entertained him in Egypt, he left the symbols of his authority as a Roman governor behind. He had, perhaps, learnt enough from Caesar's example to withhold his utter submission from the queen. He seems to have felt suspicious of her magic, to have viewed her as a temptress to be toyed with, a succubus from whom he half-wished to be prised. Egypt was a world apart from his stateman's cares, a fantasy realm to which he could retire at need but which he kept distinct in his own mind from his governorship of half the Roman world. When he finally returned to Italy for a showdown with Otavian in 40 B.C., he seems to have left all thought of Egypt behind, Despite his rival's manifest treachery, and contrary to Cleopatra's probable advice, he made a feeble peace which vastly increased the sphere of Octavian's control. Worse still, from Cleopatra's point of view, he profited from the death of his Roman wife to make a political match with Octavian's sister, Octavia. Antony was behaving like a man who feels smothered by a dominant woman and acts foolishly — even, in some degree, against his own feelings — in a reluctant effort to escape. Antony had already told Octavian that he considered himself married to Cleopatra; when he had left her, she was pregnant with his twin children. In implicitly repudiating her for Octavia he was committing an act of bigamy which, worse than a crime, was a mistake. He realised it only gradually. Over the next two years he became aware that his peace with Octavian was advantageous only to his rival, whose encroachments and insults continued unabated. At last, in 37 B.C., he resolved on a break with Octavian and a return to the policies advocated by Cleopatra. Naturally, this reversion was accompanied by a resumption of his relations with the queen.

Antony spent the rest of his life with Cleopatra. It is idle to speculate about whether they were really in love or what Cleopatra as a woman thought of his temporary desertion to Octavia. Discounting hostile propaganda, which represented them as so besotted with each other that they were rendered politically incapable, we know their partnership only as a political alliance, a marriage of convenience for the conquest of the world. Its carnal aspects were themselves instruments of policy of Cleopatra's making. Certainly, on their reunion they lost no time in the mutual recriminations of lately sundered lovers but laid their plans at once. Their only disagreements were strategic. There was no doubt of the ultimate objective. They would create a world-empire unparalleled since Alexander, turning Asia into a network of client kingdoms and the Roman state into a satellite. This was substantially Cleopatra's vision, but Antony accepted it. His disillusionment with Rome and with Octavian made him susceptible to grandiose suggestions. He did not intend to rule this super-state: he would be its tutelary deity revelling, above the cares of state, in his role as Dionysius incarnate. The government would be left to Cleopatra and her children — she the divine focus of unity at the centre, they the royal governors of the constituent kingdoms of the empire. Her children by Antony were given names and styles appropriate to their envisaged roles. Their son was now called Alexander Helios, a solar and imperial divinity's name, which was in itself a programme of conquest of the East by a new Alexander and the creation of an empire as boundless as the reach of the sun.

The first stage in the construction of such an empire lay, in Antony's view, in following Alexander's footsteps to Parthia, on the shores of the Caspian, where Alexander's greatest deeds had been wrought and where Caesar had planned a campaign which he had never been able to carry out. The appeal of a Parthian expedition was not purely romantic, though it was certain to be a hazardous adventure. Parthia was the inveterate enemy of Rome. A Parthian conquest would make Antony a hero in Rome greater even than Caesar had been. He could thus unseat Octavian without even exchanging blows and, by this oblique path, become master of Rome without incurring the odium of renewing the civil wars. Yet this first step was in effect the undoing of his plans. The Parthian expedition was hopelessly over-ambitous. Antony was defeated, his prestige wrecked, his army reduced to a pitiful rabble in a rout which he likened to the march of the Ten Thousand but which more resembled the Retreat from Moscow. He lost nearly thirty thousand men, including many of his best veterans. But for face-saving successes against Media and Armenia Antony would have been incapable of facing Octavian in the final encounter that was now his only means of redeeming his fortunes.

Disaster in Parthia made him totally dependent on Cleopatra. It was only her resources that enabled him to salvage a new army from the wreck of his old one. Egypt's wealth and diplomacy and efficient government could procure allies, men, provender and treasure. Antony had no other adequate source of any of these vital needs. His total political reliance on his mistress was mirrored in increasing emotional dependence: if ever Antony really loved Cleopatra, it was now, in his decline, when he needed her most. The story that she feared his return to Octavia (whom Octavian was still shuffling around the Mediterranean chessboard like an ineffectual pawn) and feigned a complex syndrome of amorous neurosis to keep him is probably an invention of her enemies. But she certainly used her influence with him to exhort him to confront Octavian, who continued to build up his power on the frontiers of Antony's jurisdiction, on the Adriatic and in the Balkans. In her desire for war against Rome Cleopatra was motivated by more than personal revenge on the senators who had insulted her and the triumvir who had disinherited her son. Nor was she seeking only her own dream of a new Alexandrine empire. She was representative of sentiments circulating throughout the eastern Mediterranean world — sentiments of detestation of the Roman yoke, expressed in prophecies of a great Asiatic resurgence, and a return, through Cleopatra and Alexander Helios, of the mythical Golden Age of peace and plenty. Most of the Asiatic client-states supported Cleopatra's call for war, even though they must have been suspicious of her motives.

Octavian heaped up provocations but Antony remained reluctant to the last to resort to arms. Until 32 B.C. there was still a chance of resurrecting the triumvirs' old entente. Although his foreign mésalliance was the object of ribaldry and suspicion in Rome, although his exotic dreams were distasteful to Romans and incompatible with the republican shibboleths the Senate revered, yet Antony was still valued as a general and useful as a foil against the ambitions of Octavian, who was growing dangerously overweening in his increasing security. In 32, however, Octavian abandoned all pretence of legality and carried out a coup d'état, expelling Antony's partisans from Rome. The flight of 300 senators to Anthony's side showed the continued strength of his party back home.

By now, however, Antony's home was with Cleopatra and his sentiments had taken root there. He took no advantage of the advanced state of his mobilisation to invade Italy, but still shunned the role of aggressor, waiting for Octavian to attack his jurisdiction. The years of the triumvirate had reversed the rivals' relative strengths. Antony, the dominant partner at the start, was now outmanned and short of ships. In a series of rapid manœuvres his enemy reduced his rallying-point at Actium to a state of siege by land and blockade by sea. Back in Rome the issue of the war may have been thought doubtful: a tradesman was said to be training two ravens, one to acclaim Octavian in the event of success, the other Antony. But on the field, the experienced soldiers and subordinate commanders knew that

Antony had no chance. They deserted in their thousands. Roman propagandists blamed Cleopatra. All their characteristic male hatred and fear of power-women poured out in their pamphlets. She was a witch, a whore, a debaucher of men, who had enfeebled Antony's will and emasculated his generalship. His generals left him because they were sick of the unnatural dominance of a woman at the war-council — and, what was worse, her strategic advice was not even good advice, but, coming from a woman, was of course always wrong. Cleoptra deserved none of this abuse. As paymaster of the forces, she was entitled to a voice in the council. And no single general was to blame for Antony's plight. His military predicament was simply irresoluble. If any errors were to blame, they were political errors he had made long before, when his complacency and neglect of affairs had given Octavian his early chances.

At the end of August, Antony's fleet made a desperate bid to break the blockade. The object was probably to retreat with as much of the host and treasure they could carry and erect new lines of defence in Egypt, where they might have a better chance of withstanding Octavian's onslaught. But the result of the battle of Actium seems to have exceeded Antony's worst fears. His army was cut off, his fleet destroyed. He and Cleopatra barely escaped with their lives. It was one of the most decisive battles in the history of the world, not only in the clarity of the outcome on the field but also in its long-term effects. It settled the fate of Egypt, which was now bound to become yet another Roman province. It settled the fate of Rome, which was now bound to become a despotic state at Octavian's mercy. It settled the fate of the Mediterranean which henceforth for centuries would be an unchallenged Roman lake, the vital artery of the Roman empire. It silenced forever the whisper of an Alexandrine *risorgimento* that Cleopatra had dared to utter.

Of course, in a shorter term, it also sealed the fates of Antony and Cleopatra. The romantic calumny that Cleopatra fled the battlefield and that Antony abandoned the scene for love of her has no reliable basis in the evidence. But that both were covered with shame and despair by the outcome is probably true. Antony reacted with the lassitude characterisitc of his disasters. He hardly felt it was worthwhile bothering to try to defend Egypt. Cleopatra's response, typically, was more spirited, more colourful, and more imaginative. She dreamed of founding a new Ptolemaic empire beyond the Red Sea, whither she despatched her eldest son with all the treasure she could stow (but later, after her death, the boy was betrayed to Octavian and executed). She tried to negotiate with Octavian to secure some positions of honour and authority for her children. According to one story, perhaps derived from Octavian himself, she even tried her now rather mature feminine allure on him, hoping to beguile him into a political settlement as she had beguiled Caesar and beguiled Antony.

In the event, her phrenesis was as useless as Antony's resignation. The most Octavian would allow either of them was a chance of honourable suicide, rather than the ultimate degradation of enslavement, public humiliation and execution. Both accepted this fatal option unhesitatingly, Cleopatra dying almost certainly in the way traditionally assigned to her, enclosed in her mausoleum, accompanied in death by her two faithful maidservants, killing herself in queenly fashion with the venomous fangs of an asp. The serpent was the emblem of the Dionysiac mysteries, which she had continued, in Antony's company, to practise until their last days. It was also the symbol of pharaonic power and divinity, which had risen to strike Egypt's enemies in thousands of examples of pharaonic art, and which now, with its bite, extinguished the last sovereign of independent Egypt.

Like most power-women, Cleopatra was a personal success and a political failure. Her success consisted in getting and keeping power in a world of men. She achieved it by the mixture of masculine ruthlessness and feminine artfulness that became the pattern for women of power after her time. Her failure came from deficiencies in the deployment of that power once she had got it. To some extent, these deficiencies sprang from her sex. As a woman, she could not be her own general, and was forced to rely on Antony's erratic gifts. As a practitioner of sexual wiles, she was forced into the same trap as every woman who uses sex to get her man: she had to compromise all her resources before achieving any return. Thus Caesar was able to withhold from her the political prizes she most desired, and even Antony was able to resist her up to a point, until he became her client as well as her lover. But her difficulties were ultimately connected with vast historical forces that no Egyptian monarch, man or woman, could have overcome and which she made a remarkable and heroic effort to resist. The relentless advance of Rome can be seen, with hindsight, to have been irreversible.

But she should be credited with one lasting influence, which was perhaps no less important than her failures. This was her influence on the image of the power-woman, transmitted by literature. She inspired men with fear. She stirred up all the vindictive jealousy and loathing with which men have traditionally responded to power-women. Because the historical record and literary image have been made by men, they have been distorted by the insertion of a totally unreal Cleopatra, whose force and virulence men have sought to disarm — one might almost say to emasculate — by reducing her to a mere sex-object, or to a fool who was unable to distinguish political interest from lust. Ancient historians made her a slut to deride, modern tragedians a protagonist to be pitied. But none gave her her due.

CHAPTER TWO

Late Antiquity from Pulcheria to Amalasuntha

The civilisation of Europe in the late antique and early medieval periods was a blend of traditions, all more or less hostile to women in power. Vestiges of Rome persisted, especially of Roman law and political ideas, which had inherited (ultimately from Athens) the disabilities they imposed on women. Onto the Roman legacy were grafted Christian and barbarian traditions which in their different ways were equally inimical to the idea of entrusting a woman with state-wide authority or responsibility.

Christian antipathy to power-women is well-known today, thanks to modern controversy about the propriety of ordaining women and the oft-quoted strictures of St. Paul. Writing to the brash and contentious Christian community of Corinth, with its pushy females and fractious families, Paul felt obliged to enjoin on women obedience to their husbands and decorum in Church. He saw woman as 'a reflection of man's glory... created for the sake of man'. But he still upheld the inter-dependence of the sexes and the equality of men and women before God. No contradiction was apparent, in the early days of the church, between this fundamental equality and the exclusion of women from office. In the latter respect, Christian practice merely reflected the conventions of society at large. In the former respect, the church was a liberating influence, which spared women from the tyranny of dependence on male guardians. It hallowed their choice of virginity — an attractive alternative to the hazards of childbirth. And it offered them a vocation of divine service which, even if it brought no political rewards, gave them a chance to make a distinctive contribution outside women's traditionally limited roles. If the church failed to question political discrimination against women, this may have been simply because civil society was an irrelevancy to the early Christians who, seeking a kingdom not of this world, viewed politics with contempt.

Christianity in late antiquity was particularly attractive to women, as it was to most underprivileged classes in the Roman Empire. Yet the conquest of women by Christiantity coincided with a period of female emancipation in the third and fourth centuries A.D. This might have made women and Christ less mutually accessible. Its most marked feature, for instance, was easier divorce, which the clergy abhorred. In practice, however, no rift seems discernible. A divorcée like Fabiola could be welcomed into the church by a purist like St Jerome and, indeed, lionised and almost canonised. This suggests that it was the Church that wooed the women, as much as the other way round. Their emancipation made them important, and bishops, eager for converts and bequests, concentrated their spiritual fire on them. Women could use their new-found social and economic clout, as well as their traditional influence within the household, to do the church's work — converting their husbands, or at least working at the job, baptising their children, off-loading family wealth in charity or in donations to houses of God. It was educated women like Proba, who wrote a Vergilian poem with Christ as its hero, who made the best Christians, or aggressive feminists like Melania, whose asceticism killed her still-born baby and whose charitable fervour almost bankrupted two wealthy families. Once recruited into the ranks of the church militant, women could be effective warriors for Christ.

St Augustine has left us a remarkable account of the influence of his mother on his own infantile spirituality. He was exceptional probably only in recording the experience. A patrician family like the Caeonii in Rome, for whom the old civic religion was an essential part of their longstanding role and status in society, could succumb almost entirely to Christianity within one generation, after their menfolk had taken Christian wives. Such cases explain why the clergy, having formerly outlawed mixed marriages, actually encouraged them by the late fourth century. And whether through the partiality of women for Christianity, or for women of the Church, the new creed by that time had definitely acquired a distinctly feminine character, which the clubmen of declining Rome, in doomed male solidarity, manfully resisted for a while. Volusianus, for instance, the courteous pagan correspondent of St Augustine, had a Christian mother, a Christian sister and a Christian niece. But he upheld the pagan traditions of the menfolk of his clan, despite the constant, nagging female indoctrination, until he was at last converted on his deathbed by his niece.

The Germanic barbarians who brought the main external influences, after those from the east, into the Roman Empire had no time for female rulers. The origins of their political ideas are obscure and too remote now to re-construct, but by the time of their emergence in the historical record through contact and conflict with Rome, their images of kingship were aggressively virile. Their polities functioned without supreme rulers but they acknowledged two types of leader — at least from time to time — whom the Romans called 'kings' and 'dukes'. The distinction was not necessarily clearly made, but the names seem to correspond to two genuinely indentifiable classes, both of whom were necessarily always male. The first was distinguished by a sacral character, transmitted hereditarily from the gods in the male line — like blood-right and property in their kinship systems. These kings were endued with a numinous power of communication with nature, far in excess of any political power they possessed. They were guarantors of the fertility of the soil, the benignity of weather and the fortunes of war. The second class was male for a different reason: they were the war-leaders, the field commanders, possessed (in the emergency conditions that procured their elections) of real and terrible authority, and selected by prowess, unlike their sacral counterparts whose distinguishing characteristic was called 'nobility' — that is, inherited virtue. Neither prowess nor nobility could, by definition, be found in a woman. Only Romanised women ever ruled Germanic kingdoms — and then only in the sixth century, after half a millenium of continuous German exposure to Rome. And by that time, Romanised Germans had been disciplined to accept female rule by a remarkable woman, whose story comes to life in vestiges she left in Rome and Ravenna, from where she governed Romans and barbarians alike for a quarter of a century.

In the city of Ravenna, which in the fifth century took the place of Rome and Milan as the administrative capital of the Roman Empire in Italy, stands a small cruciform building of that period. Brick-built, low and squat, under its modest little sloping roofs of rippling tiles that look as if they might belong to the house of any ordinary citizen, it presents no external ornament to attract a beholder, except for a shallow blind arcade, of only one course of bricks, to break up the bleakness of the walls. Only within does this building betray its secret. Through a narrow little aperture one enters suddenly an astonishing world of dark, hidden magnificence. Every surface is smothered with gleaming mosaics, like crusts of jewels, or rich, russet marble. Everywhere, against the dark blues and greens favoured by the artists, shines the glint of gold. In the arms of the cross stand plain stone sarcophagi. This was evidently intended as the mausoleum of someone of dazzling wealth and splendour. In fact, it was built in about 430 A.D. for one of the most intriguing power-women of history, the Empress Galla

Placidia.

Infuriatingly little is known of her, for a woman of so much importance, but a great deal can be inferred from the tomb. Its scheme of decoration is an emphatic gesture of defiance to the pagans and heretics whom it was the life's work of this Christian empress to hold at bay. Faith in salvation through Christ alone glistens on every wall. The focal point of the structure and the design is a hugh mosaic of Christ in triumph, impassive of countenance but with welcoming hands, seeming to spread about himself the golden stars that spangle the vault, as if heaven itself were closing around the inmates of the tomb. Then come the Evangelists and Apostles, transfigured in pure gold. Peter and Paul raise their arms, like patricians acclaiming an emperor. Galla Placidia evidently expected the heavenly court to resemble the one she knew on earth. Souls symbolised by scriptural emblems — harts and doves — drink from the living fountain and the water of eternal life. On other walls, the suffering of the Christian and the repose which is his reward are evoked: St Lawrence goes happily to his horrible martyrdom on the burning gridiron, while Christ the Good Shepherd feeds his sheep in scenes of sylvan bliss. Placidia's monument is a monument, too, to the qualities that brought her to exercise supreme power in a state hostile to women's rule: taste, faith, determination, courage, constant mindfulness of the two most important places in her universe — Rome, and heaven. But there are two essential qualities of hers that the pious mosaics do not reveal: ruthlessness and ambition.

Galla Placidia was born in 389. In a period when it was common for men to rise to be emperors from the humblest peasant orgins, she at least had the advantages of birth on her side. She was born in the purple of emperorship. Her father was Theodosius the Great; her mother was the sister and daughter of emperors. Her family was related by marriage to that of Constantine the Great, who had made the Roman Empire Christian and whose memory and cult sanctified and legitimised his successors. But at the time of her birth she had absolutely no prospects of power, or even of a public role save in the dynastic policy of her house or in the prayer-machine which the womenfolk of late Roman households constituted, beseeching divine favour for the activities of their men. By her father's former marriage, she had two brothers and a sister, all of whom stood before her in proximity to power. Nor was her ambition for authority formed early. Her father lavished all his attention on his sons. His wife, from whom he became virtually estranged, and the little Placidia, were relegated to a small household and court of their own, in the penumbra of palace life, where the girl had little opportunity to observe the power game in action. In 393 she took part in a great civic procession and ceremony to honour the enthronement of her brother Honorius as Augustus — that is, co-emperor with his father and brother, and therefore heir to a share of his father's power. This must have been one of Galla Placidia's earliest memories and impressed her with the pomp and circumstance that surrounded the imperial dignity. But in 394 her mother died and she was turned over to the care of tutors whose only acknowledged horizons were those of a Roman matron or a Christian virgin. It was thus a limited choice of roles that presented itself to the child Placidia. When the death of her father followed in 395, she was confided to the guardianship of a cousin and began the unhappiest phase of her childhood.

Her guardian, Serena, was wife to the most powerful man in the western Roman empire, a barbarian soldier named Stilicho who had risen to supreme command of the army, won the confidence of Theodosius and now exercised a virtual regency during the childhood and adolescence of the new emperor. The experience was important for Placidia: the theme of the imperial Roman woman behind the powerful barbarian man was to recur in her own life. She would attempt later to construct for herself a role similar to Serena's. Whether from female envy or childish revulsion she conceived an intense hatred for Serena, a hatred she cherished against a remote prospect of revenge. For the present, all she could do was get on with the programme of education recommended by the external conscience of the imperial family, St Jerome. Like many celibates, Jerome idealised women. He saw them as naturally virginal. They were angelic messengers who could communciate the tender virtues beloved by God — clemency, love, chastity — to turbulent men. His first requirement for a girl's education was therefore that she should be kept pure — no foul words, no profane songs, no boys, just 'the sweet music of the psalms'. 'The shell-dyed wool, who can bring back its pristine whiteness?'

Jerome had practical recommendations, too. He advocated teaching a girl to read through play: letters carved from wood or ivory could start as toys which an infant could gradually learn to combine in words — Jerome suggested the names of apostles and patriarchs — and sentences. For reading, only the Holy Scriptures and a few Church Fathers of unimpeachable orthodoxy could safely be recommended. And even here, the Song of Songs had to be left till last ('If she were to read it at the beginning she might be harmed by not perceiving that it was the song of a spiritual bride expressed in fleshly language') and the apocryphal scriptures omitted altogether unless with great care to point out their defects. The important omission was that of the pagan classics. At about the same time, in another part of the empire, St Augustine was bemoaning their frivolous and corrupting effects: years after he was made to learn it, he could recall Terence's fine line about Jove's golden shower landing in Danaë's lap. In common with many of his well-schooled fellow-saints, Jerome was warned off the classics in an angelic vision. But in fact, their influence and allure were irresistible. Jerome continued to model his own style on Cicero, his own imagination on Vergil. Placidia's tutors almost certainly imbued her with the works of the Greek and Roman poets from Homer onwards. And a bit of political education may have crept into her upbringing. In adulthood, she showed some acquaintance with Roman history, law and political thought. On a more domestic note, Jerome's emphasis on household education ('Let her also learn to make wool, to hold the distaff, to put the basket in her lap, to turn the spindle, to shape the thread with her thumb') was certainly embodied in the curriculum to which Placidia was subject. With their own hands, she and Serena wove a coat for the emperor's horse.

Throughout her adolescence Placidia was kept hovering uncertainly between two equally obscure fates. Her upbringing and naturally pious inclinations equipped her for a life of virginity, dedicated to prayer. Alternatively, she might have been married off in the dynastic interests of the imperial clan. Both roles had political aspects: prayer could be effective in a wordly way. The right marriage could also contribute to the stability of the state. In fact, she remained throughout her teens uncommitted to any particular course. No marriage project came to anything. On the other hand, consecration to permanent virginity was indefinitely postponed. She was something of a stranger within the imperial family: no one seems to have regarded her as important. She was left out of account. She thus happened to be free to make an independent intervention in the political scene when the first opportunity presented itself — apparently quite by chance — in 408.

At the time, she was living in Rome, secluded and under-employed, far from the seat of government (which had been removed from the ancient capital), virtually ignored by the greater members of her family who were pre-occupied with terrible political crises. Sections of the army were in revolt. Stilicho had been assassinated. The co-emperor Arcadius had died. The heartlands of the empire in Italy were being devastated by invading barbarians. And a marauding army of Visigoths under their terrible prince, Alaric, sworn to 'the extermination of the Roman name', was advancing on Rome itself. There were only two resident members of the imperial family to whom the citizens of Rome could look as rallying-points in their plight: Serena and Galla Placidia, living in proximity and mutual odium in their chaste palaces on the Palatine Hill. The absence of their menfolk gave the women a chance to make a political impact. Their dislike of one another — if it is fair to suppose that Serena reciprocated Placidia's hatred — gave them a peculiarly feminine motive.

As the relict of a barbarian tyrant, Serena was extremely unpopular in Rome. With a barbarian army approaching the gates, barbarians were seen as the incarnation of enmity. Stilicho, moreover, while he had lived, had allowed Alaric's Goths considerable licence, probably because he hoped one day to harness their power in the service of Rome; his indulgence of them, however, was now seen by the Roman people as treachery, in which Serena was popularly thought to be implicated. The Senate, meeting in terrified apprehension of the coming of the Goths, impotent to resist, resolved to sacrifice Serena as a scapegoat. But they hesitated to commit lèse-majesté against a member of the imperial family without indemnifying themselves against the possibility of future imperial reprisals. Placidia was therefore invited to share with the senators the responsibility for condemning Serena to death. Placidia's first intervention in politics was an act of spiteful revenge against the woman who had played in her childhood a kind of 'wicked stepmother' role. The death sentence was represented as a common resolution of Placidia and the Senate.

It is unlikely that any strictly political calculation can have entered into Placidia's concurrence in her cousin's execution. But, in practice, the Senate's appeal made her a person of political consequence in Rome for the duration of Alaric's siege, or for as long as she remained in the city. She was exercising what was effectively an imperial vicariate. She seems to have found this sudden experience of power to her liking and quickly to have developed a taste for it. It is curious that she should have joined without compunction in encompassing a judicial murder. But no power-woman has ever succeeded without a streak of ruthlessness, and the piety inculcated by St Jerome's curriculum was strangely selective in practice. Placidia was as familiar with the Roman law principles of realpolitik as with Christian maxims of mercy. She knew the safety of the state as the highest law and was evidently able to convince herself of the identity of the public interest with her own volition.

But before she could indulge further her new-found power-lust, she passed into Alaric's hands as a hostage, either during the siege or just after the capture of Rome. The death of Serena had not extinguished within Rome the party that wanted to treat with the Goths. Assisted by the rigours of siege life which severely afflicted the usually pampered citizens, the appeasers gained the upper hand in the Senate in the autumn of 409 and probably placed Placidia under restraint. It may have been at this point that she became Alaric's prisoner, or it may be that she stayed in Rome until the Goths finally tired of the political oscillations within the walls and seized the city in August, 410. The submission of eternal Rome to a barbarian horde was a traumatic disaster for the whole empire but it did not last long. Driven on by lack of provender, the Goths departed quickly, taking Placidia with them on the start of what for her would be seven years of rootless wanderings between rough-and-ready camp-sites and enervating campaigns.

It was a tough finishing school for the political débutante. But it seems to have taught Placidia all she still needed to learn about power. It also gave her a chance to apply what she had observed of the model of Serena and Stilicho in her childhood by domesticating a barbarian war-lord to serve her own ends. She set out to captivate her captors. The courtship was long and must have been hazardous but, probably in 414, she ended by marrying Athaulf, Alaric's successor. It was an astonishing match in many ways. Placidia was old for marriage by the standards of her day — twenty-four or twenty-five. A spinster, especially one of such a pious background, might have been expected to resign the rest of her life to God by that age. Alternatively, had Placidia desired marriage for its own sake, more likely suitors could be found in the civilised world for an emperor's sister. Though militarily effective, the Visigoths were not a numerous or wealthy tribe. And Athaulf, though dignified with the title of king, was little more than a chief of marauders. Moreover, his reputation for ferocity, at least in the early part of his career, exceeded that of all Alaric's other henchmen. He had sworn to obliterate Rome. Yet Placidia weaned him from savagery and turned him into an admiring paladin of Rome with pretensions to a more exalted role in the service of the empire. She had shown herself to be a ruthless woman in getting rid of Serena. She now showed herself to be a redoubtable woman in taming this Goth.

She hoped to make of her husband a second Stilicho. When they had a son in 415 she named him Theodosius and at once began to prepare him, one day, to be emperor. Her political ambitions had still not fully matured. She was now aiming at supreme power, but she still expected to exercise it with and through men — her husband and her son. Even when the untimely deaths of both these intended instruments of her authority forced her to adapt her plans, she still sought to harness her career to a man's. In 417 she married Constantius, a long-time suitor, who had vied with Athaulf for her hand, and whose military genius had helped keep the Goths in check. This eminently suitable husband was reluctantly espoused. Only the forbidding alternative of a barren widowhood, which would have been politically sterile, convinced her to make the step. Once she had married him, she made the most of him, as she had done of Athaulf. Over her husband she wielded every advantage that superiority of birth and beauty brought. She had him in her power. She could cajole him into any course by threatening — as she frequently did — to divorce him. She converted him to parsimony, as she had converted Athaulf to love of Rome, and ensured that his political programme of self-advancement was supported by hard cash. Fortified with the confidence of the emperor and the hand of the emperor's sister, Constantius was able to gather the government of the western empire into his own hands in the two or three years following his marriage. Surviving letters of Galla Placidia's show that she was playing an active and independent part in resolving questions of state that fell within his sphere of arbitration. Though she had as yet no formal position of authority in the empire, she was effective co-ruler of half of it. Eventually, in 421, the Emperor Honorius gave *de iure* sanction to the *de facto* situation by consenting to a formalisation of Constantius's position. Galla Placidia had been scheming to contrive this for four years. Now her husband was enthroned as co-emperor with Honorius and she at last was an empress in name — Galla Placidia Augusta.

Even more important than this formal confirmation of her status was the guarantee for the future afforded by the birth of a son, Flavius Placidus Valentinianus, on 2nd July, 419. As Honorius had no children, this boy stood closest in the west to his inheritance. And though the empire was still technically elective, the supreme office had in practice become fixed in the imperial dynasty and transmitted more or less hereditarily. Placidia now stood to rule the empire one day in earnest. Skilful puppeteer of husbands, she would surely have no difficulty in managing a son.

In 421, Constantius died. In one sense, this opened prospects for Placidia greater than ever before, as she could now hope to enjoy power unshared. But in the short term, it left her in a precarious position. She now worked on her brother with the same feminine wiles that had previously wheedled both her husbands into submission. The court was shocked by the affection she lavished on Honorius, giving him the friendly reassurance and comfort he needed in his lonely eminence as emperor, frequently kissing him on ,the lips. But there was no impropriety. Honorius was an almost sexless creature who hated amorous encounters. And for once — perhaps because of the emperor's imperviousness to sex — Placidia's charms failed to work. Honorius did not protect her from the growing opposition of senators, courtiers and generals who suspected her ambitions and still associated her with the barbarian enemies of the empire. She had lived among the Goths for years and was tainted by the association. She had been the wife of Athaulf. She had converted Constantius to a broadly pro-Gothic policy and now she swaggered round Ravenna with her entourage of Gothic bully-boys. All this was resented. Placidia found herself increasingly the object of hostile rumours and demonstrations. In 423 she decided to abandon the futile policy of cajoling Honorius with ineffective blandishments. She tried instead a bold stroke. She fled to the eastern empire, to try and establish a new power-base there from scratch and reconstruct her plans to dominate the empire on a totally revised basis.

On her arrival in Constantinople, she could not expect, and did not receive, a particularly warm welcome. Though the Roman Empire was in theory a single state, its eastern and western moieties had been divided by uneasy enmity for many years. Placidia's best hope of winning the friendship of her eastern kinsfolk lay in associating herself on their side in their feud against the west. But if there was no immediate support for Placidia in Constantinople, she did find there a useful political example from which she could learn. For it was not only the exclusion of women from the imperial succession that debarred them from power, but also the fact that Roman law did not recognise the concept of a regency. Thus a woman could not be envisaged juridically as exercising imperial authority on behalf, say, of an infant son or an incapacitated husband. The usual route of access of power-women, in other words, was closed to the women of Rome. A juridical formula, however, which amounted to a regency in effect, had been devised in Constantinople in 414 to enable a woman to rule. On his untimely death in 408, the emperor Arcadius left two children, a daughter, Pulcheria, aged seven, and a son, Theodosius, aged five. While the latter succeeded to the imperial title, effective authority was discharged by a guardian. Pulcheria succeeded to the guardianship herself when she reached the age of sixteen and it was in this capacity that she ruled the empire perhaps for about two years until her brother was old enough to assume responsibility for himself. This created an important legal precedent and perhaps broke a psychological taboo. A woman's rule was seen to work. It is doubtful whether Pulcheria's brief tenure of power was really autocratic: ministerial guidance and help were probably vital to her. But she was a genuinely political animal — or became so as a result of her unique experience — and remained politically influential for the rest of her life, again easing Placidia's path by her example. In character, she could not have been more different from most power-women of antiquity. Her piety was in her ruling passion. She was uniquely innocent both of blood and sex, running her court like a convent, surrounded by chaste and prayerful women in a kind of divine purdah. But into a life consecrated to Christ she fitted cares of state, caring particularly for the church and the spiritual well-being of her people. After relinquishing nominal authority, she remained her brother's closest adviser. And when he died in 450, she made an impressive sacrifice by consenting nominally to marry his successor, Marcian, without compromising her virginity, thus dignifying the new emperor with the prestige of the old imperial house.

To begin with, the east seemed impervious to Placidia's intrigues. She was treated as an errant member of the family and excluded from the charmed circle of imperial favour, denied the titles of honour — to say nothing of the actual power — she had wielded in the west. Theodosius and Pulcheria still hoped to succeed in their policy of controlling the western empire directly, without having to rely on their cousin's services. Their hopes were enormously enhanced by the death of Honorius in 423, which left both moieties of the empire briefly reunited in Theodosius's hands. But Placidia's charms, adapted — no doubt — to suit the obsessively chaste Pulcheria and the haughty Theodosius, were gradually winning her cousins to her side. When it became apparent that the west could not be controlled from Constantinople, when revolts, usurpations and crises had demonstrated the necessity of locating a devolved centre of imperial authority in the west, Galla Placidia and her son again became useful to the dynasty. In 424 their titles were restored. Valentinian was additionally honoured with the traditional name of Caesar, reserved for the immediate subordinates and successors of the emperors. To him and his mother Theodosius gave arms and resources for the reconquest of the west in the name of the Empire.

It is astonishing that Placidia should have pulled off such a tremendous diplomatic coup. Her fortunes were completely reversed. She had turned failure and humiliation into glorification and success. The bargain she had extracted from Theodosius was almost entirely to her own advantage. For all he was providing, he was getting little except nominal allegiance in return. Furthermore, he promised for Valentinian the hand of his daughter, Licinia Eudoxia, who was his only heir. Placidia thus had added to an immediate prospect of power in the west a remote but real chance of ruling the entire empire through her son.

The first stage of this programme was accomplished with surprising ease; the second was doomed to frustration. The armies which attacked the western empire in the name of imperial unity conquered Italy for Placidia and Valentinian without encountering much opposition. In the midst of the crises of death, bankruptcy and invasion which the western empire faced, the inhabitants seem to have rallied in desperation to the standard of legitimacy, which brought with it the prospect of divine approbation. By the middle of 425, Italy was in Placidia's power. But, like many women of power, she was better at getting it than using it. It was as if she had used up nearly all her political skill and energy in gaining the prize for which she had so long grasped and schemed. This victory was her last great success. From now on, she was confronted by insuperable problems in her attempt to govern, on her son's behalf, the more decadent moiety of a decadent empire. The cause of Rome in the west was by now virtually lost. There were too few resources, too many barbarians, too long a frontier, too small a class of devoted servants of the empire, too little ancient civic virtue. The best that can be said for Placidia, once in power, is that if she did not stop the empire's decline and fall, at least she did not speed it.

The technical problem of setting up and exercising a regency was conveniently met by reference to the example of Pulcheria. But in practice, Placidia's power was immeasurably greater than her exemplar's. Her son was still very young. He was utterly under her domination: Placidia, who tolerated no insubordination from her husbands, was even more absolute in her tyranny over Valentinian. She had none of the court rivalries, bureaucratic delays or ritual and institutional checks on her acts of will that had impeded Pulcheria in the more sophisticated east. And it is probably fair to say that compared with Pulcheria she was less trammelled by conscience. On the other hand, Placidia's reach was short. The machinery of government was so tumbledown, and in places so exiguous, that the laws and ordinances she issued with élan were feebly or fitfully felt in the provinces. Great tracts of the empire were abandoned by retreating Roman armies, doing their best to retrench on interior lines and salvage something from the slow wreck of the empire. Other provinces fell into the hands of usurpers or were ruled in virtual independence by generals whose acknowledgement of Placidia's authority was purely nominal. And even where the imperial writ still ran, proto-feudal bosses were setting up virtual principalities on their own estates as substitutes for the inadequate structures of government still available to imperial officials. Placidia's predicament was not unlike that of the Empress of China confronting the Boxers. In a world of warlords, military qualities were needed in a ruler to bring them to heel. Placidia yielded nothing to men in the arts of intrigue and the skills of politics. Yet the one thing her sex prevented was the one thing she needed most. She could not command armies in person. Her regime was always in danger of being overshadowed by the political depredations of successful soldiers, of whom the greatest, Aetius, ruled Gaul much as it pleased him for most of Placidia's reign. Whenever he was free to intervene in Italy or appear at the imperial court, his military ascendancy left the empress powerless before him. Within a few years of having gained the position of supreme authority she had craved, she must have come to the bitter realisation that the real substance of that authority was pathetically small.

Thus though she toyed with imperial tradition, representing herself as a great lawgiver in the line of Constantine and Theodosius the Great, playing at legislation with a programme hopelessly unrealistic in its scope, and striving without success to play off the warlords and barbarians against each other, the real arena in which she was increasingly confined was the imperial court itself. She could not prevent her son growing to manhood but she had to stop him from growing up in a political sense if her own position were not to be forfeit. Characteristically, she adopted a daring approach to this little domestic difficulty. She decided to let him marry young, while his betrothed spouse, Eudoxia, remained a child: thus, far from introducing a rival woman into the court, she would be able to dominate them both. The marriage therefore took place in 438, when Valentinian was eighteen and his bride only twelve. Placidia's interest coincided with that of her realm in this: by bringing the western and eastern empires into closer entente, this marriage would enable the west to call more freely on eastern help. Yet by now, after thirteen frustrating years at the head of a crumbling state, her vision was narrowing. She was probably less concerned with the broad strategy of imperial survival than with the bunker — the beleaguered court amid the marshes of Ravenna — in which she would spend her old age tying knots in the leading-strings that bound her son to her. From this point of view, too, Eudoxia was a good choice — a devoted wife and, more importantly for Placidia, a dutiful daughter-in-law.

And yet, as Placidia grew old — she was fifty when her son married and had twelve more years of life, — there was one horizon which did broaden before her. She came to see the worsening troubles of the empire as spiritual in their causes and religious in their remedies. She fell back on the desperate but not wholly irrational course of trying to placate God with an ever more intense piety, an ever more lavish bestowal of propitiatory gifts. Unlike so many of the power-women of history, Placidia had no time for magic strictly understood. In fact, she hated it. When her husband Constantius was alive, she made him slaughter a magician who came to court claiming to be able to conjure away the ills of the empire. She had prevailed, despite the fact that Constantius hmself was susceptible to hocus-pocus. Like the conventional good Christian she was, she abhorred occultism and impiety much more than bloodshed. The mystery she sought to deploy in the service of the empire was godly. She frequented and flattered the holy men with whom the late empire was strewn. She invested the diminishing wealth of the throne in the erection of churches and the endowment of religious foundations. In Rome, for instance, the restoration and decoration of St Paul-outside-the-walls was completed by the empress and celebrated in the inscription, 'The pious mind of Placidia rejoices at the resplendence of her father's work...' In Ravenna, she built the Church of St John the Evangelist to adorn that increasingly splendid city and spent lavishly to enhance the Cathedral and the Church of Santa Croce. And of course she built the magnificent mausoleum intended for her own remains.

While Placidia built churches the edifice of the state crumbled away. While she kept her grip on the court, the empire's hold on the provinces weakened. By the time of her death, which came suddenly and peacefully on 27th November, 452, she had done little to prepare Valentinian to carry on without her. And she bequeathed him the worst crisis the Roman Empire had ever faced. Attila's Huns were wreaking a terrible devastation that the political structure of the empire would barely survive. It survived, indeed, only in an attenuated form, for less than a generation.

It was not because she was a woman that Placidia failed to cope with the problems of ruling the state that fell to her care. The long, grinding process of the decline of the Roman Empire was probably irreversible, whatever the ruler's sex. Nevertheless, Placidia's equipment was defective in the vital sphere of war precisely because of her sex. And it is remarkable that exceptional skill and determination, such as has often brought power-women to positions of extreme authority, has not sufficed to bring them success thereafter. Placidia's career illustrates the reasons for this clearly enough. For a woman to achieve power in a man's world requires exceptional talent in intrigue and manœuvre: these are the arts of which all power-women have been *cognoscente*. But then to go on to rule successfully the states they have appropriated by stealth would require more experience, more prowess and more specific education for empire than women normally have access to in societies dominated by men. Placidia's achievement was entirely in wresting power, not wielding it. Yet that achievement should not be eclipsed by the disasters that befell the empire under and after her rule. It remains worthy of renown. In the partly Roman, partly Germanic, increasingly Christian world of the late empire Placidia overcame the prejudices of three cultures to exercise supreme authority for more than a quarter of a century.

It was in a state that was the most perfect fusion of Roman, Christian and Germanic influences that a woman came to power in the early sixth century A.D. And Amalasuntha, the woman concerned, was in her own character a unique representative of the blend of three traditions that made up the Ostrogothic kingdom in Italy, which she came to rule. She was born in 498 A.D., the daughter and only legitimate child of Theodoric, a barbarian king of exceptional prowess and sagacity, who founded in Italy a kingdom nominally within the Roman Empire, but effectively independent: one of the first forerunners, in fact, of the nation-states of Europe that ultimately succeeded Rome. The political methods by which he created a state that was at once Roman and Gothic and preserved peace within it despite the differences of culture, law, religion and interest which divided its main constituent peoples, is symbolised in the monumental mausoleum he erected for his interment at Ravenna. This mighty sepulchre embodied his own maxim, 'The Roman when in misery imitates the Goth and the Goth in his misery imitates the Roman.' It was built in the eclectic style and monumental materials typical of the tombs of the late Roman aristocracy: but it was surmounted by a single great hemispherical tumulus of ashlar, for which no precedent existed in Roman architecture but which evoked the burial mounds of the ancient Germanic tribes. This atavistic reversion showed how Theodoric was faithful in death to his Teutonic origins.

Throughout his state, the Roman and the Gothic were juxtaposed in equilibrium. The two communities lived together in tense but close co-operation. The king preserved the legal distinctions — the differences both in privileges and responsibilites — between Romans and Goths, but contrived at the same time to treat both peoples equally.

But if Theodoric's realm was therefore more harmonious than most of the sub-Roman kingdoms of barbarian tribes, there remained areas of special delicacy or sensitivity, tensions which could not be perfectly resolved. The first of them centred on religion. By one of the most pregnant of historical accidents, most Germanic barbarians had been converted to a form of Christianity which Romans considered heretical. Arianism denied the equality of the members of the Trinity. Because of the long exclusion of Arians from communion with the orthodox, the sect had accumulated its own saints and festivals. In practice, it probably made little difference. Co-existence was possible. In the churches of Theodoric's capital at Ravenna, where Arians and Catholics lived side by side, the two communities adorned their churches in similar styles, albeit in depicting different saints, and copied one another's inconography. The Arian Baptistery at Ravenna, endowed by Theodoric, is closely based on that of the orthodox. The scenes of the baptism of Christ with which their domes are decorated are doctrinally indistinguishable. Catholics happily consulted Theodoric about their choice of Pope. But there were dangerous moments, as in 524, when Theodoric threatened to devastate the Roman Empire in reprisal for sanctions inflicted on the Arians of Constantinople. In 526, he threw the Pope into gaol — less, perhaps, for conscientious reasons than because he doubted the pontiff's political loyalty. These storms blew over without bloodshed between the rival communions. But the peace between Arians and Catholics was an uneasy peace, and toleration was waning when Theodoric died.

Also insoluble, for all Theodoric's skill, was the problem of relations between the Ostrogothic kingdom and the ultimate source of all political authority, the Roman emperor. In 476, the predecessor whom Theodoric overthrew, Odoacer, had deposed the last Roman emperor in Italy. This left Constantinople, formerly the seat of the eastern co-emperor, as the only surviving centre of imperial legitimacy, while the Ostrogothic kingdom, a self-proclaimed 'Kingdom of Goths and Romans', occupied a twilight position between submission to and secession from the Empire. It was impossible for the inhabitants of Italy to conceive a world in which the Roman Empire had ceased to exist. Indeed, such a consummation, as St

Augustine had predicted, would mark the final domesday. Thus after the Goths had expunged the reality of Roman power from the peninsula, the Empire's phantasmagorical existence was protracted by the irremovable force of an *idée fixe*. Thus the succession of Roman consuls continued as it had always done. Gothic kings and princes were invested with Roman titles of honour by imperial grant. The Senate sat on. The civic calendar was uninterrupted. And the cults of Unconquered and Eternal Rome comforted a people who had been made subject to foreign barbarians by concealing an unpalatable reality. Theodoric was happy with all this. Indeed, he revelled in it: it legitimised his own usurpation of power, assured him of the Roman people's submission and gave him a sense of belonging to a tradition he viewed with admiration, even with awe. He was content to leave the relationship of Constantinople and Ravenna clouded by fancy and ambiguity, as long as the Emperor left real Gothic control of Italy unabated and recognised 'the exalted King to whom the power and responsibility of government is committed'.

Not everyone, however, was equally content with the compromise. Many Goths resented the Romanisation of Gothic manners which Theodoric fostered in court and city life. The military aristocracy of the Goths resented the continuing power of the scholarly senators on whom Theodoric relied for the personnel of his administration. And there was a faction among the Roman patricians who were scheming for a direct restoration of imperial rule and the expulsion of the upstart barbarians. The contrasting predicaments of two of Theodoric's patrician civil servants, Boethius and Cassiodorus, illustrate the dilemma of Romans under Gothic rule. Cassiodorus saw himself as one of the last of the best, standing on the shore of classical civilisation before the advancing tide of barbarism, regretful but resigned. He did what he could, like an antique Metternich, to prop up mouldering edifices. He would strew his missives to provincial administrators with Vergilian quotations which their readers could hardly appreciate. He urged on Theodoric the standards of Roman comportment. He represented his illiterate master as a philosopher-king and the Goths as longstanding and respected members of the community of the Romano-Hellenic world. In short, he made a virtue of necessity. Boethius, equally saturated in the classics, was unwilling to give the old civilisation up for lost. He was, perhaps, unjustly implicated in the conspiracy to unseat the king in favour of the emperor. But there is no doubt that his sympathies were on the plotters' side. Defending a fellow-patrician arraigned for communicating with Constantinople, Boethius pointed out that a senator's ultimate loyalty to the empire was inescapable. 'The whole senate,' he declared, 'including myself, is guilty.' Condemned to death for his complicity, he wrote from his cell one of the seminal works of European literature, *The Consolation of Philosophy*, in which he distilled and transmitted to posterity the Platonic tradition that had contributed so much to antiquity. Theodoric's judicial murder of Boethius and his colleagues was one of the king's most dramatic gestures of repudiation of Rome.

These things show something of the nature of the realm and problems Theodoric bequeathed to Amalasuntha. She was brought up in Ravenna, in the shade of the mausoleum of Placidia, with whom her contemporaries would compare her, and given, at Theodoric's behest, the classical education of which he personally felt the lack. Her Constantinopolitan ways and high culture made her an object of suspicion to the Goths but equipped her well to understand the Romans. Yet it is doubtful whether her father envisaged her upbringing as a preparation for power. He sighed for a son and was dubious of the capacity of a woman to suceed him. Having brought Amalasuntha up to be — at least, to think and feel — like a Roman, he decided to marry her to a thorough-going Goth. In arranging her marriage he pursued the policy of Romano-Gothic equilibrium which guided all he did. And he sought a man like himself, an adherent of Arianism, to counter-balance the Catholicism of Amalasuntha; a strong man, whose prowess would hallow his kingship, as Theodoric's had done; a virile man, who would resist the mawkish luxuries so readily available to corrupt Germanic purity in Italy; a Teuton, who would keep the Goths true to their traditions; in short a man not only to succeed him but to continue his work. As events would later prove, for virility and strength he need hardly have looked beyond Amalasuntha herself.

In 515, Theodoric felt he had found the right husband for Amalasuntha. Eutharic, son of Wideric, was of royal — even, according to the old pagan genealogies — divine ancestry, and had served Theodoric's kinsman, Alaric, King of the Visigoths. Ironically, this wedding that was supposed to have redressed the balance of the Italian kingdom in favour of the Goths was followed by a pro-Roman reaction. In 519, Eutharic's asumption of the consulship celebrated with the most Roman of entertainments, lavish circuses. The prodigious array of wild African beasts drew gasps from the mobs of Ravenna and Rome. Even a visiting embassy from Constantinople was impressed. Eutharic, the Germanic champion, was capable of Roman civic indulgence on an expansive scale. Whether he would have been able to cope with the problems of *Kulturkampf* with which the kingdom was beset must be doubted, in view of his reputation as an intransigent Arian. But the conferment of the consulship in traditional style suggests that Amalasuntha was already at work on the Romanisation of her husband. But the process was frustrated of completion. In 522 or 523 Eutharic died, pre-deceasing his father-in-law by three of four years and leaving the way open for Amalasuntha to wield supreme power herself.

Nevertheless, Amalasuntha could not succeed to the throne in her own right. In 516, she had borne a son to Eutharic and it was this infant, Athalaric, whom the Gothic nobility now acclaimed as heir to his grandfather. Shortly before his death, Theodoric had presented the boy to the Goths for their approbation — an ineluctable formality retained from the Germanic traditions of elective kingship.

On that occasion, Amalasuntha appeared at her son's side. There could be no clearer indication that she intended to pursue an active regency. Theodoric urged continued amity with Rome. There could be no clearer indication that the policy Amalasuntha represented had the old king's blessing. Despite Theodoric's long years of assiduous entente with the Romans, however, complete reconciliation had still not been achieved. A false move could precipitate civil war in Italy or an invasion from Constantinople. Theodoric's posthumous prestige could hardly stave off disaster if Amalasuntha mishandled her task. Before Theodoric's time, it was characteristic of the policy of Gothic kings, not only among the Ostrogoths but also among the kindred Visigoths, to swerve wildly from reign to reign between fawning adulation of Rome and implacable hostility. The factions among the Gothic nobility that had been responsible for these sudden oscillations remained active and intact. There was every possibility that on Theodoric's passing the old instability would be revived.

It is not known how hard it was for Amalasuntha to wrest the regency for herself, but it must have required considerable determination and force of character. It is inconceivable that she can have been other than reluctantly accepted. But she evinced from her first days of power a confidence that suggests she must have trounced her adversaries. There was no serious male rival of the royal line, and she was therefore free to play hostile factions off against each other. She embarked at once on rapprochement with the Romans. She restored to their heirs the forfeited possessions of the senators Theodoric had put to death. She promised equal favour to Goths and

Romans. She invited Catholics to pray for Athalaric. She courted the Senate. She promoted Cassiodorus, and she wrote to Constantinople in ingratiating terms, calling for 'old hatreds to be sealed up in the tomb'. But she went too far in insisting on a classical education for her son. To the Gothic aristocracy, their future king's immersion in poets and grammarians would be disastrous. It would incapacitate him for his real job as war-leader. It would open a chasm of misunderstanding between him and his subjects. It would alienate him from his natural peers and align him with the senators and civil servants. It would enslave him to the arbiters of classical elegance in Constantinople. It would subject the kingdom to foreign values and foreign rule. It would make a future reversal of Amalasuntha's policies impossible — and it may be that those policies were only tolerated in the hope that they would be short-lived.

According to legend, it was when Amalasuntha flogged the young king for some childish offence — another sign here of her toughness — and induced unmanly tears that the opponents of her choice of curriculum found a pretext for action. A deputation approached her. Later rhetoricians put into their mouths a suitable message, which may well be close to what was actually said:

> 'Arms and letters are very different things... A boy who one day must dare great deeds and win great glory has to be free of the fear of schoolmasters and practised in the wielding of weapons. Theodoric was utterly unlettered. Yet he was a mighty king. He would never let the sons of Gothic warriors go to a grammarian to study, but always said, 'If once they come to fear a tutor's rod, they will never behold the sword or spear unflinchingly.' Therefore, lady, have done with the old schoolmen and pedants. Give your son young comrades in arms who will introduce him to men's work, so that when he grows up he will know how a king of Goths should rule.'

Amalasuntha knew the classical apophthegm, 'Hasten slowly'. She was too good a politician to ignore the limits of the art of the possible. She was probably aware that the gossip of the intriguers accused her of plotting her own son's death to free her hand for a more personal tyranny. She therefore acceded to these demands with every apperance of graciousness. In fact, however, she was probably already planning a desperate and terrible counter-stroke. From the serpent-woman of Macedon to the 'Iron Lady' of modern Britain, all the great power-women of history have been associated with images of toughness. They have had to assume or affect enough virility to compensate for their sex. They have had to show ruthless, and even sanguinary resolution when necessary. Amalasuntha was no exception, even though all the sources from her time depict her as a model of feminine virtue. She was deeply religious, solicitously maternal, modest in demeanour, jealous of peace and retiring in her preferences. But she was willing to kill to keep her power.

Her concession over her son's education had not appeased but emboldened her opponents. It did Athalaric himself no good. With his young companions, free of schoolmasterly discipline, he abandoned himself to debauchery. Drunkenness was a social convention among the Gothic nobility and it undermined his fragile metabolism as well as corrupting his feeble character. While he subsided into terminal alcoholism, his mother's enemies demanded her abdication of authority into his hands. Amalasuntha responded with a kind of coup d'état. Cleverly mobilising whatever support she retained, she was able to exile three of her leading adversaries to the provinces. She then made plans for an even more daring gesture and preparations in case of failure and flight. Letters were despatched to Constantinople asking for a refuge if necessary. The royal treasure — some 40,000 pounds weight in gold — was shipped to a safe haven across the Adriatic. And assassins were engaged to make a decisive example of the exiled recalcitrants.

The murders secured her authority. Not for the last time, a woman ruler had been forced into bloodshed to show she had the stomach of a king. But if internal opposition was temporarily quelled, the position of the kingdom as a whole was precarious. Theodric's prestige had kept an uneasy peace between Italy and its neighbours, but now there was no deterrent powerful enough to stop a potential aggressor. The favour of the Roman emperor was vital for the Goths, even if Amalasuntha's personal inclinations had not led her to court it. She was actually considering a plan to abdicate in favour of a direct restoration of imperial rule in Italy when the sudden death of her son threw the entire kingdom into the crucible and endangered her own position of control.

It was now that she made her first mistake in the power-game she had so far played so well. She was in no position to usurp the throne herself — indeed, so radical an idea probably never occurred to her. The regency she

A feast of Bacchus (Gerard de Lairesse Cassel 147).

had exercised was barely palatable to her subjects. A female king would have been an intolerable absurdity. To abandon her power to the emperor would have been a hazardous undertaking, certain to provoke resistance from the Goths, and was distasteful to her personally since it involved her total withdrawal from the life of power that she had come to love. She therefore attempted a third option which was to prove disastrous. In central Italy lived her only surviving male kinsman, a Romanised Goth named Theodahad, who was reputedly uninterested in politics but whose sole concern was the accumulation of vast wealth at other people's expense. His estates had grown by the eviction of his neighbours through litigation or force. Men said that he thought it a misfortune to have a neighbour. And Amalsuntha had earned his enmity for attempting to restrain his rapacity. She should have had nothing to do with him. He was abysmally unpopular and he had cause to hate her. But now, through the fatal weakness of feeling she needed a male partner in order to retain power, she appealed for his help. She offered to make him king in return for a share in the exercise of the royal right. In 534 they ascended the throne as joint rulers. Amalsuntha had achieved a pinnacle of authority that had not been hers while merely regent. She was now queen in her own right, albeit only in association with a man.

If she hoped to dominate that man she was soon sadly disabused. The titbit of power that Amalasuntha had flung him seems to have aroused Theodahad's appetite. The anti-Roman party among the Goths, especially the kingsmen of Amalasuntha's victims, saw an opportunity to exploit the king's corruptibility and resentment. Moreover, the danger of direct imperial intervention in the kingdom's affairs was growing. Amalasuntha was still in touch with the emperor, who ambassadors were a recurrent nuisance and embarrassment to the Goths: the increased frequency of their appearances in the course of 534 betokened renewed imperial interest in the affairs of Italy. Under the influence of the pressures and tensions, the balance of power in the Gothic court was suddenly overturned. Within a few months of Theodahad's rise, Amalasuntha was horrified by the murder of various supporters. She fled to an island in the lake of Bolsena and planned to continue her flight to Constantinople, but her isolation proved insufficient protection. Theodahad and his new, ill-assorted friends were apparently uninhibited by the threat of imperial reprisals. On 30th April, 535, the queen was strangled in her bath.

A mystery still surrounds this murder. Theodahad's partisans had motive enough but a contemporary writer implicates the emperor's ambassador. According to this story, the empress in Constantinople, a would-be power-woman herself, was jealous of Amalasuntha and fearful of the role she might play in the politics of Constantinople if she ever got there. The example of Placidia's flight in the same direction more than a hundred years before may well have been in her thoughts. Amalsuntha was certainly a dangerous woman. Regal and beautiful, she appears in her only surviving portrait clad in the jewels that an empress might wear. It is certainly possible that the empress, who was not above murder for political or amorous gain, could have wished her dead. Encouragement from the imperial ambassador would also explain why the usually indecisive Theodahad was willing to take the risk of emcompassing his kinswoman's death. And it may be that there lurked behind the whole murky story a strictly political motive in Constantinople: Amalsuntha's fate gave the emperor the pretext he needed to make war on the Goths and recapture Italy from them.

That reconquest, indeed, was the posthumous consummation of Amalasuntha's story and, in a way, it represented the culmination of her pro-Roman policy. But it can hardly be ascribed to the Gothic queen as a creditable achievement. Like Galla Placidia, she had presided over the decline, and very nearly the ruin, of her state. She had shown more skill in gaining the name of power than in wielding the reality. She had, in short, been a typical power-woman — a heroic failure. Within a few years of her death, the Gothic kingdom which she had struggled and schemed to control against so many difficulties, was extinguished forever.

CHAPTER THREE

China and the Empress Wu

Cleopatra, Placidia, Amalasuntha: the record of women rulers in the west until the sixth century A.D. had been uniformly disastrous. Each had precipitated the dissolution of her realm. It is not surprising that this fatal reputation stifled the careers of most power-women in the western world for centuries thereafter. The only exception was in Francia, where the influence of Roman and Christian conventions, newly experienced in that frontier territory on the fringe of the barbarian world, enabled mannish queens of unusual ferocity, like Fredegund, Brunhild and Balthild, to carry out successful and bloody usurpations of authority by way of a regency or the weakness of a husband, for short but destructive periods. In general, however, the tradition of power-women, extinguished in the west, was kept alive during the dark ages only in Byzantium and, more improbably, in China.

It is hard to think of a society less conducive to the emergence of power-women than that of China. The Chinese conception of women has always veered between inimical extremes. They have been seen in fiction and philosophy as weak, timid, sexually exploitable on the one hand, and dangerous, menacing and sexually insatiable on the other, but rarely, if every — and never before the Ming period — as normal or even directly comparable with men. Certainly they were never regarded as fit to rule. The maxims by which they were judged were Confucian. Confucianism was at all times a prevalent or dominant tradition of the ruling élite in China, which was always composed of scholars and gentlemen, the two classes to whom the philosophy was addressed and whose interests it sought to harmonise. It was a system of thought reflective of the values of the early sixth century B.C., when China was ruled by a mixture of arms and letters, a feudal aristocracy increasingly allied with a learned bureaucratic stratum. Neither arms nor letters were normally accessible to women — arms for biological, letters for social and educational reasons. Confucius's ideal ruler was necessarily male, a 'superior man' compounded of intellect, learning and experience in office, a scholar-bureaucrat or philosopher-king. Women were naturally different from and inferior to men, with a role in the management of affairs confined strictly to household economy. Equality of the sexes would untune the strings of society: 'if no distinction were made between the sexes, disorder would ensue,' as one Confucian text put it. 'Let there be men and the government will flourish, but without men, government decays and dies,' as the master himself said.

Women's literary image in early China reflected the influence of Confucian thought. By the seventh century A.D. two texts, which were collections of anecdotes of feminine life, dominated male perceptions of women and, because they were read by such few females as may have been literate, women's perceptions of themselves. Naturally, these texts — the *Nü chieh* and the *Nü chun-yu* were the work of men. They do little more than exhort women against idleness and promiscuity. A virtuous woman is represented as one who rises early and gets on with the household chores. It is likely that a thirteenth-century book the *Lieh nü chuan* is substantially derived from Han dynasty sources: here, though the range of anecdotes is broader, the overall impression of repressive didacticism is the same. In the one story in which a woman takes over her husband's role, it is only to offer her life as a sacrifice to save his — an act of definitive self-abnegation which the compiler deems suitable.

The practical aspects of the apportionment of power in China were as hostile to women as the intellectual climate. As women rarely acquired more than elementary education — if, indeed, they were fortunate enough to get any schooling at all — they were unable to enter the Confucian scholar-élite. Posts of responsibility in government were closed to them. Occasionally, empresses acquired female secretaries, who were hated by their male peers. Women's only route of access to power lay through the dangerous and densely populated imperial harem. The emperor's court, with its myriad degrees of concubinage, offered a female equivalent of a *cursus honorum,* through which one could rise, not by the ordinary canons of merit, but by ruthlessness, beauty and sex. By this means, one could get close to the sources of authority. The woman at the apex of the seraglio, the official empress, was uniquely placed to influence the fountainhead of all power, the emperor. Though strictly debarred from ruling in her own right, she could thus contrive, if exceptionally daring and skilful, to exercise a political role. But in the atmosphere of the emperor's household, where literally hundreds of concubines jostled for influence and attention, competed to sleep with the Son of Heaven, and vied to draw attention to themselves, it was only very rarely that a woman of strong enough character emerged to dominate the system fully or for long.

The first such power-woman to emerge was the Empress Lü, the widow of the first Han emperor. After her husband's death she was able to prolong the eminent position which the emperor's favour had given her in his lifetime, by manipulating the succession so that infant emperors reigned while from 188 to 180 B.C. she exercised a cruel and sanguinary regency. She set a precedent which subsequent empresses of outstanding ability repeatedly followed, down to the time of Tz'u-hsi in the present century, or even, one might argue, Mao Tse-tung's wife, Chiang Ching, in our own times. But neither she nor any of these other women contrived to rule in their own right, without need of a figurehead male — husband or son — to 'front' their activities, with only one exception. The Empress Wu, whose life covered the greater part of the seventh century A.D., succeeded not only in ruling effectively by way of a regency for nearly a generation, but also in usurping the throne and ruling directly, *sui juris,* for fifteen years. She was the only woman to hold the supreme office, the emperorship itself, in the entire history of this most ancient of political societies. This alone makes her one of the most interesting of her sex. Her character and career are correspondingly fascinating.

She was born in the year 625 to a rich and noble family. Her father had earned the title of Duke of Ying for his services to the imperial court. Her background gave her an opportunity to acquire more learning than was usual for a girl, but it was said to be simply her exceptional beauty that imparted her first great chance in life. On the strength of a rumour of her ravishing looks, the Emperor T'ai Tsung appropriated her for his harem when she was only thirteen years old. Though the emperor was already aging and was awash with concubines and heirs, Wu Chao — even at that tender age — was alert to the political allure of 'the presence of the Son of Heaven'. Despite her family's reluctance to confine her to what seemed certain oblivion in the capacious corridors of the court, she eagerly embraced her uncertain fate, and resolved to make of it what she could.

In fact, her audacity was justified. Perhaps because of the very *embarras de richesse* with which he was surrounded, the emperor was always susceptible to a new and pretty face. Wu Chao's looks did not disappoint him. She was conspicuous even in his citadel of beauty. Though initially ascribed to the court establishment as a concubine of relatively humble grade, she enjoyed frequent access to her master. She impressed not only with her looks but her precociously ruthless sagacity. The emperor was favourably amused by the alacrity with which she recommended torture, brutality and killing as means of exacting obedience: the advice cropped up, according to tradition, in a conversation about horse-training, but, said Wu Chao later, 'T'ai Tsung understood my meaning.'

The circumstances of the court happened to favour a come-lately adventuress who would stop at nothing in the pursuit of power. When Wu Chao entered the Forbidden Palace, the emperor was about half-way through his reign and the problem of the succession was already a lively and dangerous issue of court life. It was essential to the system that the favourite wife or empress and other major concubines should scheme to get their particular sons adopted as heir apparent; in practice, however, the empress had a great advantage and it was traditional for her eldest son to take precedence over his brothers and the offspring of concubines. This tradition had brought the Crown Prince Li Ch'eng-ch'ien into line for the throne on his father's demise, but his unpopularity and impatience drove him to plot to assassinate the emperor and seize the throne prematurely. Discovered in these unfilial machinations, he was degraded and soon died. The succession was now open to the competition of the younger sons and the concubines' progeny. In 643 the emperor's choice fell upon the youngest of his sons by the empress, chiefly on the grounds that the lad was blameless in his brother's conspiracy. The new crown prince, known as Kao Tsung, was a disastrous choice — a wastrel to whom duty was an encumbrance and morality a superfluity. He was easily corruptible and a slave to his own inordinate sexual appetite. Wu Chao had both the determination and the allure to capture his attention. She had followed the intrigues that led to his nomination for the throne and mastered the techniques. She now decided to set her cap at the future emperor as a means to the power she craved.

This was a course which demanded tremendous boldness to undertake and exceptional resourcefulness to execute. The life of the palace was ordained in such a way as to guard the integrity of the emperor's women against all comers. No man was ordinarily allowed access to them save the emperor and the eunuchs. In all the vast mansions and corridors, granges and gardens, outcrops and growths, caverns and eaves of the vast, sprawling imperial establishment, no other man dwelt, not even the emperor's sons. On attaining manhood they were planted out, as it were, in households of their own. But the Crown Prince had often to attend his father, giving Wu Chao a chance to catch his eye, if she were daring enough to take it. The risks would have daunted a lesser woman. And even supposing Wu Chao were able to attract the Crown Prince, and — what was more doubtful still — contrive an occasion for intimacy with him, and even supposing that such a liaison could be carried on without detection, she would still not be secure in the prospect of enjoying a glittering future, for it was a customary on an emperor's death for all the wives and concubines to be discharged and enter a state of living immolation, with shaven heads, in the walls of a convent. This was a rigidly unalterable law, which it would be sacrilege to break. Wu Chao was therefore gambling dangerously in planning a sexual intrigue with the Crown Prince.

It proved to be a calculated risk. She seduced her quarry with ease. She took a chance afforded by the only possible occasion of privacy — when the prince was relieving himself. According to the traditional version of the story, she offered him a bowl of water with which to wash his hands, and when he apologised for splashing a drop on her face-powder replied, 'Dew from heaven has conferred grace upon this person.' In Chinese, the words conveyed a *double entendre* which amounted to a sexual invitation. The relationship was strengthened by the willingness with which Wu Chao gratified the more esoteric of her lover's perverse lusts. She had taken her first step to supreme power by a means which, albeit obvious and even crude, was extremely serviceable and widely used by the power-women of history. Wu Chao, perhaps, is an extreme case of prostitution for power's sake. But she would never have succeeded in a political world so hostile to women without using every available advantage, including the exploitation of her own body.

Still, when the emperor died, she could not avoid immolation in the convent. It took her seven years' scheming to get out. Immured and isolated, she was no longer directly privy to the intrigues of the palace, but may have been in secret communication with Kao Tsung. She was able to exploit the weakness of the new empress, who, without a man-child of her own, was in perpetual fear of displacement by a more fertile concubine and was therefore willing to encourage her husband in any depravity that would distract him from her rivals. At last, in 650, when Kao Tsung and the empress paid a courtesy visit to the convent, they resolved to procure Wu Chao's release. The empress secretly advised her to let her hair grow and within a few months, she was back in the palace, on the familiar terrain of her most corrupt past success and most spectacular future triumphs. The empress throught she had gained a supporter. In fact she had introduced the deadliest and most desperate of her rivals into the most dangerous place.

Wu Chao trod carefully for most of the first two years of her re-admission to the palace. She knew she was there illictly and on sufferance. Premature offence would cause her permanent downfall. She therefore fawned ingratiatingly on the empress while covertly using all her sexual skills to enslave the emperor to her whims and poison his mind against the empress and the concubines. By 654 she felt strong enough in Kao Tsung's affections to risk an open break with her mistress. In that year she gave birth to a daughter. The empress came to her quarters to visit the child. As soon as the empress left, Wu Chao murdered the infant to whom she had only just given birth by smothering under the covers. There is something admirable in the sort of *sang-froid* that could accomplish such a hideous crime. When the murder was discovered, the inhumanity of Wu Chao went unsuspected — for she had not yet publicly revealed the horrible ruthlessness for which she would later become notorious. Suspicion fell upon the empress, whose jealous temperament was well known. From that moment, Kao Tsung determined to be rid of the empress and elevate Wu Chao in her place.

This was no easy matter. The loyalty of every official, subordinate ruler and subject in the empire would be tested to breaking-point by such an act of sacrilege. It took years of intrigue, and all the political skill of which Wu Chao was capable, to cajole the ministers and great nobles into acceptance of the scheme, or remove those who proved recalcitrant. Wu Chao met formidable opposition, but was able to overcome it because of the fissile nature of the Chinese court in which intrigue was so much a part of the system that no policy, however disreputable, could fail to secure a faction to support it. A course the emperor was known to favour developed a momentum of its own, winning the adherence of anyone who was willing to sacrifice scruples to retain power or obtain promotion. Though all statesmen of eminence and virtue — the 'old school', as it were, of imperial servants whose fortunes and careers were identified with the service and interests of the T'ang dynasty, remained unwavering in their opposition, by 655 Wu Chao had gathered enough support to risk a coup. In November of that year, an imperial decree implicated the empress and Kao Tsung's former favourite among the concubines of the court in an alleged attempt to murder the emperor. A few days later, after the degradation and expulsion of these luckless women, Wu was raised to the rank of empress. The fact that she was ineligible, as a concubine of the previous emperor, was suppressed. So was the fact that her union with Kao Tsung — after she had certainly slept with his father — was incestuous.

The new empress behaved consistently with her background of depravity. Lacking the security that might have come from legitimate power, she attempted to safeguard her precarious eminence by naked terror. The murder of the former empress and favourite concubine were among her first acts. She had them beaten with a hundred blows, and their hands and feet cut off and bound before their mutilated bodies were flung, still conscious, into a brewing vat. 'Now the two witches can get drunk to their bones!' she cried. It took days for them to die. The corpses were further mutilated and finally hacked to pieces. This act of brutality alone was enough to intimidate opposition. Her weak and lecherous husband gladly abandoned the management of business to her, except for periodic, unpredictable returns to the political arena, which were henceforth the only limitations on Wu Chao's authority. She tyrannised the court capriciously, once she had carefully removed the surviving members of the 'old school', and built up a network of clients and kin in almost every position of responsibility. The terror by which she began to rule was gradually supplemented by the grudging admiration her administrative gifts inspired. Her methods were unsentimental but effective.

She suffered fom three sources of discontent which no amount of tyranny or bloodshed could assuage. First, though the running of the empire depended on her, thanks to her *fainéant* husband, she could never be sure that a new palace intrigue or an imperial caprice would not unseat her from her throne: while no legitimacy hallowed her occupancy of it, she resorted to witchcraft and necromancy in her craving for security. Secondly, her husband, to whom she owed everything, remained a constant threat. She was already about thirty years old by the time she came to rule. She could not be sure that her charms would not mature too fast for this fickle philanderer and although she had by then borne him two sons, one of whom had been adopted as crown prince, and was to bear him one or two more, the checkered history of the succession in recent years afforded no certainty that this would ensure her safety. The hostile court annalists who accused her of desiring Kao Tsung's death may not be far from the mark. She was certainly quick to encompass the death of any girl pretty or crafty enough to threaten to supplant her. Her own niece, for example, threatened to alienate Kao Tsung's affections with a beauty and charm that echoed Wu Chao's own: at that time, when the empress was forty-one, such youthful rivalry was intolerable and the niece was poisoned by a clay with which her aunt laced her food. Finally, Wu Chao's insatiable appetite for power could never be satisifed with the mere exercise, the mere usufruct, of it. She wanted to possess it as of right and to bestow it after her death within her own house according to her own wishes. In short, she wanted to be a female emperor — Chinese thought did not admit the concept of a sovereign empress — and to found her own dynasty. Her exemplar, the Empress Lü, in the first century B.C., had attempted a similar programme, but had neither the time nor the skill to achieve it. Wu Chao now aimed not only to emulate, but also to surpass her.

If Wu Chao was a typical power-woman in her use of sex and ruthlessness, she also shared another characteristic of the genre in her deployment of magic. Her superstitious proclivities were nourished to monstrous dimensions by her insecurity and fears, and the nightmares induced by her sense of guilt. She obsessively shunned the place where she had her predecessor so horribly murdered, even to the point of changing the site first of the imperial palace, then even the entire capital. She was afflicted with ghastly apparitions of her victims dripping with blood, and practised every kind of exorcism and counter-magic to expel them, all to no avail. Fearing the murdered women's reincarnation as cats she had every cat in the palace precincts put to death and ordered her victims to be posthumously re-named 'Snake' and 'Owl' in the hope of diverting their reincarnate spirits into the bodies of creatures whom it was customary for everyone to hunt down and kill. She acquired a notoriety for sorcery as a result of her patronage of a Taoist magus, which aroused even the somnolent Kao Tsung to protest. She received critically the advice of statesmen, but was suggestible to fortune-tellers. She needed to exploit every available resource of magic and divination to encourage her in her quest for enduring safety and ultimately for the supreme prize — the emperorship and change of dynasty. She was aided by the fact that court prophecy and augury already before her rise had portended a great mutation in the state and even the sort of hideous inversion of the natural order that could bring a woman to rule. Astrologers interpreted the prominence of Venus as indicating female ascendancy. The common people were said to believe in the replacement of the T'ang dynasty by a woman ruler to be called 'Martial Prince' ('Wu Wang'). And it was claimed that the famous astrologer Yüan T'ien-kang had actually predicted of Wu Chao, when an infant, that she would rule the empire. Beneath the magnificent surface of the Chinese empire, bubbled a seething cauldron of dark and primitive superstitions, which were both a solace and a stimulus to Wu

Chao's febrile and hag-ridden mind.

The force of these obscure prophecies was not of itself sufficient to make men adjust to the idea of a woman ruler. Especially among the Confucian scholar-bureaucrats, without whom no government could rule efficiently, Wu had to project her ambitions with circumspection and skill. She made partisans of the members of this class by lavish patronage of the learned, welding a group of them into a secretariate of her own which kept all government business and palace intrigue under ineluctable surveillance. She attempted to set her own ambitions in a context of enhanced respect for women by introducing the practice of mourning one's mother during one's father's lifetime. She curried favour with the masses by easing fiscal exactions. Though she was an easy prey to every form of mysticism and magic she tried to appease Confucians by discouraging the consecration of temples and convents to esoteric religions.

Ultimately, it was pragmatism that justified her rule. She represented an almost unique source of competence within the imperial family and she was willing to kill or exile anyone who might present a potential alternative. Her

Tzu-Hsi, Empress Dowager of China, 1834-1908. She was the last Chinese Empress and came from a distinguished Manchurian family.

own eldest son, for example, who showed statesmanlike gifts was by the 670s growing into the sort of young man who promised to be an excellent successor to the ageing and ineffectual Kao Tsung. To Wu Chao, who had already probably murdered a daughter and a niece, the elimination even of this splendid youth aroused no moral scruples. In 675, he died so suddenly that the court suspected poisoning. The next eldest of the sons ascribed to Wu Chao — though it is possible that he was an imperial bastard foisted on her for seemliness's sake, now became crown prince. But he too might have been able enough to replace the empress and so was quickly degraded and exiled on a trumped-up charge of conspiracy. His death was procured a few years later. Wu Chao's third son, known to historians as Chung Tsung, was as feeble and talentless as his father and therefore made an acceptable — or at least for the time being tolerable — crown prince for Wu Chao.

She was therefore ready for the death of Kao Tsung, which at last occurred, long expected, on 27th December, 683. In his lifetime, he had been so dominated by his wife that it was natural for him to ordain in his will that she should continue to exercise a close supervision over the government of the empire after his death. He did not envisage a formal regency, but ordered the crown prince to defer to Wu in matters of dispute or doubt. In practice, Wu's hold over the new emperor was vice-like and a system of government that was a regency in effect was accepted at every level of officialdom. Chung Tsung would probably have drifted, happily inert, under his mother's tutelage, much as Kao Tsung had done in his declining years, but for the inruption into the arena of another formidable and ambitious woman, his wife, the Lady Wei. Here was an adversary of Wu Chao's mettle, who tried to knead her malleable husband into some semblance of an emperor in effect. Wu Chao's control of the political world of the palace was, however, now too strongly entrenched to be dislodged even by the most determined newcomer. Hardly a murmur of dissent in the court or the capital was provoked when Wu Chao in defiance of every constitutional convention, deposed her son as unfit for the throne and substituted the even more tractable and submissive youngest son, Jui Tsung. Some vestige of propriety was retained: Wu Chao still did not occupy the emperor's throne in person, but she was now herself a female emperor in all but name, justifying her assumption of all the emperor's duties on the transparent pretext that Jui Tsung suffered a speech impediment that compelled her to step in.

The next five years witnessed the crisis of her career, when her chances of assuming personal sovereignty and of creating a new dynasty were tested by rebellion. The threat of quiescent but ever-simmering hostility might have deterred Wu Chao from taking definitive steps, but open rebellion in fact created just the conditions she needed for success. She was able to suspend every constraint on her tyranny by the plea of emergency. She was given the opportunity to institute a secret police force and inaugurate a reign of terror that consigned thousands of her foes to horrible deaths while it cowed the survivors. But though the outcome of the years of rebellion was favourable to Wu Chao it was a hazardous experience, which her own excesses provoked. There were three main foci of opposition. First, in the central bureaucracy, there were many scholars and administrators, who, owing their offices to Wu Chao, had long been awed by her but whose sense of propriety was offended by female rule. They feared for the future of the empire if Wu Chao's increasingly obvious plans for personal sovereignty should succeed. They resented her savagery and susceptibility to charlatans and magi whose principles were offensive to Confucianism and whose power over the empress menaced the traditional rule of the 'superior men'. Secondly, despite Wu Chao's clever distribution of the fruits of her patronage, there was always a residue of malcontents in the penumbra of government, who, disgraced for corruption or incompetence, transferred to comfortless jobs in uncivilised provinces or otherwise under-employed, were always anxious for any pretext for rebellion: to this 'country party' of embittered desperadoes, Wu Chao's behaviour was a handle for revolt. Finally, the numerous Princes of the T'ang dynasty, who lacked neither the wealth nor the leisure to rebel and who saw themselves as guardians of the imperial dignity transmitted from their ancestors, were apprehensive of Wu Chao's intentions. The role of Dowager Empresses throughout Chinese history had been to intrude their own families into the privileges and functions of the ruling house and sometimes to serve as the catalysts for palace revolutions that aimed to change the dynasty. Such had been the plan of Wu Chao's closest precursor, the Empress Lü. Not only by the favour she showed to her own house in the distribution of offices, but also in the excess of zeal with which she embraced and promoted the cult of her own ancestors, Wu Chao was evidently preparing her own family for the collective deification that signified hereditary guardianship of the imperial dignity.

Together, these three sources of opposition that threatened the empress might have constituted a formidable combination. Fortunately for Wu

Chao, they remained divided. In particular, the conspiracies and rebellions of these years hesitated between the various alternatives with which it might be possible to supplant Wu Chao — some, for instance, favouring a restoration of Chung Tsung, others an unshackling of Jui Tsung, others a bogus pretender who arose in the provinces and preposterously challenged the empress with an army of ill assorted raggle-taggle. The palace conspirators were sniffed out by her internal espionage service, the provincial *hobéreaux* and malcontents defeated in the field, the Princes poleaxed by their own timidity and imcompetence. By the end of 688, Wu Chao had trounced all-comers. Her enemies were crushed. She was in a position to do with the empire as she pleased.

By now, she had already clad herself round with a thick hedging of divinity. Had she wished to choose the safest or the wisest course she could have continued to exercise an effective autocracy behind the mask of legitimacy presented by the placid Jui Tsung. But she yearned for more than power, of which by now it seems that even she was sated. She now wished to turn herself into a demigod. In 688 she erected a temple to the Wu ancestors, equal in size and splendour to that of the imperial family. Later that year a magic stone was reported as having appeared in the bed of the Lo River bearing the inscription, 'The Holy Mother has come among men to rule with everlasting prosperity.' The river was declared sacred and Wu Chao began to call herself 'Holy Mother Divine Imperial One.' In 689, the Holy Mother opened the year with a ceremony which accorded to her own Wu father the same degree of worship as was normally reserved for the founders of the T'ang dynasty. She then extracted from the Buddhist authorities a proclamation of her status as a reincarnation of Maitreya, sent by Yama to rule the earth. Propaganda concerning the signs and portents of her emperorship was doubled and redoubled. Later, she was to place the tablets of her own ancestors in the imperial temple, re-build to her own new and ostentatious specifications the most hallowed shrine of antiquity, and create a court ceremonial of greater and more lavish magnificence than had ever before been seen in China. The New Year's Day ceremony for 693, for instance, involved nearly a thousand dancers.

By then, she had achieved the consummation for which she had so devoutly wished, the climax of all her schemes. On 24th September, 690, she was proclaimed Holy and Divine Emperor. The masculine gender of the noun remained immutable even for a female occupant of the throne. In this formal traditonalism the revolution Wu Chao wrought was cloaked. The dynasty of T'ang was declared to be at an end and the new dynasty — to be called Chou from one of the Wu family fiefs — to have begun. Jui Tsung showed his customary prudence and discretion by abdicating: he indeed, had raced with the other courtiers to petition his mother to take the emperorship upon herself. He was rewarded with the title of Imperial Heir. Wu Chao's Wu relations were elevated to princedoms. Never before had the Mandate of Heaven been so outrageously arrogated in defiance of right. Yet not a murmur was raised in protest. Sixty thousand petitioners — virtually the entire Chinese élite — had taken part in the grovelling masquerade of petitioning the Holy Mother to take the step, which everyone knew she was planning in any case. In part, she had terrorised her subjects into submission. In part, her purges and patronage had created an élite of her own making, composed of her clients and creatures. In part, it was straightforward acknowledgement of her outstanding gifts that obliged the political nation to accept her. She was emperor *faute de mieux:* she had liquidated every viable alternative.

Her attainment of personal emperorship, combined perhaps with the mellowing influence of advancing age, brought a change in her character. She had achieved the pinnacle of ambition. The driving force that had engendered within her such cruelty, such savagery and such insecurity now had no *raison d'être* and began to ebb. She seemed comforted and consoled by the specious legitimacy with which she had crowned herself, the trumped-up sanctity she had contrived. The restlessness of earlier years fell from her. She grew tolerant of criticism, though she continued to be capricious and vindictive in dispensing her sanguinary brand of justice. She mitigated the rigours of her secret police. Only in two respects did her old insecurity break through this new serenity. She remained fearful of sorcery and in 693 hurriedly murdered the wife and favourite concubine of her son Jui Tsung on the strength of a rumour that they were practising conjuration against her. She also felt in her heart the fading of her famous looks, which had given her the early opportunities that had launched her political career. She jealously pampered herself with cosmetics and proclaimed her sixty-eighth year, in which she gave herself childish delight by growing two new teeth, 'The Year of Enduring Longevity'. Frenziedly hoarding whatever she retained of youth, she continued, in all probability, to take lovers well into her seventies.

But perhaps the most fortunate beneficiaries of the surprising joviality of her declining years were her two surviving sons, Chung Tsung and Jui

Tsung. Both, as surviving representatives of the T'ang line, and discarded former emperors, were natural rallying-points for the loyalties of her opponents. In view of her unsentimental attitude to the children she had already killed, they were prime candidates for her fatal wrath. Yet her parricides all dated from the time of her rise to power: now that she was on the loftiest plateau of politics she was prepared to show a motherly indulgence hitherto alien to her mental world. Her ferocity to her own family had not sprung from mere inhumanity. She had never seen her children as other than pieces in a political chess-game — a guise in which they once actually appeared to her in a dream. When she had killed them, she had been killing strangers and rivals, not creatures she knew and loved. 'I have a son, but I do not really know him,' she once mused of Jui Tsung. She now repaid her neglect and her earlier crimes by sparing him and Chung Tsung. The brothers, for their part, having picked their careful path till now around the corpses of their kin, were dedicated practitioners of the art of survival, who had perfected their charade of complete submissiveness before their mother, in order to outlive her. In their lonely side-palaces, they nurtured their numerous progeny and befriended generals and ministers against the day when they might re-emerge from seclusion.

If Wu felt enhanced security after assuming her emperor's title, she was perhaps the only person in the court who was not bedevilled by unease. Her usurpation had provided a short-term solution to the problem of the occupancy of the throne, but it had created other problems for the longer term. It was unclear what the change of dynasty really meant. The ambitions of the house of Wu had been titillated without really being gratified. For although the Mandate of Heaven had been declared to have passed from T'ang to Wu, and although Chung Tsung and Ji Tsung had both abjured the name of T'ang in favour of their mother's surname, and although all the other princes of the T'ang line had been pitilessly exterminated (save for a few who escaped detection), and although the ancestral rites in honour of the T'ang had been abandoned, all these changes — dramatic and revolutionary as they were — remained in a sense purely nominal. The former emperor, Jui Tsung, was Wu Chao's heir; his son, in turn, was called 'Imperial Grandson.' The names and ancestor-cult of the ruling house were therefore those of Wu, but the blood was still the blood of the T'ang.

The settlement Wu Chao had enforced thus combined the satisfaction of her own whims with the retention of some comfort for the loyalists. But she had intruded numerous Wu into positions of power and influence which they could only safeguard by effecting a more radical revolution, which would transfer the succession to a nephew or cousin of Wu Chao and obliterate every trace of the T'ang. The dynastic alliances she forced on the two houses, no doubt in the hope of effecting a certain fusion of interest, actually made the situation worse, as it gave some of the T'ang womenfolk, who had Wu children or grandchildren, a reason to ally with the Wu to overturn the existing order and cheat Wu Chao's sons of their right to the succession. Most of what remained of Wu Chao's life and reign was therefore dominated by factional struggles which eventually brought about her downfall.

Moreover, in her old age, she became absurdly susceptible to favourites. Again, this was a result of her attainment of a long-felt want of security. She was now relaxed enough to suspend the sort of anxious discrimination with which fear had formerly inspired her to judge all men. In choosing her favourites, she showed appalling taste. The most notorious was a charlatan known as Hsüeh Huai-i who affected to be a Buddhist sage and holy man. His trade as a peddlar of cosmetic concoctions gave him a background in the kind of specious patter that might impress the empress, who was always interested in magic arts and a keen customer for make-up and aphrodisiacs. Her religious sympathies were mercurial: anything with a mystical touch might attract her and when Hsüeh came into her life her interest in Taoism was waning in favour of Buddhism. She made him a monk to facilitate access to the palace and appointed him to the abbacy of the oldest and most venerated Buddhist shrine in China. Unhappily, he brought the ways of the gutter into the cloister, organising gangs of *soi-disant* monks from among his former cronies of the demi-monde to beat up Taoists, subject tradesmen to extortion and terrorise politicians whom he desired to influence. Wu Chao also confided to him the care of one of her dearest projects, the Ming T'ang, a reconstruction of a fabled temple of antiquity, which was intended to exceed all other temples in magnificence and honour the highest spirits of heaven. It also provided a setting for the most solemn state acts of the divine autocrat. Under Hsüeh's care, the temple was curiously vulnerable to arsonists: it was a natural target for the enemies of Wu Chao but on at least one occasion Hsüeh put it to the torch himself out of pique at some trifling disfavour the empress had shown him.

At length, even Wu Chao tired of his arrogance and indiscretions and had him quietly murdered — allegedly by some of the palace women. But within two years, in 697, she succumbed to the charms of a pair of ne'er-dowells who achieved an ascendancy excelling even that of Hsüeh Huai-i. The brothers Chang were itinerant artists. Her association with Hsüeh must have given the ageing sovereign — now seventy-two years old — a taste for the bizarre. But they were well born and amusing with their cleverly contrived silk clothes and startling make-up, pantomime clowns who could be tolerated as the empress's toys but derided as no possible political threat. At first, court factions almost welcomed them as alternative channels of communication with the empress. Gradually, however, they came to monopolise her company for longer periods. In the periods of illness which began to afflict her in the new century and which by 705 had become frequent and protracted, no one else could gain access to her bedside. They abused their influence in ways characteristic of upstart favourites, to commit vindictive outrages against established members of the élite and secure unmerited offices and corrupt wealth for themselves and their friends. The whole court feared that they might use their uniquely central position in the palace to perpetrate a coup. Indeed, they were almost bound to try some desperate stroke to prolong their influence after Wu Chao's death, for otherwise their own destruction would surely follow. Their rise imperilled Wu Chao's power because it united, as perhaps nothing else could, the factions of T'ang loyalists and Wu revolutionaries in fear and detestation of the upstarts.

As she approached her eighties, Wu Chao faced a formidable coagulation of opposition. Her age and infirmity impaired the efficiency that had always been her greatest asset in securing support. The imminence of her death — as always in any autocratic system — animated the factions whose candidates aspired to replace her. The insecurity of court life led everyone to yearn for change. The pent-up rivalries of the factions, increased by the ambiguous and changeable arrangements she had ordained for the succession, were nearing breaking-point. The tyranny of the favourites united her opponents and impelled them to act.

Not only had she hesitated between bequeathing her throne to her own offspring and her Wu cousins, she had also veered between her two sons, first nominating Jui Tsung as imperial heir, then, in 698, restoring Chung Tsung, who had the support of the majority of legitimists, to the dignity of Crown Prince. This act had been followed by many manifestations of loyalty to Chung Tsung among the people at large. Only in the name of the Crown Prince, for example, had it been possible to raise adequate levies against the barbarians. In 701, Wu Chao received petitions from the highest levels of the bureaucracy in favour of her abdication on Chung Tsung's behalf. It is a sign of her mellowing that her reactions were dismissive but bloodless.

By 705, her eightieth year, Wu had achieved a kind of contentment. No unfulfilled ambition was left to her. When at last her enemies screwed their courage to the sticking-point and launched a coup on 20th February, 705, she was ready to abdicate and retire. Her first minister led the conspirators who suborned a reliable core of the palace garrison and induced the impressionable Chung Tsung, perhaps by trickery, to accompany them in arms to the presence of the empress. In an antechamber, her favourites were discovered and decapitated. 'Well, well: the two boys have been killed,' remarked Wu Chao on emerging from her apartments. She did not even mourn them: they had engaged her ravenous sensuality, (and even she must by now have outgrown that) and perhaps also her sense of humour, but they had never really alienated her affections. She accepted the conspirators' demand for her abdication with mingled scorn and relief. She turned her back on them and retired to her bed to sleep — perhaps for the first time since she had plunged into the troubled world of Chinese politics sixty-seven years before — with utter serenity.

It was with utter serenity that over the next few months she watched the factions who had united to overthrow her prepare to tear themselves apart. She took only a detached interest in affairs, enjoying the gingerish courtesies paid to her by Chung Tsung who visited her with every honour and deference two or three times a month. She was treated with all the reverence owed to a retired emperor, and even with a certain measure of affection. The whole ruling class and to some extent the whole empire, had long lived in awe of her but remained beholden to her for having survived and, in many cases, having prospered. One of her old ministers, who had joined the plot to unseat her, yet wept openly to see her go. 'I served the empress for many years,' he said, 'and cannot but feel pity to see this change. Although the deposition of the former sovereign was a meritorious act, it truly moves my heart.' Wu Chao was spared the spectacle of the bloodshed and anarchy that followed from her retirement. For on 16th December, 705, China's Holy Mother and only female emperor, who by turns had terrorised and saved the state, died peacefully of old age.

Like all power-women, she was reviled by male historians, who heaped upon her so many infamies that it is impossible to distinguish the true from the false. Her extraordinary career of bloodshed may be less a sign of the strength of her character than of the mendacity of her detractors. But even if we grant that she was typical of the syndrome commonly ascribed to power-women — of necromancy, depravity and blood-lust — it is at least possible to rebut the common slander that she ruled badly, neglected affairs or ignored the welfare of the empire. In all these respects, she was a successful ruler, who left China strengthened against the barbarians, staffed with well chosen administrators — even her enemies allow her that — and with most public works in good repair, despite economic difficulties. She was an excellent manageress of the state. Indeed, it was only by dint of surpassing competence that she was able to exact obedience to herself, smack against every convention to which the Chinese elite was heir. Her achievement went beyond even this. She so warped men's expectations that female imitators arose without compunction within the imperial family, both in the generation after her death and at intervals throughout the rest of Chinese history, to try to re-construct her career. None ever succeeded. To be oft imitated and never equalled is a mark of a unique kind of greatness.

Her failures were characteristically feminine. As with Placidia and Amalasuntha, her political talent was most obvious during her rise to power, she was less effective — because more complacent — as emperor than she had been as empress. Her attempt to found a new dynasty was abortive. After her death the state dissolved into civil war and interecine bloodshed through rivalries she herself had created. Thus she exacted a posthumous revenge, worthy of the passions that had governed her own life. Her legacy was destructive. She vindicated male fears of power wielded by her sex.

CHAPTER FOUR

Irene of Byzantium

'The sight of a woman is like a poisoned arrow. The longer the poison remains in the soul, the more corruption it produces.' On the surface, Byzantium was among the most misogynistic of civilisations, as Antiochus's characteristation of woman suggests. The Byzantines — scrupulous guardians of classical learning in their fastness of Constantinople throughout the dark ages — inherited much of the woman-hatred of the Athenians, to which their ferociously austere Christianity and susceptibility to monastic influence added a deep suspicion of sex and marriage. This in its turn generated more anti-feminist literature. Women were seen literally as the devil's agents, diabolically manipulated to entrap men in relationships that imperilled their souls. Women encouraged illicit sex, violent passions, wasteful expenditure and frivolous vanity. Almost daily for hundreds of years Byzantines were bombarded from the pulpit with images of feminine depravity, as in the sermon which on one occasion in the sixth century drove the haughty empress Theodora from the cathedral of Constantinople, shamed and angry at the preacher's condemnation of excessive cosmetics and monstrous hair-dos. Monks struggling to stay celibate or keep silent condemned women for promiscuity and chatter. Patricians striving to conserve family fortunes excoriated them for their expensive tastes. A male society that prized, at different extremes, togas and hair-shirts, naturally deprecated the scented silks, dripping jewels and embroidered purple in which women dressed. Their face-paint, powders and rouges were only the outward signs of a deeply dissembling nature. They were 'daughters of mendacity'. According to St John Chrysostom, women possessed nothing that could commend them to men except their sexual serviceability; hence God, compensating for their despicable characters, gave them the sexual allure without which they would never get husbands. According to John Moschus, the only good woman was one who never showed her face. Contact with the Muslim Arabs from the seventh century reinforced this attitude and consigned many ordinary Byzantine women to conditions approaching domestic purdah.

Even women admitted many of the common prejudices against their own sex. One of the most cultured and enlightened women in all the thousand years of Byzantine history was the writer — and political aspirant — Anna Comnena, an emperor's daughter, privileged with every social and educational advantage. Yet, though she led a relatively emancipated life — much freer, certainly, than that of most Byzantine women — and although she actually nourished ambitions of political influence, even perhaps of supreme power, for herself, she could not escape from anti-feminist stereotypes in her own voluminous writings. No doubt subconsciously exempting herself, she limits the sphere of women's competence to household management and mourning, for which their natural lachrymosity equips them. In general, Anna regards her own sex as unfit for power. Women are 'leaky vessels', incapable of refraining from domestic gossip, let alone guarding secrets of state. Her father, she admits, was culpable for entrusting the regency of the empire at one point to a woman.

When Anna does praise her fellow-women, it is for one of two virtues: modesty, which is an abnegation of femininity, or manliness, which is a substitute for it. Thus her mother's political prominence is justified by her manliness 'like that woman sung of by Solomon in Proverbs... She showed no womanly feelings'. 'She had a manly mind' and on the death of her beloved husband 'especially did she play the man' by stifling her grief and staunching her tears. As for her modesty,

> for the most part she was a stay-at-home, and did her own works, I mean the reading of books of the Saints... and when she had to make herself public, for some urgent need as empress, she was filled with modesty and straightaway blossomed out in a blush on her cheeks.

Anna then tells the story of a female pupil of Pythagoras who was said to have replied to a compliment on the beauty of her forearm, 'But it is not public.' 'So the empress my mother,' Anna went on,

> image of dignity, repose of holiness, not only disliked to make her forearm and her glance public, but did not even wish to let her voice be heard in unfamiliar ears, such a great and wonderful portent of modesty was she.

The shadow of the purdah fell even in the palace, the most liberal of Byzantine milieux.

Anna's treatment of women was broadly consistent with that of male authors. The only women who attracted praise in early Byzantine literature were those who suppressed their femininity — the 'disguised' transvestites, the female saints. Most of them, on experiencing a 'conversion' — that is, a reform of their lives along saintly lines — changed not only their apparel but also their personality and even their name. Some of them even destroyed the female characteristics of their bodies. Of Hilary, who became Hilarion, we are told, 'Her breasts were not like the breasts of other women. On account of her ascetic practices they were withered; and she was not subjected to the illness of women, for God had ordained it this way.' Anastasia the patrician had 'breasts like dead leaves'. The saintly princess Apollinaria, who became Dorotheus, reduced her once beautiful body 'to the semblance of a tortoise's skin'. Moschos praised a nun who had gouged out her own eyes because they had inspired men with lust. These women could gain merit by posing as men — generally as eunuchs — even at the cost of inviting scandalous embarrassments, like Matrona/Babylas, who became a novice in a male monastery, and Marina/Marinos, who was accused of paternity in the case of an innkeeper's daughter casually impregnated by a soldier. It was not of course the dissimulation that was meritorious, but the genuine masculinity attained or signified thereby. Apollinaria was endued by Christ with 'manly virtue'. Eugenia/Eugenios was 'a virgin in body and a man at heart'.

When, from about the tenth century onwards, writers began to see women as taking a distinctively feminine path to sainthood, it was still by way of another kind of disguise — the modesty of the cloister, the purdah or the veil. Athanasia of Egina turned marriage from a snare for the soul into a means of salvation — but only by converting her husband and persuading him to enter a monastery. Thomais of Lesbos, 'a woman in body, but more manly than men in her virtue and austerity', remained a virgin in marriage and was a martyr to her husband's petty retaliations. It was only gradually that a thoroughly feminine life, encompassing marriage and childbirth, was acknowledged (as one author put it) 'as no impediment to attaining God's glory'. But even the sources most sympathetic to women — two funeral orations by sons in praise of their mothers, one of the eighth and one of the eleventh century, — reflect many of the ingrained prejudices. Theoctista, born in Constantinople in about 740, dressed demurely, ate sparingly, averted her eyes from comic entertainments and shunned sorcery. She devoted herself to good works, wifely submissiveness and household management. But even she was dissatisfied with this blameless — indeed, exemplary — life and decided to retire from marriage, disperse the household and become a nun. She draws praise from her own son for the 'diamond heart' with which she drove away her own children. Three hundred years later, Theodota, mother of the accomplished littérateur and administrator, Michael Psellus, led a broadly similar, if slightly more emancipated life. Her husband's retiring nature forced upon her a paternal role in the home and frustrated her ambition to retire to a convent. But the death of her daughter, when the rest of her family were grown up, freed her to consummate a lifelong ambition, for which she had prepared by years of austerity and charity and countless visits to the houses of monks and nuns. Cropped and veiled, she retired from the world, refraining at first from taking final vows because of a conviction of her own unworthiness but eventually succumbing to the will of Providence before dying, admired and venerated by the whole of Constantinople.

Above Byzantine society perched an ideal of womanhood, like an idol on a totem pole. The Blessed Virgin Mary was the empire's special patroness and unrivalled cynosure. Almost more than a demigod, she was a virtual deity, the *Theotokos,* Mother of God, on whose intercession in countless crises the survival of the empire was genuinely believed to depend. If the Byzantines' warped view of women was redeemed by one example it was that of this supremely redeeming woman. But the example of Our Lady was by definition unique. Its social significance consisted in its inimitability. The imperfections of women were cast in sharper relief against the contrast of this unattainable ideal, whose perfection was granted in despite of womanhood, not because of it.

In such a cultural climate, where even praise of women despoiled them of their femininity, it is amazing that women should ever have attained political authority. Yet powerful empresses who influenced events through pressurising their husbands were common. Female regencies occurred frequently. There were three instances of women who attained sovereign power in their own right and one — only one — of a woman who, in a career curiously parallel to that of Wu Chao — seized the emperorship for herself. The comparison with China suggests why this may have been so. The Byzantine and Chinese states present remarkable points of similarity. Both saw themselves as universal empires, divinely ordained. Both were ruled by mandarin scholar-élites whose assumptions were all hostile to the idea of female rulers. But both were centred on elaborate courts in which purposeful women could inveigle their way into power. In Byzantium, as in China, the laws of succession to the imperial throne were rudimentary, perhaps because it was assumed that God would always provide an emperor. The hereditary principle was broadly observed, but, as in China, there were no precise rules and intrigue within the palace or pronunciamientos by the troops were, as in China, the main determinants of the descent of the sceptre. The field was open to tough dowagers or elder sisters to exercise regencies and to domineering wives to control weak emperors.

Moreover, Byzantine empresses and princesses were on the whole better equipped and better placed than those of China for entry into the political arena. Byzantine emperors were rigidly monogamous: re-marriage was discouraged even in widowerhood. The competition within any one generation of palace women was therefore always much more restricted than in China. Educational opportunities for women of the imperial family were far more plentiful. Anna Comnena knew more of history and rhetoric than many members of the scholar-bureaucrat class, and loved to show off her mastery of this virile curriculum in her writings. Anna Dalassena, her grandmother, was celebrated for her intellectual attainments. Irene, her

Annunciation. Byzantine.

mother, could converse with the learned and profit from books. Wu Chao's problem of penetrating the conceptual world of the élite that served her and resisting the superstitious hocus-pocus of quack politicians did not necessarily afflict all the imperial womenfolk of Byzantium. And the environment of a Byzantine palace was much less restrictive than that of the court of the Son of Heaven. Vast, convoluted, sacred and eunuch-bound, it was nevertheless open to the world. The Gynaeceum or women's quarters, was no seraglio, though it was under women's management and could enclose all manner of secrets, like the heretical patriarch who was kept hidden there by the palace women for twelve years in the sixth century, or as when the evil empress Theophano hid her husband's assassins there in the tenth. The world flowed into the Gynaeceum — husbands, relatives, soldiers, lovers, petitioners, priests, administrators and ambassadors. And the women had frequent occasion to sally. A new empress made a ceremonial outing to the baths after her marriage. She had to be present at all court festivities. She participated in the reception of guests of both sexes on Palm Sunday. She presented herself to the people for regular acclamations at the Hippodrome. And she had her own public procession to church every Sunday. Within the limits prescribed by conventional modesty, the role of a Byzantine empress was thus a relatively wordly one.

Moreover, the empress shared some part of the numinous aura of her husband. This is surprising in view of the random or capricious methods employed in the selection of an empress. It was usual when an imperial heir was in want of a bride to send officials all over the empire to gather the most beautiful girls from good families. The candidates were then assembled in Constantinople for an extraordinary bridal beauty-contest more appropriate in a fairy tale than to a serious matter of state. But this was the accepted custom: it evoked no surprise and, apparently, little embarrassment. When this method was not employed, an imperial match might be effected for the sake of dynastic alliance, but it was as likely to be a love-match with a girl almost literally plucked off the street. The most famous or infamous of all Byzantine empresses, Theodora, wife of Justinian, was raised to the purple from the murkiest of backgrounds as an actress and a whore by the heir's whim. But once chosen, by whatever means, the empresses were exalted to a pinnacle of sanctity and splendour which conferred, if not an actual share of sovereignty, a place on its very threshold. Theodora, whom Constantinopolitan society despised in her teens as a trollop, was depicted in her maturity in the mosaics of Ravenna as a semi-devine creature, with a symbolic stature exceeding that of all men except her husband, with whom she was depicted equal, and a halo about her head. Like the emperor, the empress was called 'God-crowned' and was independently acclaimed by the people. She received the same form of obeisance from subordinates — prostration and kissing of the feet and knees. It was acknowledged in the written tradition on conventions of government that in default of an emperor, an empress could nominate a successor. Thus, in sum, Byzantine empresses had more opportunity to exercise power than their Chinese counterparts, and their political interventions were more readily intelligible to their servants and subjects.

Yet the only woman to take full advantage of the chances the Byzantine system afforded to female ambition was the Empress Irene, who ruled the empire from 780 to 802 and from 797, like Wu Chao, called herself 'emperor', using the masculine noun in token of her explicit claim to unqualified sovereignty. Her career was one of the most spectacular in the entire history of power-women, and yet also at the same time in many ways one of the most representative. She arose in a real sense from nowhere, for she was an orphan of whose antecedents and early life nothing is known. But in Byzantium, obscurity was not necessarily a bar to greatness. Peasants could and did become emperors. A prostitute could become an empress. For Irene, whether she was chosen by means of one of the 'beauty contests' from which imperial consorts emerged or by some even more whimsical caprice, ascent to the throne presented no insuperable obstacle. That she came from Athens is known; that she was of surpassing beauty may be inferred. That her wedding to Leo, son of the Emperor Constantine V, must have impressed her with its sumptuous festivities and heady solemnities may be guessed. The obscure orphan had been clothed in cloth of gold and adorned with jewels by an emperor's hand. She had been crowned by the Patriarch. And she had been adored by all the noblemen and high functionaries of the empire. It was a dazzling introduction to the world of power to which she devoted the rest of her life.

But she could hardly have succeeded in gaining a monopoly of sovereignty had not the circumstances of Byzantine history at the time themselves been extraordinary. Religion was always the key factor in Byzantine politics. The entire society was a prey to religious obsessions. Constantinople was populated by amateur theologues. From the fifth century, when Gregory of Nyssa joked about the ubiquity of theological disputation in Constantinople, even in the market-stalls and over the shop-counters, every doctrinal fashion, every dogmatic fad inspired conflicting passions that divided the city and the empire into factions. In Irene's day, the empire was convulsed by one of the deepest and most violent controversies of all. Many attempts have been made to explain the modalities of the Iconoclastic conflict, as it was called. Most modern explanations have tried to find some obvious class interest at the basis of the divisions between the iconoclasts and their enemies, but the evidence does not support them. The configurations of the struggle cut across class lines. To assume that religion was merely a pretext, or provided a language, for the elaboration of conflicts that were social or economic in origin is to misunderstand the nature of Byzantine society, which was primarily characterised by intense religiosity. Byzantines' primary aims were genuinely spiritual, where ours are material. In a sense, religious issues were implicitly political, because the whole Byzantine polity was built on religious foundations. Byzantium justified its claim to universal empire by reference to the state's role as the guardian of Christian verity. Orthodox observance was to Byzantium what the propitiation of the spirits is to a primitive society: upon it the success and even the survival of the state depended. As one of the fundamental law-codes of the empire put it. 'We are aware that Our State is sustained more by religion than by official duties and physical toil and sweat.' To define and teach orthodoxy was the job of the Church. To enforce it was the duty of the emperor.

'It is Our will,' wrote the emperor Justinian in the sixth century, in a law that was transmitted to all his successors,

> that all the peoples who are ruled by the government of Our Clemency shall practise that religion which the holy apostle, Peter, handed down to the Romans... We command that all who keep this law shall embrace the name of Catholic Christians. The rest, however, whom we adjudge mad and demented, shall endure the infamy that belongs to heretical doctrines. Their congregations shall not receive the name of churches, and they shall be smitten first by the vengeance of God and secondly by the justice administered by us and dispensed according to God's will.

This was clear enough in some respects. Dissent was insanity, like opposition in the Soviet Union today. It was also to be treated as a crime against the state. These contradictions are commonly paired by intolerant authorities. But the law left unclear the crucial question of what orthodoxy was, apart from acceptance of the doctrine of the Trinity. The kaleidoscope of 'true' doctrine was re-shaken by every generation, and though its contents always remained the same, they appeared from time to time under the semblance of markedly differing patterns. Patriarchs and emperors themselves frequently held opinions that might subsequently be judged heretical by the theological consensus. And for such a consensus to be established was itself a rare event. The Byzantine hierarchy was repeatedly riven by disputes concerning the nature of the Trinity and, in particular, the nature of Christ. If there was a single thread, a single contrast of fundamental attitudes, that ran through all the frequent differences, it lay in a profound ontological problem that was inherent in Christianity and in Greek thought. As a Greek-speaking Christian people, the Byzantines could hardly escape this heritage. We meet this problem already in the pages of the Gospel, in the story of the Greeks who wanted to 'see' Jesus, and in the subtle abstractions of St. John. It is the problem of the relationship of *esse* and *percipi*, of symbol and reality, of apparent form signifying being. Greek philosophy was a sparring-ring of empiricists, who believed that knowledge was verifiable through the evidence of the senses, and metaphysicians who distrusted appearances and believed that reality was reflected at best imperfectly by its perceived symbols. In an extreme form, this latter approach led to gnosticism, which postulated that matter was unreal, symbols deceptive and knowledge accessible only through initiation into esoteric mysteries. Christiantity, with its mystical tints, its dogmatic defiance of the ordinary canons of epistemology, its peculiar rituals and its unseen God, was highly vulnerable to gnostic infiltration. In the sixth century, for instance, a Byzantine emperor, along with innumerable subjects, fell victim to the heresy that Christ did not 'really' suffer on the Cross but only 'seemed' to suffer: a conclusion which goes a long way to negating the whole point of Christianity and which betrays an obviously gnostic conception of reality. Similarly, from the fifth century, a heresy that infected imperial and patriarchal circles from time to time postulated that Christ was not 'really' human at all, but only divine, or that his nature as man did not 'really' subsist in his incarnate form. Again, gnostic influence was apparent in this doctrine, which captured the allegiance of almost half the empire.

In a sense, the iconoclastic contest of the eighth century prolonged some of the themes of these earlier disputes. The iconoclasts, who denied that Christ and the saints could be worshipped in painted or graven images, stood in a tradition which stretched back through the monophysites to the gnostics. For the basis of their objection to image-worship was not puritanical delicacy or scriptural fundamentalism, but the belief that divine reality could not be captured, as it were, by men's sense-perceptions. Defenders of the use of icons were, of course, not conscious idolaters, but viewed icons as similar to relics: in the holy images, part of the virtue and personality of Christ or the saint resided. It was therefore proper to use them as aids to devotion, to venerate and embrace them, to address prayers to them or through them. The God of the iconoclasts was altogether transcendent, imperceptible, beyond ordinary knowledge. To the iconodules, the whole essence of Christianity was that God had made Himself intelligible to men in concrete images: the incarnate Christ, the Church, the saints, the Holy Icons. Orthodoxy has subsequently vindicated the iconodule point of view — although the persistence of Protestantism in our own world reminds us that there are still Christians for whom esteem for God's images seems idolatrous in the light of their conviction of his transcendence. In the eighth century, the question was an open one.

In trying to understand the force of this theological problem in the Byzantine world, it is helpful to remember that Christianity had undergone a sea-change at the time of its reception as the official religion of the empire. In its origins, Christianity was the faith of the poor and ignorant, the lowest and most under-privileged classes who were indifferent to ontological or epistemological problems. They cared little about the logical consistency of their faith, or the elegance of its scriptures or the compatibility of its teachings with classical philosophy, as long as it satisfied their need for an intelligible God and a hope of salvation. In conquering the empire, however, Christianity had to conquer the élite. It had to become a religion that educated men could respect. It had to master and use the subtle language of the mandarins, with its rich, polysyllabic vocabulary, its nice philosophical distinctions and its word for every abstruse and intractable concept the ancient Greeks had identified. The transmutation was alchemical. In contriving an appeal to intellectuals, Christianity became a religion of a different kind, pre-occupied with philosophical respectability. Influences were introduced from which all the doctinal heresies that troubled the Church for centuries were derived. The iconoclasts were by no means all intellectuals, any more than the Protestants are, but they included some of the spokesmen for the most aggressively intellectual approach to the analysis of Christian faith.

Although no straighforward socio-economic analysis of the parties in the iconoclastic conflict is possible, some broad generalisations are useful. The iconoclasts were mainly easterners: the strictly European lands of the empire remained loyal to the images. The mob of Constantinople was fickle and happy to join in orgies of image-breaking when the chance arose, but in general, the urban lower classes and peasantry liked the comforting intelligibility of sanctity embodied in material, tangible form. Iconoclasm tended to be a mandarin creed; the ill-educated, like Irene herself, tended to favour icons. And significantly, icons seem to have been a special predilection of women. Monks and nuns, who in their scores of thousands constituted a numerically strong as well as an enormously powerful and rich minority in the empire, were the most zealous defenders of the images, of which they were often custodians and whose sacral properties added substantially to the monastic armoury of influence. Indeed, some historians have seen the iconoclastic movement as a secular attack on the privileges and wealth of the monasteries. In any event, when the imperial dynasty was seduced into support for iconoclasm, there was a vast body of opinion prepared to support any reversal of policy in the direction of orthodoxy. It was this that gave Irene her chance to win acceptance, in spite of her sex, as the arbiter of the empire. She rose as champion of the images.

Iconoclasm began in 726, when the emperor Leo III ordered the destruction of one of Byzantium's most celebrated statues of Christ. But popular resistance moderated imperial zeal and it was not until the second half of the century, under the emperor Constantine V, that destruction of icons was unremittingly pursued as a prime objective of imperial policy. A council of 754 cursed 'the evil art of the painters' and forbade images to be made or kept: these were to be civil offences. The jurisdiction under which offenders fell would be that of the emperor, not the ecclesiastical courts. Relics were included along with icons in the anathemas. A wave of destruction and vilification of images followed. In churches they were replaced with innocuous nature paintings; churches became 'fruit stores and aviaries'. Iconodulists were exposed to persecution and a campaign of terror. Famous painters had their hands chopped off. Constantine V took the opportunity to profit from the dispersion and dispossession of monastic communities who clung to the old ways.

But the religious conservatives of the empire nourished hopes of the princess Irene. Like all other important people in the empire, she had been obliged to submit to an oath against the icons exacted by Constantine V. But her secret sympathy with iconodulism was widely suspected. Until the death of Constantine V she had to tread warily, but when her husband came to the throne in 775, a less rigid and vigilant regime set in, thanks to her influence, and she was able to begin to build up a party of supporters of a return to the veneration of the icons. She still had to exercise caution: the emperor sent armed guards to search the premises of the Gynaeceum for images — and on one occasion a pair was discovered. In April, 780, several of Irene's accomplices were put to the torture on suspicion of harbouring images. Had the emperor not died in September of that year, the persecution might have touched Irene herself.

In fact, however, her husband's death unmuzzled her and enabled her to emerge as the leader of the iconodulists. This was a double stroke of good luck. It gave her a chance of power, which she now exercised as regent for her infant son, Constantine VI. And it ensured that the monks and a great part of the clergy would fawn on her as the defender of orthodoxy. Her ruthlessness, her crimes and her power-lust were overlooked by the clerical makers of the historical record. Her alleged piety, selflessness and wisdom fill their pages. Yet though there is no reason to doubt the sincerity of her devotion to images, it is apparent that the praise of her admirers was overdrawn. She was as amoral a politician as any of her fellow power-women. She had to be in order to rid her administration of the determined iconoclasts who held office under her husband. There were male rivals — the late emperor's brothers — to dispose of: she forced them to take holy orders, thereby excluding themselves from any claim to the throne. And, gradually at first, she purged, disgraced or killed the elder statesmen and replaced them with creatures she could trust.

After two or three years of power she began to restore the old devotions in public rites. She took back to the churches of their shrines some of the most famous of the relics which the depredations of the previous regime had removed. She went in procession to the cathedral to return the virgin's crown filched by her husband. She ceremoniously replaced relics which had been miraculously recovered after Constantine V had cast them into the sea. In 784 she removed from office the iconoclastic patriarch who had served the image-breakers' ends and placed a secretary of her own, a layman and a client, on the patriarchal throne. And in 786 she moved to complete the iconodulist revolution by summoning a council to re-define orthodoxy along lines — she presumed — to be dictated by herself. In the event, she was sadly disabused. She had hurried too recklessly, with insufficient preparations, and reckoned without the army's hostility to a woman who was doing all she could to reverse the policies of the revered commander, Constantine V. Troops burst into the chamber where the bishops were debating and ejected Irene's partisans at sword-point. They may well have intended to carry out a putsch. But Irene escaped and managed to rally the empire by contriving a war-scare and packing the recalcitrant soldiers off to the front. It was a narrowly fought day. Irene's plans had suffered a temporary setback. But she emerged wiser and perhaps stronger. The following year, by convening the council in a provincial town, she was able to avoid a repetition of the debacle. The religious settlement of Constantine V was completely overturned by the new council. The icons were resurrected to their former glory. The iconoclasts became in their turn the victims of anathema. The monks were triumphant. And Irene was acclaimed as 'the Christ-supporting empress.'

In some respects, this moment marked the zenith of her life. So far, she had executed only quiet outrages in pursuit of her aims. No scandal marred her achievement. Her pose as Christian champion was artfully sustained. Henceforth, however, success seems to have completed her corruption. Exposure to absolute power, and awareness of the vicious responses required to keep it in a society profoundly prejudiced against women rulers, filled her with a revulsion against all the standards conventionally expected of her sex. She resolved to put womanliness aside and beat men in the power-struggles of Byzantium with their own methods. She gloried in the 'masculine spirit' attributed to her by her propagandists. She came to see her own son as a political enemy. Constantine VI was a weak and relatively inoffensive boy, brought up in such total subjection to his mother that she might have continued to dominate him well into his adulthood. In 788, despite his own preference for a foreign dynastic marriage, she selected and forced upon him a bride produced by the traditional method of scouring the empire for beauty-contestants. He had submitted without demur. Yet the mere fact that he was growing up made him a threat to his mother's power. Disaffected soldiers and courtiers might use him as a figurehead in an attempted coup. The élite of the empire might feel that a regency was no longer required. The boy himself might come to feel the need to assert his imperial dignity against the humiliating tutelage of his mother.

She kept him on a tight rein, secluded in private quarters of the palace. Access to the emperor's presence was controlled by her. When he was about eighteen, Irene realised that she must make a definitive choice between her son's rights and her own ambition. There was no doubt which she would choose. She rounded up his particular friends, with any enemies of her own who had escaped earlier purges, and put them to the torture on charges of plotting a coup. While they were imprisoned or exiled, the young emperor himself was beaten with rods like a schoolboy and kept closely under guard. The fear of losing her authority had induced horrors of almost paranoid intensity in Irene's mind. Like Wu Chao, she did not share the sophisticated culture of the traditional ruling class and sought counsel outside their ranks from soothsayers and stargazers, who were all too ready to play upon her fears and ambitions to earn their corrupt fees. She was encouraged by prophecies similar to those which had deluded Wu Chao. She was assured that God hated her son; that her orthodoxy had won for her a divine grace that was permissive of any crime committed in God's name, and that the auguries portended her own personal assumption of sovereignty. Immediately after striking her first great blow against her son and his friends, she demanded a new and startling oath of allegiance from the army: 'So long as thou shalt live, we shall never acknowledge thy son as emperor.' It was patently a conscious step towards outright usurpation of the throne.

By thus proclaiming her unnatural ambition, Irene provoked the very reaction she had feared. The army rebelled and insisted on the admission of the legitimate emperor to all his rights. Irene was compelled to submit and see iconoclasts and enemies restored to positions of favour and influence. But four features of her downfall redeemed it from total disaster. In the first place, she escaped with her life: she was thus able to fight another day. Secondly, she retained her dominance over her feeble son: even after the inhuman treatment he had received at her hands, he seems to have cherished a quite unreciprocated affection for her, or perhaps he was merely still cowed. This gave her a chance to recover her ascendancy gradually, and work towards the undoing of her enemies. Thirdly, those enemies were divided among themselves. They included legitimists, whose main concern was no more than to see the rightful emperor on the throne; iconoclasts, who wanted a return to the policies of the previous reign; and partisans of rival pretenders of the imperial family, who were suspicious of the continued favour Irene enjoyed with her son. The clever and malevolent woman was able to play these parties off against one another, feeding their mutual suspicion, dividing them and annihilating them one by one. Finally, she could count on the support of the majority of the inhabitants of the empire whose religious loyalties were iconodulist. From the moment of her removal from political supremacy, Irene plotted her comeback.

Her scheming had, as its main target and focus of enmity, her own son. For he was the greatest single obstacle between herself and the recovery of her power. Her aim was to isolate him from his supporters and to exploit the rivalries of the factions among her enemies to set them against each other. She began by poisoning the emperor's mind against the generals who had carried out the coup against her. This was relatively easily done, as they had already given ample evidence of their dangerous posture towards the civil power in the unseating of Irene. The degradation and judicial blinding of prominent army men alienated the young emperor from the affections of the army, who had been the instrument of his ascent to power. Next, Irene convinced Constantine of the threat from other male members of the imperial family, who in consequence suffered blinding or the excision of their tongues — with the object of incapacitating them for the role of rival emperors — at the young man's command. By these means, Irene set her foes at loggerheads.

Having isolated her son, she sought a pretext for his overthrow. Given the priorities of Byzantine politics, this had to be religious. Young Constantine, who had never been enthusiastic about his mother's choice of a wife, conceived a guilty passion for a lady of the court, which Irene, anxious for his disgrace, was happy to encourage. When in 795, Constantine forced his wife into a convent and went through a form of marriage with his paramour, the whole church was scandalised. Monks and patriarchs upbraided the emperor with outspoken self-righteousness which Irene secretly stimulated. Finding it impossible to appease this clerical indignation, Constantine began to renew the secularist policies and anti-monastic purges that had bedevilled his grandfather's reign. This not only outraged the devout, but also raised anew the spectre of iconoclasm. Constantine was seen as an oppressor of the Church and fautor of heretics, in contrast to the alleged piety and orthodoxy of his mother. Monks blabbered darkly of blood-letting and martyrdom in confrontation of the 'new Herod'. In secret intrigues at court, Irene rallied the partisans of the church and the images to launch a counter-coup and restore her power.

She suborned members of the imperial guard by bribery. In the emperor's entourage, she could rely on the assistance of some of the eunuchs, who had enjoyed unparalleled favour as a class during her régime and longed for a restoration of their prosperity. In the spring of 797 the emperor's absence from the capital, preparing a campaign against the Arabs, gave her a chance to complete her preparations. She tricked him into returning without his troops to cope with a feigned emergency. On 17th July, the conspirators sprang their trap, ambushing the emperor and attempting to seize his person, while Irene with a few reliable soldiers took possession of the palace and the organs of government. But the ambush was bungled; Constantine escaped and fled towards the nearest units of the army. All seemed lost. For a moment — but only for a moment — Irene contemplated capitulation. Yet it would have been out of character for her to admit defeat. No woman ever rose to power in a man's world by weakness. She recovered her nerve and hazarded a typically bold stroke. She warned her fellow-conspirators that she would denounce them all in the event of failure. Confronted with the stark choice, effectively between success and death, they somehow managed to salvage their tottering scheme when it already seemed too late. At the second attempt, Constantine was seized and brought back to the palace as Irene's prisoner.

With unsentimental efficiency, Irene ordered the blinding of the son who had indulged her so much. It was an unmotherly act. But it was consistent with the utterly selfish political expediency that power-women have to practise to succeed. She proclaimed herself emperor in her own right — 'great *Basileus* and *Autocrator*'. Like Wu Chao in China, she had to style herself with a masculine name because of the conceptual absurdity of a female sovereign, for which the Greek language had no word. She appeared attired in the personal regalia of the emperor, which she had not dared to don in the days of her regency, to receive the acclamations of the crowd.

This unique revolution was not achieved without inspiring qualms. Even the adulatory clerical chroniclers felt an inkling of horror at the contemplation of Irene's deeds. The sun was said to have been blotted out by cloud at the moment of the emperor's blinding and to have foreborne to shine for seventeen days. Some annalists tried to exonerate Irene by claiming falsely that she was ignorant of the outrage. In western Europe, where the authority of Byzantium was not acknowledged but where the superior dignity of the emperor enjoyed respect, Irene was not accepted as a true emperor. In distant Aachen, Charlemagne planned to take the title of emperor for himelf, at least in temporary trust while Irene's usurpation lasted. In a sense, without Irene, Charlemagne's imperial coronation in 800 would have been unthinkable. Yet within the boundaries of Byzantine territory, there was surprisingly little resistance to the usurpation. Like Wu

The Empress Theodora, wife of Justinian I, Eastern Roman Emperor. She rose from being born a bear-trainer's daughter to the most powerful position in the Empire of Justinian I. She is known to have caused the death of many hundreds of people.

Chao, Irene had demonstrated her claim to the throne pragmatically. Her opponents were cowed. And it was better to have a woman as emperor than an iconoclast. The servile support of the monks, the *faute de mieux* acceptance of the iconodulists were sufficient for the time being to keep Irene on the throne.

She was not destined for a long tenure of power, such as Wu Chao had enjoyed. The religious divisions which had brought her to the throne were still lively enough to unseat her. She began resolutely, disgracing, killing or exiling the surviving princes of the imperial family. At the same time she took more positive measures to secure her popularity, remitting taxes and distributing doles to the poor. Her propaganda machine was already well oiled. Iconodulist preachers and writers were ready to lavish any praise upon her, irrespective of her merits. She bolstered her reputation with the opinion-makers by lavish endowments to monasteries and to the shrines of the holy icons. But success had come too late for her. She was already growing old. And, like so many power-women, her lust for authority ebbed once she held it in her grasp and the days of intrigue and anticipation were over. She was content to leave the administration to the eunuchs. She toyed dreamily with the idea of alliance with Charlemagne — perhaps to be cemented by a marriage between the rival emperors of the east and the west and the restoration of the vanished unity of the old Roman world. But this hopelessly unrealistic scheme shows how her ambition was casting around desperately for some worthy object, now that her heart's desire had been attained.

Thus when the end came, she was hardly inclined to fight it. Just as Wu Chao's undoing had been the odium inspired at court by her favourites, so Irene's reign was threatened by the irksome rule of the eunuchs, whom all parties resented. In the palace, a coalition gradually formed out of a combination between great nobles, who detested the favour shown to upstarts, and iconoclasts, who viewed the resurrection of the images with abhorrence. It was an esoteric conspiracy. The ordinary people remained loyal to the female emperor, from whose rule they had benefited enormously through the remission of their taxes and the restitution of their benign icons. But when the plotters struck, Irene no longer cared enough to appeal over their heads to the people. At the time, she was holidaying in the resort of Eleutherion, where she loved to spend as much time as possible. The duties of government were being discharged by the eunuch Aëtius, who was widely suspected of harbouring his own designs upon the throne. As Irene aged and sickened, the palace was a prey to rumours about the succession, in the absence of any obvious heir. The soldiers who joined in the coup at Constantinople may have believed that it was only directed against Aëtius. Certainly, the conspirators showed them forged letters, purporting to come from Irene herself, authorising action which was represented as intended to forestall a possible usurpation of authority by the eunuch. Meanwhile, however, a detachment of the conspirators had invaded Irene's holiday palace and taken her into custody. They hurriedly proclaimed as a makeshift emperor the minister of finance, Nicephorus, chosen because he was unacceptable to no faction but blandly inoffensive to all. The monkish party was flabbergasted. 'God in His wisdom — which passes all understanding — let it come to pass to punish the sins of mankind,' said the best of their chroniclers. In any other terms, the fall of an orthodox ruler seemed unintelligible. In return for her life and the promise of comfortable old age, Irene refrained from exploiting her popular support to the discomfiture of the victors. She withdrew from power with a grace she had never shown in getting it. As with Wu Chao, her vanquishers triumphed almost by her sufferance. It was 31st October, 802. Her sole and sovereign reign had lasted barely five years. She had only ten more months to live, spent in insular exile in Prinkipos and Lesbos, amid the pious consolations afforded by her precious icons.

Like Wu Chao, she was emulated but never equalled. Byzantine empresses repeatedly exercised power in traditional ways, but Irene's achievement remained unique. On two occasions in the eleventh century, women wrested sovereign authority: first, the empresses Zoë and Theodora jointly in 1042, and then Theodora solely from 1055 to 1056. But these sisters called themselves 'sovereign empresses', not emperors. Their first reign was conscientiously a caretaker-administration, lasting only a couple of months during a crisis in the succession, while a new emperor was sought. Theodora's brief sole reign, although purposefully undertaken and distinguished by the seventy-year old lady's refusal to associate a man with her as emperor, was loudly resented as unnatural: it was shameful, according to the Patriarch Cerularius, that a woman should rule the empire. Nor was either woman of Irene's mettle. Zoë was a frivolous marionette, easily manipulated by men; Theodora was tough and characterful but too pious to undertake the dirty work inseparable from successful statesmanship in medieval Byzantium. Neither was a power-woman in Irene's class.

It is surprising that Irene's example of female emperorship should have gone unrepeated in the subsequent history of the state. In China, for instance, Wu Chao's example was a perpetual deterrent to would-be imitators, for the historians had heaped every abomination on her name. In Byzantium, on the other hand, Irene was represented *à parti pris* as a glistening paragon of orthodoxy. Her remains were translated, when the orthodox tradition at last triumphed over iconoclasm, to the imperial mausoleum at Constantinople. Anyone consulting the historical record would find that a woman's rule had attracted the highest praise. In reality, however, Irene had been far from successful. Her reign severely dislocated the machinery of the Byzantine state. A generation of instability followed. The office of emperor was tossed around from upstart to upstart and only gradually did the rhythm of dynastic succession re-establish itself. Moreover, Irene's great handiwork, the object of all her policy, the resurrection of the icons, did not survive her. The iconoclastic reaction which followed her reign lasted until 843, when the holy images were finally and definitively restored to veneration under another female regency. After Irene's day, the Byzantine empire was almost uninterruptedly a battleground. Military emergencies became the principal and unremitting pre-occupation of government and for these, whatever women's other accomplishments, female leadership was useless. Even Anna Comnena assures us that no woman would stoop to engage in war: that would stamp her as a barbarian. Thus after her death, Irene's example became partly a snare and partly an irrelevancy. In any case, it was effectively eschewed. In the long run, it did nothing to enhance the reputation of power-women.

To us, it appears at once admirable and terrible. The blinding of her son was unjustifiable by the moral standards of any society and puts her almost on the level of Wu Chao, the murderess of her own children. It is possible to plead reasons of state on both women's behalf. The autocrats of China and Byzantium were regarded by their subjects as genuinely absolute — that is, unconstrained by any of the laws whose infraction they might punish in their subjects — as long as the welfare of the people was served. If one accepts that both women sincerely believed the emperorship was rightly theirs — whether because they were misled by phoney astrologers or merely maddened by their own craze for power — they were therefore acting consistently with the laws and prevailing political philosophies of their times. But their willingness to sacrifice morality for *realpolitik* remains unqualified. If their misdeeds can be exculpated at all, it is simply because they were women. To discard maternal feelings to the point of committing horrible outrages against one's own offspring is the most powerful and explicit rejection of femininity of which a woman is capable. And it was the societies in which they lived that impelled women like Irene and Wu Chao to such extremes. By insisting that masculinity was an essential pre-requisite of sovereignty, they invited their women rulers to make dramatic and bloody renunciations of womanhood. To get a chance of power, the women had to outstrip men in the unfeeling ruthlessness that power-struggles demand. That is why the most vicious and hideous acts of power-women have been called forth in the least emancipated societies. In modern democracies, where prejudice against female politicians is somewhat attenuated, they still have to be tougher than men; but their sacrifices can be less sanguinary, and their moral senses less constrained.

CHAPTER FIVE

Latin Christendom
and the Rise of the Power-Women

Despite the conspicuous positions Wu Chao and Irene occupied in China and Byzantium, the power-woman in modern times, outside primitive societies, has been a western phenomenon. Women rulers — as far as they have occurred at all — have generally governed western countries, or lands to which western culture was exported in the colonial expansion of Europe. The origins of the modern power-woman, like so many features of the modern world, have therefore to be sought in the crucible of the west — that is, in medieval Latin Christendom, the arc of lands washed by the western Mediterranean, Atlantic and North Sea, where prevailed the Christian religion (practised according to the Roman rite) and Latin as a medium of learned communication, for over a thousand years after the disintegration of the Roman empire. During the middle ages, the civilisation of Latin Christendom, although fundamentally hostile to female authority, gradually became accustomed to the exercise of control by women rulers. Fitfully, grudgingly, never with more than reluctant acceptance, men submitted to female regencies and at last to female sovereignty. Yet in contrast with China or Byzantium, female sovereignty in the west, when it was eventually brought to pass, was no one-off experiment: it became rooted as part of the received nature of things. Arguably, but for the achievements of this phase of women's history, power-women might never have been tolerated when democratic societies came, in more recent times, to succeed dynastic ones. The story of how this improbable effect came about is long, checkered and bloody, but lightened and enlivened by the careers of a number of colourful and impressive women.

Women started the middle ages severely encumbered. Their 'press' — their literary image — was thoroughly bad, warped by the celibate distrust of scrupulous church fathers. 'I am not giving permission for a woman to teach or to tell a man what do do,' wrote the Apostle Paul to Timothy, 'A woman ought not to speak, because Adam was formed first and Eve afterwards, and it was not Adam who was led astray but the woman who was led astray and fell into sin. Nevertheless, she will be saved by childbearing, provided she lives a modest life.' Patristic writers took their cue from the apostle. Augustine denied that women bore the image of God. Ambrose advocated the unexceptionable subjection of women to men. The models most writers adopted to express the relationship of woman to man were models of subjection and service. Dominating all men's perceptions of women was the image of Eve, the temptress, man's undoing, of whom — more than of all other creatures who threatened only physical harm — he should be wary. Eve was the prototype of those 'wikked wyves' whose cautionary stories the Wife of Bath had to endure. Women were the 'Devil's gatekeepers', posing permanent peril to men's souls. These images endured throughout the middle ages (as the Wife of Bath's competent struggles against them shows). Even a kind husband in a relatively emancipated late medieval century, the *Menagier de Paris* who has left us the book of household management he wrote for his wife, compares a wife's position in the household to that of a dog. Given that they were both dangerous and inferior, like dogs, it seemed only fitting that they should be kept in their place, as dogs are confined to kennels — like dogs, they could, in their restricted sphere, win affection and even merit. Like dogs, they were lawfully beaten at home. The law encumbered them further, limiting — though never wholly denying — their rights of free disposal of property and free access to the courts.

The problem at its most elementary level was, as the Wife of Bath pointed out, that the image of woman was man-made:

By god, if wommen hadde writen stories
As clerkes han with-inne hir oratories,
They wolde han writen of men more wikkednesse
Than all the mark of Adam may redresse.

The image was further cheapened by the obscene depiction of women, as degraded as on any inner-city news-stand today, on the lintels of brothels and the portals of churches. One can still see the vestiges. A grotesque whore grasps a dildo in a late medieval carving in a Cambridge street; a tarty Magdalen smirks nastily from outside the south transept at pilgrims approaching the shrine of St. James of Compostela. Whether calculated to incite or deter lust, these images are pornographic in the strictest sense. They show women at their most susceptible and most debased.

The Queen of Stephen pleading with the Empress Matilda (1102-1164) for her husband's release — After J. G. Hulck.

Although the ideology of female abasement persisted for a long time, it was vulnerable to practical constraints which gradually emancipated women from the worst rigours of their theoretical inferiority. But in the early middle ages, the examples that were to hand of the practical exercise of power by women were hardly encouraging. The disastrous reigns of Cleopatra, Galla Placidia and Amalasuntha were admonitory beacons, gleaming faintly from a half-forgotten past. There was no tradition of female learning or female solidarity to re-write the record. Amalasuntha's servant, Cassiodorus, had even blackened Placidia's memory in order to make his mistress seem less bad. Among the successor-states of Rome women rulers were shunned after Amalasuntha's time, except in Merovingian Francia, where the iniquities of the queen-regents Fredegund, Brunhild and Balthild only heaped further infamy on the reputation of power-women. They were sexually exploitative viragos. They achieved queenship — in Balthild's case from origins as a slave-girl — by sexual allure: it took no little sexual talent to get and keep a kingly husband in a court which was virtually a brothel and in which the irrefragable sanctity of marriage was a joke. They got their right to rule in their husband's absence or death through an almost magical process whereby part of his virtue was thought to be transmitted by fertile coition. And they asserted that right by 'girding manfully', as the great chronicler of the time, Gregory of Tours, puts it. They affected virility, shed blood freely, were denounced as Jezebels and were toppled from their contentious thrones by emulous men. Brunhild's death — tied to the tail of a mad horse lashed into frenzy — showed how she had forfeited any consideration due to her sex.

It took a long time for the image of female authority to recover respectability in the west. Most of the law-codes of the sub-Roman Germanic kingdoms of western Europe at the start of the Middle Ages mitigated the disfavour shown to women by Roman legists. But all restricted their rights in some respects. The most conservative code was that of the Lombards, which prevailed in northern Italy: here women were kept under the close tutelage of their husbands' kin. But where the Burgundian and Visigothic laws were observed — in Spain and the south of what is now France, women were free to inherit and manage their own lands; they could also share in the administration of family property or, as widows, assume control over it. It was in these same areas of relatively emancipated womanhood that female inheritors first came to exercise major social influence. They also became the earliest nurseries of medieval power-women.

In the tenth century, arguably, the first signs of a revival can be discerned. The fortunes of women marched, in a sense, *pari passu* with the progress of western civilisation generally. The chronic emergencies of the Dark Ages, the times of Moorish, Viking and Magyar invasions, left no room at the top of society for 'civilian', much less womanly, rule. The hour called forth war leaders. But as Europe emerged from that protracted crisis, women were in (or came to occupy) a position from which a bid for power by a woman might have some prospect of success. They were not yet free of thoretical impediments, but seem to have been better able to subvert them in practice. In tenth century Saxony — of whose women the historian Karl Leyser has given us a vivid sketch — 'custom treated female heirs better than the Law', which subjected widows to the guardianship of their husbands' male kin. The critical factor in making women's fortunes in this period was their advantage of greater life expectancy over men. In the family of the emperors of Germany, in the six generations beginning in the mid-ninth century, wives had a three-to-one chance of surviving their husbands; among broods of siblings of the same family, sisters were more than one and a half times more likely to be the last to die than brothers. This pattern was characteristic not only of the imperial house but of the aristocracy generally. It shows that the hazards of war and the feud — incessant drains on aristocratic and royal blood — outweighed those of childbirth. The result was that women occupied a vital point in the transmission of property across the generations — and, concretely, of land, the unique source of all wealth and power in the early middle ages. By outliving their menfolk, they outflanked the hindrances with which property law encumbered them.

Correspondingly, in the same period, we can see the womenfolk of the imperial house grasping at the fringes of power. Bishops were summoned to attend *en masse* when a princess was veiled, much as when a male heir was acclaimed or a prince knighted; the ceremony might be performed by an archbishop, like a royal confirmation or unction. In 995 the Empress Adelheid summoned the bishops of the realm in her own right; in 1005, Queen Kunigunde subscribed an important synodal decree directly after her husband. Elsewhere, obvious prominence and influence was achieved by Queen Aelfthryth of England in the last quarter of the tenth century. In Francia, Hugh Capet's Queen Anne figured in some public acts and exercised something like a brief regency on her husband's death. In Spain, Leon-Castile had a woman to govern it — Queen Elvira, as regent for her nephew — and another woman regent, Teresa, to succeed her for more than a decade from 966. Women were intruding themselves into the ceremonial functions which signified and gave effect to power. It is against this background that we should understand the emergence of the first great power-woman of the high middle ages, Agnes, wife of the emperor Henry III.

Agnes of Poitiers was born in about 1025 or 1026. Her mother, Agnes of Burgundy had brought relatively emancipated, southern ideas on womanhood to the court at Poitiers, where she had exerted considerable influence with Count William V 'the Great' in a period when the fortunes of the Poitevin house were in the ascendant. Though the dynasty was distinguished enough to contract a royal or imperial marriage, little Agnes was orphaned in 1030 and confided to the care of collateral relations, with whom her chances of a brilliant match were slighter. But she was lucky to be the beneficiary of one of the few love-matches to occur at that period among the European ruling élite — for usually the exigencies of inheritance law enforced betrothals in infancy and marriages in the early teens. On a visit to the court of Renard of Burgundy, the future emperor Henry III was captivated by Agnes's beauty and married her in 1043. Thus far, Agnes cuts a typical power-woman figure: her Burgundian background familiarised her with the notion of politically committed feminity; she came from a world in which women often inherited fiefs or administered them in widowhood. She had used her beauty — in the time-honoured manner — to ensnare a man who would introduce her to politically enchanted circles. But Agnes was no Cleopatra. She was charismatic — but the source of her charisma was spiritual. She insisted on an austere wedding, without the usual vulgar junketings. She led a devout, prayerful life reminiscent of Pulcheria's, surrounding herself — increasingly as she grew older — with like-minded noblewomen, forming an intense sorority. She enthralled the great theologue Peter Damian into the most extraordinary adulation. He called her 'the chamber of divine treasure' and wrote to her, in terms which anticipate the most abject courtly love-lyrics of the next century, of how he 'sighs with unfelt sorrows on being parted from my heart' on leaving her. Jean de Fécamp dedicated to her a mystical treatise on the contemplation of God. The Pope likened her to one of the Maries who were the first witnesses of Christ's resurrection.

These remarkable spiritual gifts, however, and her fancy Burgundian feminism, availed little in the cold, virile world of German politics. As recently as 1037, the emperor Conrad II had forbidden women to succeed to feudal inheritances in his dominions. When, on her husband's death in 1056, Agnes became the first German empress to assume the regency, she aroused almost immediate opposition — some principled, some opportunistic. Female administration of lesser fiefs had occurred even in Germany, and even royal female regencies were known further west and further south. But not all Germans were inclined to follow such decadent examples. The Empire was incomparably the most important polity of the day — the super-power *par excellence*. Agnes began well enough, repressing revolts in Flanders, Franconia and Saxony. She fostered the efforts of the monastic order of Cluny to purge the Church of the corrupt and profane influences attracted by ecclesiastical power and wealth. She intervened to resolve a dispute over the Hungarian succession. But she soon showed that she lacked the mettle to rule with the ruthlessness a power-woman needs for success. Exhausted by the problems of controlling such a vast and disparate realm, Agnes, confiding too much in the good faith of the emperor's vassals, devolved jurisdictions and intermediate powers on a dangerously lavish scale into the grasp of ambitious dukes. The great duchies of Swabia, Carinthia and Bavaria, which earlier emperors had struggled to incorporate in the crown, were alienated to usurping hands. The new Duke Otto of Bavaria repaid Agnes's trust by entering a conspiracy to strip her of the regency, in collusion with prince-bishops who detested her policy of ecclesiastical reform. In 1062, the conspirators kidnapped her son, the young emperor, and forced her to abjure her power. She withdrew to a nunnery in Piedmont to devote the rest of her life to her pious priorities and plague correspondents with her unremittingly bitter self-reproaches. She had been a failure and she knew it. Her rule had been almost a vindication of misogyny.

Despite the Empress Agnes's failures, women were asserting themselves as manageresses and administrators, both of nunneries and of secular estates. Nunneries were important to the image of women generally — an antidote to allegations that women were a source of devilry, an answer to imputations that dated back to Eve. Some of the first queens whom we see emerging from anonymity into an important role in the world in the tenth century were imitators of nuns. Queen Mathilda and the Empress Adelheid, for instance, did vicarious penance for their husbands' sins. Mathilda performed acts of remembrance of the dead — a function specifically associated with the religious life. The prayerfulness, alms-giving and cultivation of personal sanctity by these royal women not only mitigated the harshness of life in the dark ages but also made of their lives a kind of married mirroring of monasticism. As well as setting an example by which women's image could be refurbished, the convents offered scope for talented women to exercise managerial arts, sometimes on a large scale. Abbesses of big monasteries often evinced the most startling and creative powers of mind. Hroswitha of Gandersheim was a woman as delightful as she was remarkable, kindling the flame of classical civilisation in the depths of dark-age Germany, writing delicate little comedies in the style of Plautus and Terence with the subject-matter, however, nicely adjusted to a more suitable theme, the praise of chastity. Forceful abbesses like Gerbega of Ödingen could treat with kings on behalf of their houses and win their case.

But secular life was not without opportunities for women to demonstrate their administrative competence. Even before the great open lineage came to displace the nuclear family as the unit of social organisation of the European aristocracy in the twelfth century, the medieval household was a vast and complex affair which it took great skill to run efficiently. Late medieval treatises survive to show us the range of arts involved: an aristocratic estate was not only the power-house from which a lord's authority extended over his tenants and his vassals, it was also a factory in which vast amounts of food and clothing were processed or manufactured and large quantities of manpower deployed. It ingested as well as radiated energy. Poor communications called for meticulous long-term planning. And the mistress's responsibilities extended beyond the walls of the house into the gardens and orchards, the home farm and the dairy. And when the lord was away, the entire management of the estate devolved upon his lady. Every aristocratic wife was accustomed, as it were, to a little regency of her own within her husband's property, even before female regents became common at the apex of society. Indeed, in a natural extension of the civil and common-law principle that a husband's responsibility devolves upon his wife in his absence, the origin of the gradual acceptance of female regencies in the middle ages probably lies. A king's office, in common with other offices, was conceived in the early middle ages as a form of property. It was only logical to treat it in practice in the same way as an aristocratic patrimony.

Wifely tutelage of great estates was common enough. Just about every fief in the French monarchy was governed by a woman at some time or other between the twelfth and fifteenth centuries. Eileen Power has written,

> While the lord was away at court or war, who looked after his
> manor and handed it back again, with all walls in repair, farming

in order and lawsuits fought when he returned? And when the lord got himself taken prisoner, who collected the ransom, squeezing every penny from the estate, bothering archbishops for indulgences, selling the family plate? Or when the lord perchance got killed, who acted as executor of his will and brought up his children? The answer to these questions in nine cases out of ten, is — his wife.

The circumstances in which royal regencies arose were exactly parallel.

In most cases of the substitution of female for male authority, whether in husbandry of an estate or regency over a kingdom, the vacancy — so to speak — arose from war. Thus although war was *par excellence* the activity from which women were by nature generally excluded, and which therefore incapacitated them for one part of a ruler's responsibilities, it nevertheless created certain opportunities for women. It was not unusual for women to acquire war experience under siege. Countess Matilda of Tuscany — a magnificent spiritual firebrand of a woman who sometimes sallied from her prayers into the battle field — was an excellent siege-captain behind the forbidding walls of her castle at Canossa. El Cid's widow continued to command the defences of Valencia after her husband's death. Alice de Montfort proved a stout garrison chief in her husband's absence. Nicole de la Haie, the 'crone most cunning', tipped the balance of the civil war of 1216 by her stout defence of Lincoln Castle for King John. Joan of Blois, during the Hundred Years' War, defied her own father in defence of one of her husband's castles. These examples could easily be multiplied. The ethos of the female chatelains is best summarised in the words of Alice Knyvet, uttered from the ramparts of her husband's castle to a royal official who had come, on the king's orders, to seize the place:

> I will not leave possession of this castle to die therefore and if ye being to break the peace or make any war to get the place of me, I shall defend me, for liever had I in such wise to die than to be slain when my husband cometh home, for he charged me to keep it.

Against this background, acceptance of female regents was an inexorable process, arising naturally out of analogy between kingdoms and lordships and evolving inevitably from the practical circumstances that thrust women to the fore in defiance of their theoretical inferiority. At one point in the early twelfth century there were female regents in eleven states of Latin Christendom. After the hesitancies of the eleventh century this sudden blossoming was spectacular. The pennants of these female rulers fluttered coquettishly over the tourneys of an increasingly romantic chivalric ethic. The image of woman was being changed — and perhaps even, in some respects, her social position emancipated — by new ideas.

This 'twelfth century female emancipation' did not touch the inequalities women suffered before the law. Indeed, in Germany, it is clear that the privileges men enjoyed as claimants to inherited wealth were being enforced against women with a rigour not discernible, for instance, in the tenth century. Yet there was an important shift of mental emphasis. For the first time, women were attracting images of lordship rather than of service: they were being seen as served rather than serving. This was the achievement of the troubadours, whose patrons were often women. The inversion of the traditional model of women as servants of men was beautifully expressed by Bernard de Ventadour, the most famous of all the troubadours, in lines probably addressed to that most powerful of power-women, Eleanor of Aquitaine:

Donna, vostre sui e serai
Del vostre servizi garnitz,
Vostr'om sui juratz e plevitz,
E vostre m'era des abans.

The language is knightly: the lover is his lady's 'man' 'sworn and pledged' in her 'service' and 'arrayed' to perform it. The troubadours concocted such lines all over western Europe but especially — and originally — in the luxurious and matriarchal courts of southern France and northern Spain, in parts of the world where men of lofty social rank chose to identify themselves by their matronyms and where women presided, sometimes over all the business of great inheritances but always over the elaborate court-games in which 'trials of love' were acted out with the matrons as judges. Beyond the relatively restricted span around the western Mediterranean, where women enjoyed something approaching equality under the law, the powerful ideology of chivalric romance was spread all over Latin Christendom.

The code of courtly love, in which a knight 'served' his (usually married) lady as a vassal serves a lord, and fought for her 'favours' and

Blanche of Castile, 1187-1251, Queen of Louis VIII of France, and niece to King John.

prostrated himself before her in abject longing in a way that reversed, with the mocking force of a gigantic satire, the traditional relationship of women to men, was a product of the sexual tensions of the increasingly complex households where young knights dwelt. In competing for the attention of their lord's wife they were challenging a social order that condemned them to subjection. In response, society rapidly evoked an equivocal code of sexual morality. Amorous encounters in the street or meadow — usually with anonymous 'shepherdesses' who eagerly submitted to knightly embraces — were applauded in verse. But adultery by a lady was the deadliest form of dishonour. Chastity became a characteristically aristocratic virtue. Yet the treason of Guinevere remained the dream of many a young knight. If translated into fact, it could have revolutionary effects within their little worlds.

A woman's verses illustrate this admirably. Marie de France was not a professional poetess, but she wrote sparingly and well for the court of Henry II of England. She captured faithfully, from a female perspective, the spirit of the *trouvères* in her fables and lays. The characteristic themes of the adulterous love of a young knight for his lord's wife, of lust frustrated because of its social ambitions, dominate her poety. Tristram, the hero, is exiled by the jealous King Mark for love of the queen:

> Li reis Mark esteit coroucié
> Vers Tristran son neveu irié.
> De sa terre le congea
> Pur la reine qu'il ama.

Tristram suffered fearful love-pangs:

> Ne vous esmerveilliez néant
> Car qui aime moult lealment
> Moult est dolenz et respensés
> Quant il nen a ses volentés.

Eventually the lovers contrive a reunion with predictable results:

> Dedans le bois celui trouva
> Qui plus l'amoit que rien vivant.
> Entre eus meinent joie moult grant.

The poetess employs irony which in her day was conventional by extolling the mutual 'faithfulness' of this adulterous pair.

If the confections of the troubadours assailed the traditional image of women from one direction, a quite distinct attack was mounted by religious literature, which in the twelfth century promoted the liberation of affective emotions in a sentimental revolution inspired by the tender, loving and essentially feminine figure of the Virgin Mary, as also by a vision of man bereft of *machismo* — and better for it: the vision, that is, of the suffering Christ. The poignant crucifixions created by twelfth century artists open this world for us, as the Christ they nailed with such highly charged realism to their crosses opens his very human embrace. He is a Christ no longer remote, no longer aloof, no longer a cold *pantokrator* sitting in judgement over men. He is one of us, emphatically a man of woman born, sharing with us the experience of the womb and all the mundane horrors that follow. Anselm was one of the most sensitive devotional writers of the age, and he put it like this: 'He entered a mother's womb, was born of woman, nourished with her milk and other human food and — not to mention many other things which seem inconsistent with God's nature — suffered weariness, hunger, thirst, blows, crucifixion and death among robbers.' Naturally, therefore, the context in which twelfth century artists and writers best loved to imagine Christ, after the Crucifixion, was in His mother's arms. Never before had the 'Madonna and Child' motif taken root in western art. Its reception had to await this affective revolution, in which God's real, deep humanity could be heartfelt. Thus the Virgin Mary, the intimate, carnal vessel of God's humanity, became for twelfth century Latin Christendom a patroness as perfect as she had been for Byzantium. But in the process, her image was changed. From the *Theotokos* — almost a goddess herself, staring impassively from numinous icons, she became a real woman, depicted with every nuance of facial emotion that artists who wallowed in sentimental effects could achieve.

Mary seemed to step out of the statues and paintings and prayers to enter men's lives. From the twelfth century, writers began to gather stories of her miracles, in which little graces are lovingly conferred on a personal, human scale to individual suppliants. Her love is just like a woman's — it embraces sinners out of an entirely subjective type of concern. She rescues a drowning priest on his way to an amorous assignation or a thief who is lawfully hanged but had revered her even at the height of his crimes. She is even capable of feminine jealousy — spiriting away from his honeymoon bed a devotee who had broken tryst with her by marrying. The new honour and veneration in which Our Lady was held in the twelfth century benefited her entire sex for centuries thereafter.

> Our Blessed Lady bereth the name
> Of all women wher that they go,

as the slightly later English poem of *The Nut Brown Maid* neatly put it.

But perhaps as much from the assertion of the troubadour-image of womanhood, or the influence of the new cult of the Virgin Mary, women were liberated in the twelfth century by their access to education. This was a period in which letters as well as arms were an increasingly important part of statesmanship. Neither was a traditional part of women's equipment, but educational opportunities at least seem to have multiplied for women of high social rank at the time and literacy became a not infrequent female attainment. Marie de France was only one of a *nouvelle vague* of female littérateurs. Perhaps the greatest of them was Heloise, paramour and wife of Abelard before her enforced retirement to a convent of which she became abbess. Her letters have been ascribed to male authorship, but the case for their authenticity remains convincing. They constitute one of the most original works of literary genius of all times. Heloise propounds an entirely novel idea of love — novel, that is, for the time but familiar to us because the power of Heloise's creativity has captured the mainstream of western culture so that we have taken over her conception and made it our own. In reply to Abelard's conventional lamentations on a past he evidently regrets because of the burden of sinfulness he feels, Heloise regards their love, albeit technically illicit, as sanctified by the sincerity of their emotions. She cannot bring herself to the *de rigueur* responses, — shame, contrition, penance — which were thought to be necessary for salvation, because in her heart she cannot acknowledge the sinfulness of what she has done. She glories, where Abelard merely feels guilty. She loves on, unregretting.

Of course, there had been isolated female luminaries before, especially, as we have mentioned, during the renaissance of the tenth century. But in the twelfth century, while still flinging up individuals of genius like Heloise, women as a class were making great eductional progress. Nunneries and unaided autodidacticism were no longer the only outlets open to them. Abelard first seduced Heloise during the lessons he was employed to give her. Few girls can have had such expert schooling, but mastery of letters was coming to be considered a normal accomplishment in the *haut monde*. A heroine of Robert of Blois in the thirteenth century

> Knew well how to play chess and board games,
> To read romances, tell tales and
> Sing songs — all things a well bred
> Lady ought to know.

Many great women read their own psalters — some of which, lavishly illuminated, have survived, like those of Queen Margaret of Scotland, Countess Matilda of Tuscany and Judith of Flanders.

Perhaps the greatest of all medieval theologians, Peter Lombard, reflected the twelfth century emancipation of women when he reversed the traditional interpretation of the story of Adam's rib — which had seemed to earlier generations to confirm women's status as the second sex, formed for man's sake to do him service. God did not make woman, the Lombard said, from man's head, for she was not intended to be his ruler, nor from his feet, for she was not meant to be his slave, but from his side, to signify her status as fellow and friend. André le Chapelain — writing, it must be admitted, *à parti pris* since a patroness paid his keep — expressed a similar idea even more graphically, using the images of courtly love, which was indulged as a game and a cult in the court of Blois where he lived and worked:

> It is evident — and clearly enough, to my mind — that men are nothing. They are incapable even of drinking from the source of all worth unless they are led there by women. At all events, since women are the origin and cause of all that is good, and since God has privileged them so highly, it follows that they should behave in such a way that the virtue of men who do good under their inspiration should in turn arouse others to do the same. If their radiance illumines no man, they are like a light under a bushel, which neither atrracts nor pursues. Thus it is manifest that each man must strive to serve ladies, so that he may be enlightened by their grace. And the ladies must do their best to harness the hearts of good men for good deeds and must honour good men for their virtue's sake. For all the good men do in their lives is done for the love of ladies, to enlist their praise and display their favours, without which nothing is achieved in this life that is worthy of praise.

If in the late eleventh century female rulers multiplied, in the twelfth and thirteenth they positively pullulated. With one or two exceptions, they ruled only as regents or custodians or guardians of their realms, not normally as sovereigns. The outstanding exception was Doña Urraca, titular sovereign of León and Castile from 1109 to 1126. Prior to her accession, this kingdom had only once experienced female rule — a spell of regency during a king's minority in the 960s and 970s. But the law in general was sympathetic to female inheritance of property, which was normally understood to include offices. Nor did the Visigothic laws, from which those of León-Castile were derived, distinguish the royal patrimony from other types of property. Thus Urraca encountered little opposition to the advancement of her claims. But, on the other hand, her pretensions to the thrones of other, more conservative kingdoms of the Iberian peninusula were violenty rebuffed. Even within León-Castile, the custom was generally preferred, which prevailed in the other peninsular kingdoms, of confiding the government to a husband or son when a woman inherited. A similar practice for the avoidance of female rule can be observed in the kingdom of Jerusalem: when Queen Sybilla inherited the crown in 1186 it was the husband she took, Guy of Lusignan, who became king, in both name and deed. The unacceptability of female sovereignty in England was amply demonstrated by the rejection of the Empress Matilda in favour of Stephen of Blois in 1135 — and this in spite of the fact that Stephen's claim to the throne came through a female line. Yet when Matilda was able to offer her son as an alternative candidate, his sex made him universally acceptable. If, however, the power-women of the twelfth century did not succeed in acclimatising their age to the notion of women as sovereigns, the authority they exercised short of full sovereignty was no less real for that. Their sheer number is impressive as is their geographical spread over every part of Latin Christendom from the Atlantic to the Levant. A few examples must do duty for all of them.

Eleanor of Aquitaine, in a life that lasted for nearly three quarters of a century experienced every department of political life, but only ruled a kingdom for a relatively brief period from 1191 to 1198 when her son Richard I was fighting in the Holy Land or languishing in an Austrian prison. She performed with great credit and an energy suited to the emergency. 'Eleanor by the wrath of God Queen of the English' her documents proclaimed her. The unusual and sonorous style was well chosen. She successfully contended with the rivals who hoped to profit from

Richard's absence — the ambitious Prince John and rapacious King Philip Augustus of France. She forestalled attack by fortifying Richard's border castles. She travelled tirelessly, despite her advanced years, and wheedled affirmations of loyalty from all her son's important vassals. And when a ransom of 150,000 silver marks was demanded for the king's release from confinement, she raised this unprecedented sum and saw it — in person — safely delivered to its destination. In short, hers was one of the most politically flawless regencies in history. It reflected arts she had developed over many years — first as heiress of the greatest fief in Christendom, the duchy of Aquitaine, then as consort to the Kings, first of France, then of England. Her first marriage she contracted as an act of political sagacity, to safeguard the duchy she had only just acquired, but she conserved considerable independence from her husband. She regarded the marriage as an equal partnership and herself virtually as a queen in her own right — for the Aquitanians traditionally regarded themselves as a 'nation' and their territory as a 'monarchy'. Her dominions were in fact more extensive and more wealthy than those of the king her husband. Fittingly, therefore, she played an influential part in the government of the Franco-Aquitanian state she had helped to create. Indeed, her independence was such that, when it suited her, she had her union with the French king dissolved — probably by agreement but almost certainly on her initiative — and made a daring re-marriage to Henry of Anjou, a young Adonis ten years her junior. She used her legendary beauty — she was the favourite subject of the troubadours — to good effect in her relations with men, but her choice of Henry was no feminine caprice. It was not his youth or good looks but his political destiny that attracted her. With him she created an Angevin empire that dwarfed and almost surrounded her former husband's relatively paltry dominions. But not even in this second marriage would she sacrifice her independence. In 1171 she led her sons in a rebellion against her husband. She was beaten, and tardily reconciled; but she had shown in that audacious act the ruthless determination that was to make her an extraordinarily successful power-woman when the exile of Richard I at last gave her an opportunity to wield untrammelled authority.

A more representative — because less spectacular — power-woman was Melisende, Queen of Jerusalem, a product of that displaced troubadour society, the colonial world of Levantine Outremer. The crusaders shocked the Muslim writer, Usamah, by the licence they allowed their womenfolk and the public activities in which 'Frankish' women engaged. The early queens of the crusader realm were never formally associated with the Government, though periodic interventions in dynastic politics, diplomatic negotiations and the raising of troops gave them opportunities to make their presence felt, until in the 1120s Melisende necessarily became heiress presumptive to the crown in the absence of any obvious male heir. It was not yet possible, however, that a woman should succeed in her own right. Melisende was therefore acknowledged only as joint-heir with the husband she took in 1129, Fulk of Anjou. In the early years of their reign, her husband completely eclipsed her. Her name scarcely appears in the records of the time but she was deliberately thrust into the background by Fulk. Towards the mid-1130's an event occurred which gave her an opportunity to break this unwelcome confinement. Her husband, allegedly suspecting her of a chivalresque liaison with the greatest of his vassals, provoked a war with her partisans among the magnates. The inconclusive outcome enabled Melisende to insist on stringent peace-terms, which included her re-admission to the inner councils of the kingdom. Therefore, as the Hierosolomitan historian William of Tyre wrote, Fulk 'never tried to initiate anything, even in trivial matters, without her foreknowledge'.

For the rest of Fulk's life, she was formally associated in all his acts, though it is impossible to say how far she prevailed in the making of policy. Her husband's death in 1134 left her with an unquestioned right to administer the kingdom, in trust for and in association with her thirteen year-old son, Baldwin. She was effectively regent. All royal powers were concentrated exclusively in her hands. But she was not sovereign in her own right: Baldwin's name, with hers, headed all her documents. Only during his minority would she be able to exact regal obedience. It was not the throne itself but only the management of the kingdom which, as William of Tyre said, 'corresponded to her by inheritance.' This obnubilated authority, however, was insufficient to satisfy her. Like most power-women she had steeled herself for politics to the point where a share of power only whetted her appetite for absolute control. She aspired to usurp her son's position and concentrate all the rights of the crown solely in her own hands. Thus in 1145 she neglected to celebrate the attainment of his majority in due fashion and showed no sign of complying with custom by yielding power to him. On the contrary, she dealt with him as Fulk of Anjou had formerly dealt with her, manœuvring him out of every place of influence, omitting his name from public acts. By 1152 his resentment had reached the point where he complained to the high court of the kingdom that his mother would not let him rule and demanded that the realm be divided between mother and son. The nature and duration of this division are uncertain; it was an expedient only briefly tolerated, for the kingdom of Jerusalem was under constant threat from the revanchism of its Muslim neighbours and any protracted disunity might be fatal. Melisende had powerful supporters, especially in the moiety of the kingdom she was alotted in the south. She had been an efficient administrator while Baldwin was growing up and the partisans of pragmatism rallied to her banner, much as the mandarins had swallowed their distaste and accepted Wu Chao. Legitimacy, however, ensured that Baldwin should command the greater support and it required only a brief campaign for him to overwhelm his mother's army, seize her territory and besiege her in the cramped confines of the Tower of David in Jerusalem. The success of his coup, despite the unfilial animosity with which he had challenged his mother in war, brought neither indignities of any description nor even a total political eclipse for Melisende. Like Wu Chao and Irene, she continued to enjoy the respect of the son of whom she had made a political adversary. She occupied an honoured place as one of his closest advisers until her death in 1161.

Melisende had demonstrated considerable resources of character, exceptional determination and sagacity in intrigue. But the period of her ascendancy was disastrous for the kingdom of Jerusalem. It brought irreversible Muslim successes, procured by the genius of the atabeg Zangi — himself rumoured to be the offspring of a western virago, the Margravine Ida of Austria (who, it was said, took the field with the crusaders but was captured and immured in a harem). Zangi and his successors wrested great tracts of crusader territory under cover of the divisions with which Melisende had troubled her realm. Jerusalem would never again experiment with the divisive and disastrous rule of a woman. Dowagers were excluded from future regencies. When in 1186 a woman actually inherited the crown, her husand was effectively elevated to rule in her stead.

It is remarkable that as time went on power-women seem to have got more feminine. The chivalric image of woman was no doubt responsible for this. Once women were esteemed for their womanly qualities, the necessity to ape men became less marked. Metaphors of virility, of course, continued to be ascribed to power-women. The late middle ages occasionally threw up 'transvestite' heroines in male guise, like Joan of Arc — throwbacks to the types extolled, as we saw, in early Byzantine literature. But the image a power-woman might choose to project of herself in the thirteenth century was as likely to be of beauty, elegance and civility as of the affected martial prowess of an ersatz male. The seal of the most renowned woman of that century, Blanche of Castile, demonstrates this to perfection. Her willowy figure, depicted full length, face outwards, is all sinuous, seductive curves — at once lissom and voluptuous. Even in the clumsy wax impression, she comes across as a ravishing beauty, swathed in tactile, sensuous fabrics that excite uncomplicated admiration. Yet this was a woman who, without sacrifice of femininity, and without recourse to any of the crude expedients or ruthless cruelties demanded of her predecessors by the adverse circumstances in which their political careers were made, ruled France for a total of thirteen years in two widely separated spells, and exercised enormous influence over the political fortunes of two generations.

She was born in Palencia on 4th March, 1188, and selected by Eleanor of Aquitaine, whose grand-daughter she was, to be the bride of the future King of France. In conformity with the custom of the time, she was brought up in the household of her spouse's family, but never lost touch with Castile or the close ties of affection that bound her to her Castilian kin. At the court of France, she was educated alongside her betrothed and was lucky to have one of the outstanding scholars of the day, Amaury of Bène, as her tutor. Under his guidance she became an accomplished pupil, endued with considerable rhetorical flair. In adult life she took a hand in the composition of much of her official correspondence, conversed with prelates and ambassadors on terms of intellectual equality and had a love of scholarly debate. In short, she talked and wrote the language of the mandarins — a redoubtable advantage in an increasingly bureaucratic age. On one famous occasion in 1240, she presided with much relish over a formal disputation between the leading Christian and Jewish scholars of Paris concerning the authenticity of the Talmud. Her interventions in the argument — in the interests of strict logic and fair debate — were uniformly felicitous. Probably no earlier power-woman could have held her own in such company on such a subject with such skill.

But her education did not turn her into a sexless intellectual. She retained the passions and intuitions typical of a woman. At the age of twelve, when she was already a child-bride, and when princesses were supposed to behave as adults, St Hugh of Lincoln found her in a fit of childish melancholy, streaming with mute tears. She would neither explain her grief nor accept consolation from anybody, but the saint took her aside for a heart-to-heart which was eventually effective since thenceforth, according to Hugh's hagiographer 'her looks and heart were of the happiest'. Still, her passionate nature endured. When, for example, her father-in-law failed to succour her husband with money and reinforcements during one of his campaigns against the English, she threatened to give her own children in pledge to raise the sums required. When the husband with whom she had grown up and whom she had come to love died in 1226, she might have killed herself on the spot on hearing the news if not restrained by her entourage. When her eldest son, whom she loved 'more than all else in life' married, she surrendered to feminine envy: according to the Sieur de Joinville, author of one of the most intimate and curious royal biographies of the middle ages, 'The Queen Blanche would not suffer more than she could help that her son bear his wife company except it be at night when he did go to bed with her' and the young wife is said to have exclaimed to Blanche on her bed of sickness, 'Alack! You will not suffer me living or dead to see my lord.' Some contemporaries felt that Blanche let her femininity influence her politics. Matthew Paris, the English monk-chronicler, whose nation was inimical to France and whose opinion was therefore partisan, denounced her as 'hot-headed by nature with womanish impetuosity.' In fact, her temperament was complex and if politics could make her fiery, religion could make her meek. She was lavish in charity, even by the standards of her age. Her special devotion was for the most austere of the religious orders, the Cistercians, to whom she commended herself on her deathbed, although she was susceptible to the pleasures of splendour, inducing, for instance, episcopal disapproval of the lavish style in which she once proposed to go on pilgrimage, or delighting to bestow costly croziers of delicate magnificence on favoured abbots and abbesses. Yet, despite the secular emphasis of her life and the absorbing extent of her political pre-occupations, she did find the time and the grace to radiate a certain spirituality. She gave birth to a brood of heroes and saints. Her royal crusader son, Louis IX, was canonised primarily, perhaps, in recognition of his achievements in holy war, but her daughter Isabella was a saint of more conventional cast, who had to be induced to eat by promises that her mother would give more charity to the poor. She was 'mirror of innocence, model of penitence, rose of patience, lily of chastity, fountain of mercy,' according to her first biographer.

In a political sense, Blanche made a brilliant impression on her age. Her reputation as a power-woman who not only gained power but knew how to use it equals that even of her extraordinary grandmother, Eleanor of Aquitaine. She was much favoured by circumstances. Thirteenth-century

France was heir to the rich political legacy bequeathed by Blanche's father-in-law, Philip Augustus, one of the greatest politicians of all time. It would have taken exceptional incompetence to undo the good start that had already been made. Yet Blanche did more than conserve past achievements. She consolidated and extended them. Her first regency — or more strictly guardianship or custodianship of the realm — was assumed on her husband's death in November, 1226, as the old king had wished. It opened purposefully, with the coronation of the young Louis IX being hastened to pre-empt any cavil at the prospect of a child king or woman ruler. For Blanche was well aware that even at this late date there were forces that found female dominance unpalatable. Only a few years before, she and her husband had received letters from noble malcontents in Castile, asking French help to overturn the feminine regency in that country of Blanche's sister, Berenguela. The queen was therefore on the alert for similar misogynistic scruples among the French nobility. Nor were her fears unfounded, for the first serious emergency of her regency occurred within a few months of its inception, when the Count of Brittany, Peter Mauclerc, led an insurrection. Blanche suppressed the rebels, but they planned to oust her by means of a coup — ambushing and kidnapping the young king, in the way Otto of Bavaria had ousted the Empress Agnes. Blanche thwarted them by appealing over the heads of the nobility to the townsmen who spontaneously raised a rough-and-ready militia to rescue the king. This was an act of far-seeing statesmanship: Blanche was harnessing in the service of legitimate authority the new social and political forces — commercial and municipal above all — who would play an increasing role in French history in the coming centuries and whose alliance with the crown would last, almost continuously, until the Revolution of 1789. She continued to cultivate and at times mobilise the towns during the rest of her first period of regency, which was dominated by the rebelliousness of restive magnates. The authority of the king of France in remote feudal principalities, like Brittany in the extreme north or Toulouse in the extreme south, was tenuous; it could be preserved and asserted only with difficulty and danger. Blanche made peace with the Count of Toulouse, who had been at war with the crown for the best part of twenty years, to counter the more imminent threat from Brittany. She gradually whittled away Mauclerc's support among the magnates. Just as she used the townsfolk to fight them, she exploited her beauty to cajole them. In prising the Count of Champagne from Mauclerc's party, she swept him of his feet in a wave of chivalresque sentiment. 'My Lady,' he ended by declaring, 'my heart and arm and all my land are yours to command.' She had detached her adversary's chief ally and ensured the victory of the monarchy by a nice blend of policy and charm.

Blanche duly allowed her son to accede to royal power as he grew up. By the mid-1230's he was exercising authority on his own. But Louis IX continued to seek his mother's counsel and rely on her experience. As Joinville wrote, 'he did all things by the advice of his good mother by whom he was always guided.' In the events of the subsequent decade Blanche's influence continued to be paramount, discernible alike in the energy with which the English invaders were repelled in 1242 or the moderation with which the crown intervened in the wars of the nobles in the south, advancing royal interests in the area by degrees.

But she was yet to be recalled to the principal place in the kingdom for another spell as regent when Louis departed on crusade. He resolved to do so in 1244 on recovering from a sickness that was thought likely to be fatal. Blanche felt she had recovered her son only to lose him again. As he took the cross, witnesses observed in her 'as much affliction as had she seen him dead.' But despite her efforts to dissuade him he would not be deflected from fulfilling his vow. In 1247 he departed, entrusting the kingdom to be cared for by her, as that of Richard I had been cared for by her grandmother. 'Mother most sweet,' he said,

> by that allegiance that you owe me, I bid you return henceforth. I leave my three children for your wards. I leave this realm of France to you to govern it. Truly I know that they well guarded and it well governed be.

Blanche's mastery of policy in her second regency was, if anything, even more brilliant than in her first. It was no mean feat to keep the royal patrimony together amid competition from emulous members of the dynasty and feudatories always eager to usurp what they could. In 1249 Blanche, in one of her most important acts, completed the absorption of the midi into the French state by claiming the County of Toulouse, on the old count's death, for her absent son, Alphonse. She had made possible this immeasurable extension of the ruling dynasty's power by the terms of earlier agreements she had concluded with the Toulousain ruler, whereby Alphonse would marry the count's heiress, whose rights would be transferred to her husband. Here Blanche was serving the interests of her country rather than her sex. It would have been consistent with the customs of Toulouse for the heiress to succeed in her own right alone. Indeed, the subordinate nobles of Toulouse would have preferred such a course of events and resented the sleight-of-hand by which Blanche foisted her son upon them. But by acting with characteristic energy to make her claim and enforce it, Blanche secured the county. As a result, the kingdom of France assumed more closely the shape and appearance of the modern French state. The process by which France grew from a relatively small heartland in the north to occupy the whole western salient of continental Europe from the English Channel to the Mediterranean had been carried forward in an important respect. The outlet to the warmth and wealth of the south, through Mediterranean ports, which French kings had always craved, was at last assured.

Blanche was to die only three years after this achievement, but not before carrying out a characteristic last gesture. In freeing the imprisoned serfs of Orly, whom the wordly monks of the local abbey had gaoled for failure to pay extortionate tallage, she went to the prison in person and smashed the bolts with a cudgel. For a sixty-four year-old woman, it was a remarkably assertive act. Denying usurped authority, liberating the poor, acting in person — every aspect of the affair was representative of longstanding themes in her work. She did not live to see her beloved son return from crusade. But when she died in November, 1252, she could take comfort from the evidence of political success with which she was surrounded. 'The realm', on the other hand, as even her critic, Matthew Paris, acknowledged, 'was inconsolable.'

The passing of a power-woman of proven success and admitted renown must have advanced the cause of the sex. In many respects, the remaining centuries of the middle ages represented a downturn in the emancipation of women. The chivalric image of women, in the fourteenth and fifteenth centuries, was subjected to satire and smut. The *fabliaux* — works of popular literature whose heroines were shrews and nymphomaniacs — displaced the troubadour songs and sullied the reputation of the sex. But at the highest levels of politics, women progressed from the mere exercise of regencies or similar offices, like those of Agnes, Eleanor, Melisende and Blanche, to the possession of full personal sovereignty. The age of female regencies was over and the proper era of the 'monstrous regiment' was about to begin.

CHAPTER SIX

The Catholic Queen and the Dawn of 'Monstrous' Rule

If female regencies originated in the feudal law of property administration, female sovereignty was probably an outgrowth of the law of inheritance. It was a relatively short step from the inheritance of other forms of property by women to the transmission of sovereignty to them. Indeed, it was in parts of Europe where the laws on female inheritance were most liberal that the era of power-women dawned. Female sovereignty was also facilitated towards the end of the middle ages by the growth of respect for indefeasibile hereditary right as a means of determining the descent of crowns. Though succession laws everywhere in Christendom gave male heirs priority, it was impossible to deny female heirs any place in an order of succession once the divine right of kings was acknowledged to be conferred by blood-right. Women always had a better chance of power in an hereditary than an elective system of government, until democracy and female emancipation enabled women to contend for chief executive positions in the states of our own times.

Yet it was no easy matter for women to win acceptance as potential sovereigns. The favourable impression made by Blanche of Castile was mitigated by other less successful regents. In 1384, Leonor of Portugal was turned out after only one disastrous year. In the same period Agnes of Austria did little for the meek reputation of her sex by putting 1,000 of her subjects to death at a stroke. And apart from the influence of these bad examples, social and ideological attitudes towards women were anyway less favourable in the fourteenth century than they had been in the thirteenth.

To some extent, at the highest levels of intellect, this was a result of a new reception of classical Greek prejudice by western writers. The renaissance of the high middle ages consisted largely in a re-absorption of much lost Greek learning into mainstream western culture, principally through the medium of Arab learning — itself representative of a culture in which women were hardly emancipated. Even while Blanche of Castile was accomplishing great things for her sex, St Thomas Aquinas was re-writing the basis of western political thought with a copy of Aristotle's *Politics* at his elbow. Thus he was able to fortify the long tradition of clerical hostility to women with Aristotle's convictions of feminine political incapacity. This combination of traditions continued to influence all opinion-makers for the rest of the middle ages. Aristotle, whose monopoly as the source of philosophical orthodoxy was so complete in these centuries that he was referred to as 'The Philosopher' *tout court,* was of almost unquestioned authority. And it was not only the hostility of the *Politics* that afflicted women, but also the pseudo-biological explanation of female inferiority of another text of his that became widely known in this period, *The Generation of Animals.* Nature, according to Aristotle, seeks always to produce a male; only imperfect conditions for procreation vitiate the reproductive act and a defective creature — the female — results.

At a more popular level, the same retreat from emancipation to re-enslavement of women is noticeable after the expansive and generous mood

Reason, Rectitude and Justice appearing to Christine de Pisan (1364-1431) and promising to assist her in writing La Cité des Dames. *From an illumination of the Library of the King of France.*

of the twelfth and thirteenth centuries. In some works, writers fought back on women's behalf against the debasement of the chivalric ideal, as in Martin Le Franc's *Champion des dames,* set to music in the mock-chivalric court of Burgundy. In two seminal works, which formed the starting-point of most late medieval polemics about women, Boccaccio gave rival points of view of equal but opposed extremity. In his *Labyrinth of Love* he grossly libelled the entire sex: it was a work of literary revenge bred of sexual envy, as vehement as Catullus and as wickedly funny as the *Decameron.* But the author thought better of it. In his *Famous Women* he offered a counter-weight in the form of a rather solemn compendium of biographical vignettes of saints and heroines. In the fifteenth century, women had a professional champion of their own sex in the brilliant Christine de Pisan, who made a living in widowhood from her *belles lettres* and has a claim to be reckoned the first blue stocking in history. In Spain, when female sovereignty emerged in the person of Isabella the Catholic in the 1470's, a troubadour revival was in progress. But these isolated and sporadic reactions serve to emphasise that the general tenor of popular prejudice was swinging against women. The ideal of the troubadours, in which woman had been an object of service, was warped by late medieval writers who made her an object of sex. Even noble ladies were put down from their pedestals and put on the level of the courtesans and shepherdesses who had typified the pornography of the twelfth century.

Nothing illustrates this better than the textual history of one of the best-known of love allegories, the *Roman de la Rose.* The first version, written by Guillaume de Lorris early in the thirteenth century, is saturated in the troubadour ethic. The expanded version completed by Jean de Meung at the end of the century inaugurates a new age, in which the same ethic is mocked mercilessly and corrupted shamelessly. In Guillaume's text, the lover encounters Love, to whose service he is bound, dancing in a garden. He meets Love's blessings — Hope, Sweet Thought, Sweet Speech, Sweet Look. After much self-steeling, he purposes to pluck a rose from the Lover with the aid of Bel-Acceuil, son of Courtesy. But now Danger, Ill-of-speech, Fear and Shame intervene. It is time for Venus and Reason to appear on the scene and resolve the issue. Thus far, nothing could be more decorous — one might almost say, more bland, even more conventional. But in the hands of Jean de Meung the rest of the poem becomes a riot of outrage. Most of Meung's additions are excursions — rambling frivolities barely related to the main theme. But the lines which do deal with the conquest of the garden (transformed into a castle) of the roses treat the subject as a crudely erotic burlesque. Venus promises that no woman will be left undebauched. She makes Eros promise that he will strip men of their inhibitions to facilitate the desired outcome. Nature joins the conspiracy, denouncing mankind as the only species of creature to practise sexual continence. Genius is sent to exhort Eros's assault troops with an imprecation of sacrilegious ribaldry. He anathemises virginity and condemns the chaste to hell. Paradise, where the white sheep, led by the Lamb born of Mary, feed on inexhaustible pastures, is reserved for those who obey their sexual instincts. There is evidently nothing subtle about the satire. It relies on the sheer brutality of its inversion of convention for its effect. Genius and Venus fling their torches and set the castle of the roses aflame. Danger and Inhibition flee, the castle falls, and the Lover at last grasps the rose of his choice.

Not content with the grossness of his theme, Meung exploits his ample asides to denigrate women more comprehensively. They are licentious, stupid, stubborn, self-righteous, easily duped (Meung takes advantage of this to give detailed advice on how to deceive two mistresses at once) a prey to their instincts, unreasonable, incorrigible... the deprecatory epithets could be infinitely extended.

It took a subtler satirist, Christine de Pisan herself, to make an adequate reply to the scabrous calumnies of Jean de Meung. In her poetry, Christine uses some of the same imagery to devastatingly different effect:

Ne trop ne peu au cuer me sens frappée
Des dars d'Amour qu'on dit qui font grant guerre
A maintegent, mais ne suis atrappée —
Le Dieu merci! — es las ne en la serre
        Du dieu d'Amours.
Je ne lui fais requestes ne clamours,
Je vif sans lui en plaisance et en joie:
Par amour n'aim, ne amer ne voudroie.

She replies not only to the *Roman de la Rose* but to the entire genre, drawn ultimately from traditional models, in which poets of the time put love-plaints into the mouths of girls. Christine was speaking for her sex against the usurped utterances of men. Her own love poetry, addressed always without sententiousness to her dead husband, is so enchantingly sincere that it defies satire and is impossible to mock. Conveying passion without prurience, she wrote some of the most beautiful and moving love lyrics in the world. She also attacked the excesses of the *Roman de la Rose* directly, in prose and verse, and provides alternative view of women, in her *Cité des Dames, Livre des Trois Vertus* and *Epistre au Dieu d'Amour*. She acknowledges that there are bad women, but defends the merit of the sex. Far from being evil succubi women are the victims, not the instigators, of unhappy affairs. Women should be honoured as mothers, peacemakers and — above all — as sisters of the Blessed Virgin. To besmirch them with the sin of Eve is hypocritical for Adam — says Christine daringly — was just as bad. And the evil men have done throughout history — killing, burning, oppressing and deceiving and, above all, betraying Christ himself — far outweighs that for which women are responsible. Her *coup de grâce* is the same as that of the Wife of Bath. One word, she says, suffices to answer all the infamies heaped on woman's name in literature: it is not women but clerks — men by definition — who have written the books.

A bridge between popular and learned levels of anti-feminism was provided by sermons. An idea of the character of late medieval homiletics on woman can be got from the digests of quotations compiled for popular preachers. These might be compiled, according to the prejudices of the editor, to put women in either a relatively favourable or a relatively unfavourable light, but the great majority are devoted to establishing woman's inferiority to man. Here they merely reflected the balance of the available sources. The unanimity of scripture, patristics and the classics in condemning woman to subjugation limited editors who favoured women to a desperately narrow choice. The late medieval tradition threw up some quaint variants on old themes, such as the suggestion (derived from one of the medieval theologians most highly esteemed in the Renaissance, Nicholas of Lyra) that biblical prohibition of transvestism disqualified women for male roles, or the notion of Duns Scotus that in heaven all women, except for Our Lady, must be transmuted into males. Alongside the perpetuation of images of female subjection, late medieval compilations stress female libido much more than earlier writers. The notion of woman's carnality derived much support in the period from the re-discovery of classical medical writings that claimed, in accordance with a theory of Aristotle's that women, being imperfect, actively seek to perfect themselves through sex.

It is remarkable that a power-woman should have triumphed, to the extent of achieving sovereignty, in a period of such marked anti-feminism, but understandable that it was in Castile, traditionally a kingdom where the law favoured female inheritance, that this consummation was achieved.

From the time of the Visigoths, honours were more easily transmitted to or through women in Spain than in any other part of Christendom. In the thirteenth century, the law codes of Alfonso the Wise, on which all subsequent Castilian law was based, enshrined the principle that a woman could not be deprived of her inheritance by virtue of her sex. It also made it explicit that a woman could succeed to the throne in default of male heirs: Castile's experience with Doña Urraca in the twelfth century was now clearly susceptible of repetition. In Catalonia — always more advanced — women in the late middle ages enjoyed even more favourable rights: it was normal for property to descend through their line. And Aragon — influenced both by Catalonia and Sicily, which had a quiet but persistent record of female regencies — was notorious in the late middle ages for its virile queens. Violante of Hungary, for instance, succeeded in dominating her husband Jaume I, in the mid-thirteenth century — a feat repeated with even greater vigour by her domineering namesake, Violante de Bar, who can almost be said to have ruled Aragon through her relatively pliable consort, John I, in the late fourteenth. Even after his death she continued to wield inordinate influence over her son and grandson.

Despite these preparatory experiences, when a woman at last took supreme power in a peninsular kingdom in her own right it was by accident rather than design. The mid-fifteenth century was a time of magnate revolts against royal authority and of civil war all over western Europe. In Castile, the unprincipled opposition of noble factions against the crown was eager for any champion to act as figurehead to the nobles' rather shabby cause. Their first choice was the king's nephew, the child prince Don Alfonso, whom they elevated in 1468 to a spurious regality, declaring the rightful king deposed. When their nominee embarrassed them by dying a year later with no decisive progress made in the war against the crown, the noble rebels were at something of a loss. They had gone too far for a reconciliation with the king. There were no other male candidates for the crown whose pretensions they could take up in succession to those of Alfonso. They were therefore more or less forced, willy-nilly, to adopt Alfonso's sister, Isabella, as their candidate, *faute de mieux.* It is unthinkable that they should have been driven to the dangerous, even desperate expedient of sponsoring a woman for sovereignty, had they not been *in extremis.*

This Isabella had been born in April, 1451. the messenger who took news of her birth to the city of Segovia was tipped only a third as much as when the birth of her younger brother was announced: there could be no more eloquent measure of the insignificance of a princess, compared with a royal manchild. She was not educated to rule, though she was a king's daughter, but envisaged at her upbringing as a marriageable asset of the royal house. When she was three years old, her father died and she was brought up in relative isolation, far from the political centre of things, in her mother's little provincial court. Her education was neglected. To the end of her life — even after she had taught herself in adulthood — her grasp of Latin was halting. From this untroubled infancy she was suddenly wrenched, before the age of nine, when her brother, King Henry IV, decided to keep her at his own court, where she would be under close surveillance and where the rebellious magnates whose recalcitrance was already making government difficult, could not reach her. Under her brother's tutelage, her life was regulated by the Queen, her sister-in-law, who she hated and abhorred throughout the rest of her life as 'wicked stepmother' figure who had made her life miserable.

The king's fears concerning her potential political importance to the rebels were justified. When civil war broke out openly in 1461, it was provoked by the birth of a daughter to the Queen. Widely impugned as illegitimate, this child provided the pretext for violence sought by the restive noblemen. The king was generally acknowledged to be impotent. His marriage had been fruitless for suspiciously long. His efforts to have the Queen's daughter accepted as his heir were unacceptable to many of his great subjects. Ironically — since it was this party of unreconciled objectors to the king's wishes who later formed the basis of support for Isabella's claim to the crown — one of the most distasteful things about the contentious little princess was her sex. The rebellious magnates atempted to substitute the manchild of the previous monarch first as heir and then — on the grounds that Henry was incapable of discharging his duty — as king.

Hostilities were long and indecisive. Henry made, when losing the war, concessions on which he renegued when he recovered. The outcome was still uncertain when the sudden death of Prince Alfonso thrust Isabella in an unexpectedly prominent position. When the rebel magnates came to her to ask her to take up her dead brother's cause and defy the king to arms, she rushed at the chance of political involvement — less perhaps for the sake of power than for personal reasons. She now had an opportunity of revenge on the queen she hated so much and whom she blamed for all the pain of her childhood. She was still a child: only eighteen years old, and young for her age. She knew nothing of the world she was about to enter so rashly. But she had some of the most experienced politicians in the realm as her partisans, led by the primate of Spain, Archibishop Alonso Carrillo of Toledo. The propaganda issued on her behalf was trenchantly expressed. 'You already know,' she wrote to the municipalities of Castile, 'that from the moment when our Lord disposed otherwise of the death of my lord the king [as she grandiloquently styled her brother Alfonso,] the succession of these kingdoms and lordships of Castile and León belong to me as his rightful heiress and successor.'

After several months more of inconclusive hostilities and insincere negotiations, Isabella's claims seemed to be going by default. Only progress could generate the momentum she needed and no progress was being made. As her chances of getting the throne ebbed, her supporters deserted. With her party shrinking alarmingly, she had to contrive some bold stroke to restore her fortunes. It was probably through the advice of Archbishop Carrillo and her other magnate-counsellors, rather than through any amorous inclination or political wisdom of her own, that she resolved to retrieve her position by the ingenious expedient of marriage to Ferdinand, Prince of Aragon. He was popular in Castile and would make an acceptable consort for a future queen. Isabella took enormous risks in seeking to marry him. She had to act strictly illegally — without the necessary dispensations from the pope and the king in order to complete the union with maximum speed and secrecy. She had to take evasive measures, leading a virtually fugitive life, to escape the king's agents and preserve the liberty of her person, without which she would never have been able to effect the marriage. Ferdinand of Aragon, in his turn, was plunging into a chancy business, linking himself with a princess of shady prospects. But if successful, the marriage could become a great coup for him — opening the great resources of the Castilian crown to exploitation for Aragonese purposes. In 1469, they were married and presented the king and community in Castile with a *fait accompli*. Uncertain how to react, the king wavered; the ruling élite of the realm, perceiving his hesitation, took it as a sign that Isabella's cause was again in the ascendant. The momentum of her rise was recovered.

Her marriage marked not only the resuscitation of her political career but also the start of a love affair with her husband. She had never seen him before. The marriage had been arranged for exclusively political motives on both sides. But Isabella was just emerging from an adolescence which had been sheltered in some ways and extremely precocious and dangerous in another. She was already a romantic, who luxuriated — to judge from her surviving letters — in fairy-tale images of adventure and chivalry. As her prince approached, she waited fervently. When he appeared below her window she was said to have run to see him, calling 'That is he! That is he!' Neither spouse was of much physical charm: Isabella was plain and pouting and tended to fat. Ferdinand was an inelegant youth with a small mouth and eyes and a big head. But he was the object of amorous adoration from his wife. He was incapable of reciprocating: he was an incorrigible philanderer of unlively emotions. But he was attentive, if unaffectionate, and respectful, if unfaithful.

When the old king died in 1474, with the succession issue still unresolved, the royal lovers had differences of their own to sort out before they could confront their enemies and capture the crown. Ferdinand was inclined to claim the throne himself, at his wife's expense. Aragonese law was less indulgent towards the idea of female sovereignty than that of Castile. But Isabella's Castilian partisans resented this foreign attempt to subvert their own customs. And Isabella herself demonstrated her statesmanship — or at least her diplomatic skill, by out-arguing her husband. 'My lord, ' she said to him,

'There is no reason why you should raise these matters. Where there is that conformity which, by God's grace, exists between you and me, there can be no differences. Wherefore, whatever is decided here, you as my husband are still king of Castile, and what you command shall be done in the realm... And as for the governing of these kingdoms we must remember that, if God's will so pleases, the Princess, our daughter, must marry... a foreign prince, who would appropriate for himself the government of these kingdoms and would wish to place the fortresses and royal patrimony in the power of other foreigners of his nation who would not be Castilians, or it could happen that the kingdom would fall into the hands of a race of strangers, which would be a grave charge upon our consciences, a disservice to God and the utter ruin of our successors and our native subjects.'

It was an unanswerable case. Isabella had matured with astonishing rapidity into a skilful politician. Over the next few months she and Ferdinand worked out a political *modus vivendi,* according to which all their acts in the realm of Castile would be considered joint acts. Isabella's sole sovereignty was unimpaired, but in practice her consort was able to partake of a share in it.

Before this delicately balanced arrangement could have a chance to work in practice, Ferdinand and Isabella had literally to conquer their kingdom first from the partisans of the rival pretender, then against the king of Portugal who sought to profit from the divisions of the kingdom to acquire it for himself. It cost them five years of war, and innumerable concessions to a rapacious nobility whose support they had to buy, before they got a practical grip on the whole of the realm. The fact that the reign began in war was in a sense a disadvantage for Isabella. She was confined to a largely exhortatory role, while Ferdinand took pride of place as protagonist in the field and commanded the victorious forces in the decisive battle of the war at Toro in 1476.

By 1479, however, the war was won and the monarchs could feel secure on a throne they shared in amity. The strain of disorder had told so hard upon their weary subjects and had enervated even the rumbustious nobility to such an extent that the times had never been more propitious for the introduction of firm government or its acceptance by the subjects of the crown. Ferdinand and Isabella could rule with an exceptional level of co-operation from their magnates, their towns and — loyal as ever to the monarchy — the church: in short, there was a rallying to royal leadership in the wake of the war of all who were important in the realm.

The king and queen exploited this favourable mood together, ruling in harness with such perfect contrivance that it is impossible in most cases to distinguish Ferdinand's contributions from Isabella's or Isabella's policies from Ferdinand's. At a time when it was usual for monarchs to govern through favourites, it was their secretary's opinion that 'the King's favourite is the Queen and the Queen's is the King' According to one contemporary observer they 'shared a single mind'. According to another, the Italian humanist and Hispanophile, Peter Martyr of Anghiera,

> If ever it was permitted among mortal men to say that one spirit might infuse two bodies, these are two bodies which by one spirit and one will are ruled... They have disposed that the Queen should govern in such a fashion that she shall be seen to govern jointly with her husband.

The monarchs fostered the impression of what they called 'deep love and conformity' between themselves with sedulous care. The annalists of the reign were not permitted to distinguish their strictly political roles. Almost every public instrument of the reign was issued in both names jointly. Technically, Ferdinand's power in Castile was a power of attorney, conferred upon him by his wife. When he acted he therefore bore her *persona*. It was, in other words, only by virtue of Isabella's right that he was empowered to act at all. He would have been within his entitlement had he chosen to rest on his power of attorney and to forbear to refer to his wife thereafter. In practice, however, he never omitted to seek her consent for his own projects. In effect, the association of Ferdinand in her government enhanced rather than diminished Isabella's sovereignty.

This was a dazzling reign, universally acknowleged to be one of the most important of Spanish history and the starting-point of Spain's 'Golden Age' — the century and a half when Spanish hegemony over the western world and cultural superiority were among the most conspicuous features of history. Perhaps the greatest achievements of the reign — considered from the broadest perspective — were the final defeat of the Spanish Moors and the discovery of the New World. In both these connexions, the reality and limits of Isabella's rule can be perceived.

The defeat of the Moors in the War of Granada from 1481 to 1492 was the culmination of a long process of reconquest of peninsular territory by Christian monarchs from Moorish occupants, which had dominated the course of Spanish history since the arrival of the first Moorish invaders and settlers in the eighth century A.D. But the two centuries preceding the reign of Ferdinand and Isabella had seen little progress in the Christian advance. The Moors had been left relatively undisturbed in the mountain fastnesses of their kingdom of Granada, last of the once numerous Moorish states of Spain, in the south-east corner of the peninsula. The Christian states had tolerated this anachronism much in the way China today tolerates Hong Kong: it was idealogically distasteful but commercially profitable. Ferdinand and Isabella, with vast and greedy numbers of followers to reward from the years of civil war in Castile, badly needed a rapid infusion of new resources. Unlike their predecessors, they therefore found it would be profitable to terminate the old understanding with Granada and take the beleaguered kingdom's resources by force. The war actually broke out over trivial border incidents but the Castilian monarchs made it clear that they welcomed the outbreak — 'We take pleasure in what has passed,' they told the pope — as part of their long-term ambition of uprooting the last Moorish presence from Spain. Cupidity, as so often in the history of warfare, was united with righteous zeal, in this case specifically religious inspiration. The Granada War was in the strictest sense of the word a crusade, dignified by the same sort of papal indulgences for participants and paymasters as applied to the medieval holy wars in Palestine. And like most religious violence, that of the Castilian monarchs was intemperate in its ambitions. Ferdinand declared his aims thus:

> With great earnestness we now intend to put ourselves in readiness
> to toil with all our strength for the time when we shall conquer
> that kingdom of Granada and expel from Spain all the enemies of
> the Catholic Faith and dedicate Spain to the service of God.

It was in recognition of their victory in the war that the pope conferred on Ferdinand and Isabella and all their successors the title of 'Catholic King and Queen' by which historians commonly call them, and which Spanish sovereigns have vaunted ever since.

The course of the war was slow but relentless. The Moors of Granada had no conception of the implacable determination with which Ferdinand and Isabella proposed to harry them to their end. After every defeat, they continued to hope for a compromise. Granada was like a bunker seething with rivalries impassioned by despair, which the Christians were able to exploit. Gradually, relentlessly, the Moors were pushed back into their capital, which at last fell, to acclamations and rejoicing throughout Latin Christendom on 2nd January, 1492. Unlike most areas of their activity, the conquest of Granada presented Ferdinand and Isabella with clearly defined and distinct roles. In this enterprise, their conformity was at its height and their parts were complementary. They advanced Castile's cause, as one of their court poets sang, together,

> She with her prayers,
> He with many armed men.

Isabella was happy to defer on military matters. On the one occasion when she ventured a suggestion of her own, she started with a tell-tale *captatio benevolentiae*: 'May your Lordship pardon me for speaking of things which I do not understand...'. But the religious passion to prosecute the war came more from her than from her husband, whose priorities were purely secular.

The king whom Machiavelli hero-worshipped was not the type of man to take material risks for the sake of spiritual gains. And it required all Isabella's influence with her husband to make him commit himself for so many years to a war that was far removed fom Aragonese interests in Italy and the north.

The case of the discovery of the New World shows Isabella in an even more positive light. When Christopher Columbus, as a young, rather bookish adventurer presented himself at the Castilian court in 1486, Isabella was one of the few people on whom he made a favourable impression. The project for which he sought the royal backing appeared madcap. He was an autodidact whose unsystematic cosmographical knowledge was refracted by an undisciplined speculative genius. Following a fantastic labyrinth of error — misreading classical geographers, miscalculating the nature of degrees of longitude, uncritically deploying unreliable information — he had come to the conclusion that the world was much smaller than it really is. Scholars at the time knew the size of the globe roughly correctly: the calculation had first been done by Eratosthenes, and transmitted to later learning by Ptolemy. It should hardly be necessary to refute the persistent but silly myth that Columbus introduced the idea of a round world to his contemporaries and was derided for it: every person of even the most rudimentary education in the fifteenth century knew the world was round; in fact, they tended to exaggerate its roundness, believing it to be a perfect sphere. What was at issue between Columbus and his critics was, fundamentally, the size of the globe. Columbus's underestimate led him to suppose that the western ocean could be traversed by sail, and Asia, a new continent or at least new islands discovered in the process.

In rejecting his ideas the cosmographers of the day were acting prudently. But at Isabella's court there were some who, while deriding his calculations, believed he was worth backing because of the unforeseeable benefits that might accrue from such a westward voyage. We do not know how far Isabella understood the cosmographical arguments, but she seems to have been drawn by the power of Columbus's character — his evident wayward genius, his piety, the fervour of his ideas, the boundlessness of his ambitions. She made, in fact, an intuitive assessment of him — a woman's assessment, outflanking the rational caution of her advisers. It was largely thanks to Isabella's personal will to give his proposals a chance that, after he left the court in January 1492, dejected, having received the formal rebuttal of the experts, he was dramatically overtaken on the road by a royal messenger and recalled. The effects which stemmed from the voyage he launched under royal patronage a few months later hardly need emphasis. The 'Enterprise of the Indies' — as the Castilian involvement in the process of discovery of the New World was know at the time — remained a particular interest of the queen's as it progressed from discovery to colonisation and commerce. In accordance with Isabella's wishes, the benefits of the New World were reserved in the first instance for Castilians and the royal policies for the settlement of the discoveries and the conversion of the indigenous inhabitants reflected the queen's priorities.

As married lovers, Ferndinand and Isabella were not without their little rifts. Ferdinand was unconscionably amorous and his indiscretions were legion. Soon after his marriage, his confessor warned him 'to be far more wholehearted in the love and devotion which you owe to your excellent and worthy wife.' But he went on littering the realm with embarrassing royal bastards and seducing ladies of the court. This was upsetting to Isabella not only for the usual personal reasons but also because she had set out, as a matter of policy, to purge court life of sexual laxity, such as had prevailed in the previous reign. Courtiers were liable to exile for the most inconsequential peccadilloes. Ferdinand's failure to conform to Isabella's strait-laced conception of propriety was therefore a double affront. Her biggest source of anguish, however, arose from the usual problem of the power-woman. She was unable to escape the trap of her own femininity. She was consumed by physical jealousy. As one of her court historians tells us,

> The queen loved after such a fashion, so solicitous and vigilant in jealousy, that if she felt that her husband looked on any lady of the court with a betrayal of desire, she would very discreetly procure ways and means to dismiss that person from the household, to her own great honour and advantage.

Luckily, her husband's passionless nature favoured this policy. He never cared enough about any *inamorata* to object.

On the other hand, Isabella's personal reputation for piety and chastity has been exaggerated by eulogists bent on having her canonised. She was open, if not to physical intrigues, at least to courtly love games. Her indiscretions were tepid rather than torrid but enough to excite Ferdinand's jealousy in return and cause him to treat her male favourites as she treated his women. For example, whereas Isabella contrived to have the fascinatingly beautiful paramour, Beatriz de Bobadilla, married off to one of the remotest feudatories in the monarchy (where she later had a liaison with Columbus), Ferdinand promoted the queen's admired heart-throb, Gonzalo de Córdoba, to distant commands (where he established a reputation as one of Spain's greatest captains). But most of the romance in Isabella's life came from the poetry and flattery inspired by the troubadour renascence with which she was surrounded at court.

> When we part,
> Departs my heart,

sang Alvar Bazan, echoing the common-enough twelfth century line. In more overtly flirtatious mood, Juan Alvarez Gato daringly wooed the queen:

> My soul is fasting. I appeal
> To you for aid. I'm near to dying.
> All the world knows how my weal
> Is one that you alone can heal.

Isabella relished the attentions of these versifiers. They were a fantastic form of escape from her physical plainness.

It was not, however, the vicissitudes of her love-life with her husband that wrecked Isabella's happiness, but the sad fates that befell her children. If she was a failure as a power-woman, it was because she did not pursue politics single-mindedly. Seeking the chimera of personal happiness, and investing her quest in her fragile family life, she was doomed to disappointment despite the political brilliance of her reign. The mental world of her late years is evoked by her pictures. She collected the lachrymose and dolorous paintings of the Flemish school. Tear-streaked Christs and Maries, saints bleeding profusely from glittering wounds, human pathos realistically portrayed in fantastic, sometimes grotesque landscapes — these pictures were the pensive and poignant mirrors of a doleful countenance. What made her like this — a queen so glorious in the world's eyes, so splendoured with pomp, who had conquered the goals of fame and success that the Renaissance worshipped? In part, her mawkish character generated its own pathos. Isabella reacted to the responsibilities of her traditionally masculine role not by pretending to virility but by exaggerating, as if by way of a reaction, her femininity. Where other queens

Isabella I, of Castile, Queen of Spain 1451-1504, wife of Ferdinand V of Aragon.

became tomboys, she was a self-made cissy. She affected dislike of bloodshed at bullfights and professed a willingness to watch such spectacles only if the bulls' horns were blunted. When Ferdinand was wounded by a would-be assassin, she said she 'hadn't the heart to behold the wound' and thought that her own suffering, induced by the king's plight, was at least as great as the victim's.

She was so in love with the idea of personal grief, that she succumbed to it wholeheartedly when she had real cause. At first she was fortunate in her children. She had a male heir and four daughters who survived the perils of infant mortality: these were invaluable blessings, such as many queens and many women might have envied. But from 1490, things began to go wrong. In that year, Isabella's eldest daughter was prostrated by grief at the sudden death in a hunting accident of her bridegroom of only one year. It was some consolation that two other children, Juana and Prince John, were approaching marriageable age. But both marriages would prove disastrous. It was not at once apparent, when Juana left Spain in 1496, that her husband, Philip of Flanders, would drive her to misery and madness — but the effects of his infidelities would be exposed before long. And there was

Isabella II, Queen of Spain 1830-1904, married in 1846 to Francisco, Infante of Spain.

immediate cause for anxiety when the heir apparent, Prince John, on whom were pinned all the monarchs's hopes for the future felicity of their realm, married Margaret of Austria. The Prince's health and intellect had never given much cause for satisfaction. The court physicians thought him too young and infirm for marriage but Isabella thrust their objections aside with tragic results. Contemporaries ascribed his subsequent sickness and death to amorous intemperance with his young bride, but consumption is more likely to have been responsible. In any event, the loss of her son devastated the queen and made both her and her husband apprehensive for the future stability of the kingdom.

It was now necessary to oblige the monarchs' eldest daughter, who had never recovered from her husband's death and had never doffed her mourning, to emerge from retirement and contract another marriage in the hope of ensuring the continuation of the line. Reluctantly, she espoused her duty and, with it, a new husband. Her marriage to the Portuguese King, who had long admired her, augured well when she rapidly became pregnant. But in delivering the longed-for manchild in August, 1500, she did not survive the birth, and the little prince, christened Miguel, lived for only two months. The prospects of the dynasty were ruined, and the monarchs' eldest children sacrificed in vain. The infant's death, wrote Peter Martyr, 'has profoundly affected his grandparents. They have evidently been unable to bear with equanimity so many strokes of fate.' For Isabella, it had been what another chronicler called 'the third stab of pain to pierce her heart' — the loss of her eldest son had been followed by that of her favourite daughter and now the grandson who was to have been the consolation of her old age.

Worse was to follow. The youngest daughter, Katharine of Aragon, was shipped off to England to marry Prince Arthur: when he died a few months later — allegedly as a result of the same conjugal excesses as had killed Prince John — she was subjected to virtual hostage status, imprisoned in the cold and loveless English court. At least Isabella was spared knowledge of her future fate as wife of Henry VIII. A year later, the Princess Juana, now heiress to the throne, returned to Castile to horrify her mother with the evidence of her personal decline. Exposed to the demoralising barbarity of her husband's behaviour she had become withdrawn, melancholic and depressive. Her plight was a tragic burlesque of Isabella's own — but she had the resources of character to cope with an unfaithful husband. Juana, frail and deficient in character, declined into madness.

When Isabella the Catholic died in 1504, she left Castile the most feared and respected realm in Christendom. Castilians had begun the discovery and colonisation of America, and conquered Granada and much of Italy. Castilian troops had decisively trounced their rivals for European hegemony, the French. The Spanish Inquisition had been created and the Jews expelled from Spain. The Spanish Church had been reformed and the nobility disciplined. A framework of dynastic alliances had forced a link between Castile and Aragon that would endure, with some difficult moments, for the rest of Spanish history. Fruitful relations were secured with Portugal, England and the Holy Roman Empire which would have transcendent importance in the next two generations. Isabella, in short, had been mistress of an impressive edifice. But this political success had been achieved at the cost of her personal happiness, which, in the end, meant more to her. She had been a successful power-woman without being a committed one. She was fortunate in her husband who supplied the qualities she lacked — ruthlessness, *realpolitik,* craftiness — and which most other power-women have had to supply for themselves. She was fortunate too that after their initial bout of rivalry, Ferdinand was content to rule at her side without seeking to eclipse her. Isabella had shown an ability to fend off his political rapacity at the start of their reign, but if he had chosen to renew the attack later it is hard to imagine how she could have contrived to withstand it again. She was a great reader of popular compilations of moral philosophy by male feminists — the *Book of Women* by Francisc Eiximenis and the *Virtuous Women* of Alvaro de Luna. These were typical of the output of that class of moralists who were anxious in the late medieval period to temper the prevailing misogyny of most sermons, but they were still cautionary in tone. Alvaro de Luna's book, for instance, mixed precious little useful generalisation into its tedious catalogue of epitypes of the male idea of what a good woman should be — modest and motherly, spotless and saintly, goodly and godly. De Luna was uniquely equipped to write about politics. As a royal favourite earlier in the century he had been effective ruler of Castile and was custodian of the government at the time he was writing his book. But his *Virtuous Women,* even when they are queens, are politically inert. The sort of advice Isabella might have got from his book included warnings to sit up straight at table and take care over personal cleanliness. On the other hand, it is worth quoting some of his concluding remarks, which did have some comfort to offer, by implication, to a queen beleaguered in a man's world. After pointing out that Christian tradition accords equality, in certain respects, to both sexes, praising women for their fortitude in childbirth, and citing the Ten Commandments as authority for giving equal honour to fathers and mothers, Don Alvaro continues:

> It is the intention of the present work... only to show that virtues are something men and women have in common, wherefore vices, sins and virtues, too, are — it seems — common to all the human race, that is, men and women alike. And women are no more worthy of blame than men.

On the other hand, the author is quick to modify his opinion with a few conventional masculine shibboleths: women owe reverence to men: 'the man is the head of the woman'; man is the glory of God and woman the glory of her husband; man, in the person of Adam, was not made from woman but woman from man. To escape the sentence of Eve, women had — so the pages before Isabella's eyes told her — to shine with exceptional virtue. To exercise any sort of managerial competence — yet alone sovereignty such as fell to Isabella's lot — they had to attain to a discretion that was thought uncharacteristic of their sex, even by the most favourably disposed of writers. Isabella had her little shortcomings from this exacting code — her troubadour flirtations, her frivolous, even slightly salacious literary tastes, her amorous jealousies and spite — but by the almost universal admiration she commanded in her day she did much to prise women in a political context from the odium of Eve. She had demonstrated the workability of female sovereignty. Already in her own time she had helped to inspire Anne of Beaujeu, eldest daughter of Louis XI, to exercise an informal regency during the minority of Charles VIII. The high-handed methods of this princess — unlike Isabella, she had a feeble husband whom she had to galvanise with her own iron nerves — revolted her subjects and she was vindictively overthrown when the king came of age. But Isabella's image outshone hers. The century after their deaths brought a remarkable concatenation of female rulers to power in Europe. The power-women of the early modern era were lucky to have Isabella's example before them.

CHAPTER SEVEN

The Century of 'Monstrous Regiment'

In 1529, Henricus Cornelius Agrippa, one of the cleverest of the innumerable practitioners of occult arts and pseudo-sciences who thronged the courts and cloisters of Renaissance Europe, published a tract entitled *De nobilitate et praecellentia foeminei sexus*. Its arguments in favour of woman's 'nobility' and 'excellence' were traditional. It recapitulated the feminism of Christine de Pisan and of an anonymous writer, probably of the fifteenth century, whose views are recorded in a Cambridge manuscript and who wrote,

> Woman is to be preferred to Man, to wit in material: Adam made from clay and Eve from side of Adam; in place: Adam made outside paradise and Eve within; in conception: a woman conceived God, which a man did not do; in apparition: Christ appeared to a woman after the Resurrection, to wit the Magdalene; in exaltation: a woman is exalted above the choirs of angels, to wit the Blessed Mary.

In common with other feminist champions of the period, Agrippa adds arguments 'in name' — Eve in Hebrew means life, Adam earth — and 'in order' — Eve was the last created thing and therefore the perfection of God's work. There were many more such champions of women in the sixteenth century than ever before, but their views showed little novelty, little advance. And as Agrippa admitted in his own case, most of their arguments were rhetorical exercises, narrowly conceived within the traditional framework of scholastic debate, riddled with sophistry, calculated more to entertain than instruct.

It was outside the ranks of the conventional apologists that the sixteenth-century image of woman was transformed. Women were vindicated on a practical level by the triumphs of numerous power-women who occupied thrones and exercised regencies in this century of 'monstrous regiment'. At the same time — and whether as cause or in consequence none

139

can say — men's perceptions of women were gradually but unrecognisably changed by the influence of scientific research and new philosophical influences. Science effected the more radical changes. The scientific renaissance was felt earliest and most fruitfully, among the medical sciences, within anatomy. By the early sixteenth century, experimental anatomists were dispensing with traditional inhibitions and discovering the secrets of the human interior with rapidity and regularity in Italy and Spain, by means of techniques that quickly spread to the Low Countries, France, Germany and England. Naturally, the reproductive organs and processes were a source of particular interest for the early explorers of the body. Dissection of female corpses enabled anatomists to apply rigorous tests to the longstanding assumption that the female body was merely a man's *manqué* — nature's imperfect attempting at producing a man. The revelation of the reality of the female body is owed, more than to any other individual, to Gabriele Falloppio, the companion of Vesalius in disproving empirically the shibboleths from Galen on which traditional surgery relied. His *Observationes Antomicae* of 1561, which portrayed the female genitalia with a fullness and accuracy never before attained, demonstrated the inadequacy of the Aristotelian and Galenic descriptions. Even conservative surgeons little affected by the new science were prepared increasingly during the sixteenth century to concede that women were as perfect as men in their own sexuality.

Apart from the influence of experimental anatomy, the Renaissance enhanced women's image through the reception of Platonism by moral philosophers. Not that Plato was any more generous towards women than Aristotle, whose philosophical supremacy had been almost absolute in the late middle ages. Indeed, in some ways Plato, who thought that wives should be held in common and that women could not be satisfactory companions for men, was an even more thoroughgoing misogynist than his great pupil. But in the *Republic*, in the course and for the sake of argument, he puts into Socrates's mouth the view that women should be admitted to political citizenship. And the Platonic model of love, though perhaps not intended by Plato to be understood or applied in a romantic context, was a valuable antidote, from women's point of view, to the crude distortion of *amour courtois* that had represented them as little more than sex objects in the fourteenth and fifteenth centuries. Plato, by purging the love-concept of sex, and identifying it with a loftier sentimental and intellectual relationship, enabled Renaissance writers to treat women in love poetry with a recaptured dignity. Under the influence of Plato's views on love and beauty men actually began literally to *see* women in a new light. The paintings of artists who were directly affected by Plato — like Botticelli, Piero di Cosimo, Leonardo, Michelangelo and Raphael — illustrate this admirably. They wrested from their models forms of ideal beauty that no artist had ever before perceived, or certainly, at least, never before portrayed with such sublime intensity. In Piero's most famous portrait, that of Simonetta Vespucci, mistress of Lorenzo the Magnificent, the sitter seems abstracted from the canvas to a higher level of reality, despite the fidelity — characteristic of Renaissance 'realism' — with which she is drawn. Botticelli, similarly, paints not mere women in his *Primavera* or his *Birth of Venus* or his series of seated Virtues, but noble, beautiful abstractions embodied in female contours — sometimes meek, sometimes majestic, enfleshed in women's guise. In these artists' successors of the next century their hyper-realism, so to speak, is prosecuted to the limits of its expressive power in, say, the *Virgin of the Rocks* of Leonardo, the proverbial Madonne of Raphael, or — to take examples from the world of sculpture — Michelangelo's *Pietá* or *Madonna of Bruges.*

The last gift of the Renaissance to women was enhanced education. Education was an indispensable part of the Renaissance conception of virtue. From the perspective of the power-women, it is also important that it was specifically part of political virtue. Not arms alone, but now also indisputably letters were a vital item in any ruler's acknowledged equipment and it was especially needful for women, who remained largely excluded from the exercise of arms, to deploy letters with proficiency. In the fifteenth century, only one feminist writer was a woman herself. In the late sixteenth century, Christine de Pisan had many successors.

Humanist writers on education — and there were many of them, for this was a subject central to humanist concerns — all paid heed to the educational needs of women. Whereas Isabella the Catholic, as we saw, lacked a childhood grounding in Latin, all her daughters were taught it from infancy. Mary Tudor was the inspiration for a treatise on the education of a princess written by Luis Vives. Elizabeth I, who was taught by another theorist of female education, Roger Ascham, astonished her own court with her proficiency in extemporised Latin oratory. But she was unexceptional in this. All the power-women of the sixteenth century could turn a pretty phrase. Even Mary Queen of Scots, who showed little aptitude for politics or for Latin, might in other circumstances have made a better career as a blue

Mary, Queen of England 1516-1538. The inscription on the portrait reads "Ladi Mari daughter to the most vertuous Prince Kinge Henri the Eight. The Age of XXVIII yeres."

Mary Stuart, Queen of Scotland, 1542-1587.

Mary of Guise, Queen of Scotland 1515-1560. An engraving by Harding from a painting in the Duke of Devonshire's possession.

stocking, for she was an accomplished sonneteer.

Empowered by all this new learning, emancipated by the new and favourable notions of their sex, women of the sixteenth century invaded the political arena. In 1558, when John Knox published his *First Blast of the Trumpet against the Monstruous Regiment of Women,* one woman had just succeeded another in England; Mary Queen of Scots was about to take over direct control from a female regent in Scotland; the French crown was soon to begin a long period under female tutelage; and Margaret of Parma was shortly to be elevated to the regency of the Low Countries. Never before had power-women ruled so far and wide. Never before had the 'corrupted fountein', as Knox called it — the authority of women — flowed so profusely. Knox's own objections were perhaps more circumstantial than fundamental, for all these women were enemies of the Calvinist faith which he wished to impose on fellow-Christians. But he expressed himself trenchantly enough:

> And therefore I say, that of necessitie it is, that this monstruous empire of women, (which amongest all enormities, that this day do abound upon the face of the whole earth, is most detestable and

damnable) be openlie reveled and plainlie declared to the world, to the end that some may repent and be saved.

The peculiar object of his indignation was the queen he punningly called 'Iezebel' of England. Elizabeth I was then shakily installed upon a contentious throne, an easy target of Knox's satire. In the course of her reign she would create and project an image of dazzling success, which, outlasting the effects of her many political mistakes, would make a more effective apologia for female sovereignty than the work of any number of polemicists. In singling her out for special abuse, Knox was unwittingly concentrating his attack on the most important power-woman of the age. Her birth was inauspicious. Her father, Henry VIII, had imperilled the whole realm to marry his pregnant mistress, Anne Boleyn, in the hope of a manchild to succeed him. The birth of Elizabeth on 1534 was therefore a national and personal disappointment, which contributed to Anne Boleyn's rapid repudiation and judicial murder. Motherless at the age of two, branded with bastardy by her own father, Elizabeth had the sort of hate-filled, peril-fraught infancy that must either permanently scar or immeasurably strengthen the child who suffers it.

Politically, the making of Elizabeth was her alliance with her sister, Mary. Elizabeth has enjoyed the greater reputation. For Mary's reign was disfigured by the blood-letting and burning that marred her efforts to contain heresy, while under Elizabeth, sanguinary bigotry was successfully disguised as political prudence or witch-hunting. Protestants won England's religious struggles and history was re-written by the victors. Mary's reign has none of the 'rattling good history' that great victories make, whereas Elizabeth's has been glorified as England's age of national greatness, thanks to some creditable but subsequently much exaggerated swashbuckling. Above all, Mary had the ill fortune to die young. Elizabeth reaped the benefit of a cultural flourishing that began in the elder sister's reign. She lived to be celebrated by Spenser, hymned by Byrd, painted by Hillyard and entertained by Shakespeare. Yet considered simply as a power-woman, Mary Tudor was almost the equal of Elizabeth. It was only thanks to her sister that Elizabeth achieved the throne at all. For Mary was the first sovereign queen of England: she thus created a precedent that eased Elizabeth's path to the throne. And she used her influence to uphold Elizabeth's right to the succession, which, in an age of chronic dynastic instability, was an enormous boon. Above all, she provided Elizabeth with an admirable example of what to follow and what to avoid. Elizabeth's greatness was founded on the head start Mary gave her.

Mary's accession in July, 1553, was procured by her own efforts. But it must be acknowledged that the triumph of a woman was favoured by the lack of any creditable male contender for the throne. The houses of York and Lancaster, which had disputed the crown for a century and a half, both rested their claims on descent through the female line — through Anne Mortimer and Margaret Beaufort respectively, great-great-grand-daughters of Edward III. Since the marriage of Henry VII and Elizabeth of York those claims were united — provided the principle of descent in the female line was admitted — in the Tudor dynasty. After the death of Edward, Earl of Warwick in 1499, there was no surviving representative of the descendants of Edward III in the line male. Even so, had there been a male heir in the female line to challenge Mary's claim in 1553 her right would have been hard to assert. But the only menfolk who could advance such claims — of the families of Pole, Courtenay, Hastings and Stafford — were all, for varying reasons, unwilling or unable to act at the time (though some of them made later bids for the throne). Still, the hostility in England to a female accession should not be under-estimated. Henry VIII's attempts to make legislative provision to regulate the succession had all been designed to favour heirs male of Henry VII; but in the event there were none — save, in the line of the kings of Scots, whom he specifically excluded. And John Knox spoke for a common opinion when he declared that 'Woman in her greatest perfection was made to serve and obey man, not to rule and command him.'

In the event, therefore, it was Mary's good fortune that she had only another woman with whom to dispute her throne at the crucial moment when Edward VI's death left it vacant. Lady Jane Grey was by any standards an absurd and unworthy candidate. At least a dozen possible pretenders stood closer than she in line of succession. Her rather remote descent from Henry VII came through her mother, who was still alive: it was thus impossible to admit the propriety of Jane's pretensions without illogicality, since her mother's claim must necessarily have been superior. The only constitutional points in her favour were feeble in the extreme: Henry VIII had awarded the succession to her mother's issue — but the purpose of this was to provide for the possibility of male heirs, not to give Jane the throne or disinherit her mother. Edward VI in the last weeks of his life had been made to utter a 'devise' bequeathing the crown to Jane, but this had been done on the unconstitutional advice or coercion of a self-interested minister. In any case, there was no good precedent in England for regulating the succession by means of royal bequest. The real reasons for Jane's elevation were of crude political expediency. For the latter part of Edward's reign, power had been almost totally concentrated within the grasp of the chief minister, John Dudley, Duke of Northumberland. He had ruled as a despotic vizir and knew that if he once relinquished control, his terrible record of excesses would bring just vengeance on his head. He was restrained by no scruple in attempting to manipulate the succession — as formerly he had manipulated the king and the council — to perpetuate his power. Lady Jane Grey was a weak, impressionable and immature girl of only sixteen years of age. Already under Northumberland's influence, she came firmly under his control by means of the web of marriage alliances by which he bound her to his partisans and kin, culminating in the betrothal and hasty marriage of Jane to his own son, the Earl of Guildford. Northumberland's palpable opportunism won him no friends. The magnates of England looked askance at the prospect of a Dudley regime permanently enshrined through the appropriation of the crown matrimonial. The only serious qualification Jane had to commend her was her sincere and staunch adherence to Protestantism. Most of England's ruling class, which had profited from the secularisation of Church property under Henry VIII and Edward VI, had reason to fear the possibility of a Catholic *revanche* under Mary. But confessional divisions were as yet neither deep nor even distinct in England, where Reformation and Counter-Reformation alike had so far been only faintly felt. Mary was generally expected — falsely, of course, as events turned out — to be pragmatic in matters of religion; it was at least certain that she would attempt no major unscrambling of the distribution of former church property. The appeal of the old faith, at least in its formal and liturgical manifestations, had not yet been displaced from most Englishmen's hearts by the rise of Protestantism. In just about every respect, therefore, Lady Jane Grey carried infinitely less conviction as a potential sovereign than Mary. Her rival's weakness was Mary's greatest strength.

Still, Mary's struggle for the crown demanded power-womanly qualities in abundance. Those admirable observers, the imperial ambassadors, believed she had no chance of success. She had been rigorously excluded from the circles of power during the reigns of Henry VIII and Edward VI. The religious and sexual prejudices of the ruling élite were utterly opposed to her. The expressed wishes of the previous kings and the terms of various statutes emphatically denied her a place in the succession. The organs of government were all in the unrelaxed control of her enemies. She embarked on her challenge to Northumberland's plans with no weapon save her own determination to succeed. A hundred peers, bishops and sheriffs — including almost all the most important men in England — subscribed Edward VI's will on 21st June, 1553, definitively disinheriting Mary. Early in July, knowing that her own person would be seized by Northumberland's men as soon as the king died, she fled in secret, braving the dangers of a crossing of Protestant East Anglia, where her Catholic faith was unpopular, to reach the lands of the house of Howard, one of the few aristocratic families on whom she could count for support.

Her audacity proved decisive. The mere display of resolution on her part brought out into the open the latent sympathy she commanded all over the country and exposed the fragility of the aristocratic coalition that ruled in London in Queen Jane's name. Northumberland had cowed the court, but control procured by fear is always precarious and most of the ruling élite was willing enough to welcome a chance to desert him. When he rode out with his retinue to meet Mary's forces in the field, the crowds were ominously silent. 'Not one sayeth God speed us,' he admitted. Behind him, the government dissolved into fragments as all the important ministers defected to Mary's side. Around him, the localities declared for Mary. Northumberland himself reached Cambridge before acknowledging the hopelessness of resistance to an outcome which only a few weeks before had seemed unthinkable. He made his own belated submission to Mary. In yielding, inevitably, to arrest he placed his life in pawn. In London, the defectors carried out an easy coup, arresting Queen Jane and the few supporters who remained loyal to her, while the bells rang out over the streets in jubilant acclamation of Mary's approach.

For in her bid for the crown Mary also enjoyed the advantage of popular support. Her self-proclamation as Queen inspired an uprising in her favour among the common people — arguably the last of the great series of peasants' revolts that had punctuated English history since 1381. Even in East Anglia, where the Protestant majority detested her religion, she attracted thousands of followers who took up arms to march with her to London to uphold her right. Her humble partisans are unlikely to have been motivated by legitimist scruples or Catholic fervour. Throughout her predecessor's reign, rural areas had rumbled with unrest because of the royal council's indifference to agrarian distress. Mary's cause offered a pretext to overthrow the ruling clique of the previous years who threatened, by their unprincipled attempts to tamper with the succession, to perpetuate their own power. When Mary arrived at London on 3rd August, she was attended by an impressive collection of members of the royal family, including Elizabeth: family squabbles had been shelved in the interests of dynastic solidarity. Behind this royal train was a great throng of peasants. The base and summit of the pyramid of the polity had joined forces: they made a formidable combination. Mary was queen by popular election, emblemised by the severed ears of a tapster called George Potter who had defied the proclamation of Queen Jane: Mary would soon ennoble him in gratitude.

Even before her triumphal progress to the capital, Mary's opponents had abandoned all attempt to fight. They had fled, surrendered or dispersed their forces and publicly concurred in her proclamation. The forbidding array of advantages with which they had confronted Mary at the outset of the struggle had been dispelled by her resolve, with only ancillary support from the force of circumstances. She had beaten men, and over-trumped masculinity. But like so many other power-women, she seems to have expended all her prowess in winning power. Once installed on the throne, she ruled with a kind of instinctive talent for imprudence, by a singularly infelicitous series of intuitions. She was a self-parody of a woman in power, who deserts pragmatism for petulance, reason for instinct, and policy for passion.

Her two *idées fixes* destroyed her: her Spanish marriage outraged England's nascent nationalism: her bloody religious intolerance ruptured national unity and ruinously weakened the realm. In pursuing both policies she ignored the great truth overlooked by so many power-women, that statesmanship sometimes requires the sacrifice of personal wishes, however dearly and deeply held, in the interest of pragmatic politics. Both Mary's obsessions were deeply intuitive. She wilfully allowed her political priorities to be determined by pre-occupations derived from her childhood, when she accompanied the mother she adored into exile from court life. She associated all the unhappiness of her infancy with the injustice done to her mother, Katharine of Aragon, by her father, Henry VIII. The divorce which precipitated the English Reformation had for Mary been a personal affront and a domestic treachery. Henry, who had made his wife an outcast and his daughter a pariah, was regarded by her with awestruck hatred. Her loyalty to Katharine became focussed on the two features of her mother's life that had most impressed her: her Spanish provenance and her Catholic faith. She devoted her reign to reversing the humiliation of her mother by restoring a consort of her mother's nation to the English throne and the practice of her mother's faith to English altars.

The intuitive undercurrent of her policy was feminine enough. Her choice of husband was characteristically feminine in other ways, as she admitted implicitly when she told parliament that she would not accept political counsel concerning her marriage but reserve the decision for herself alone. It is likely that she had decided on Philip, heir to the Spanish throne, before her own accession. She dropped hints accordingly — as discreet as they were secret — to the imperial ambassador within the first few weeks of her reign. Her anxiety was quickened by her own long pent frustrations. She was thirty-seven. Countless matches had been mooted for her in her youth but political considerations had stifled every prospect. To choose one's own husband in maturity was a privilege at the time normally reserved for widows. The power to share it went to Mary's head. She seems, too, to have had an ardent physical need to bear children: here her instinct coincided with reasons of state, but the urgency Mary brought to her quest for motherhood was typified by the characteristic passion of all her fondest personal designs.

Thus she rushed headlong into marriage like a schoolgirl into her first affair. It was a disaster from the political and personal points of view alike, provoking resentment from all England but evoking no love on her husband's part. Mary gave herself to her young husband with the desperate abandon of a stock-fictional 'older woman'. He responded with dispassion, almost with distaste. His attitude was exactly expressed by a poet who accompanied him on the journey to England for the wedding:

Que no quiero amores en Ingalaterra
Pues otros mejores tengo yo en mi tierra.

which may be rendered

To England, seeking love, what need to roam?
There's better pleasure in the girls back home.

Her ardour chilled by her husband's indifference, Mary sought consolation in the savage self-mockery of successive phantom pregnancies. These were not utterly unfruitful, for they inspired Tallis to write his Mass *Puer Natus,* of which a majestic fragment has survived. But they did nothing to mitigate Mary's physical sterility.

The marriage for which she brought so much personal misery upon herself cost her the goodwill of her people. It was opposed even by her closest advisers. Bishop Gardiner of Winchester, who had been instrumental at the time of her bid for the throne and was the right-hand man of her struggle for the Catholic cause, advised her against it. Both houses of parliament begged her not to marry a foreigner. Popular insurrections were sparked off by her decision, bringing the Kentish rebels of Sir Thomas Wyatt to the very gates of the City of London and imperilling the throne Mary had so lately won at such great cost. But she let nothing deter her. The resolution which helped her win the throne thus hindered her in ruling from it. Mary's petulance exposed one of the great rational scruples that underlay popular hostility to power-women in the era of dynastic rule. The advent of a queen implied a bleak array of prospects for her realm: if she remained childless, a succession crisis must ensue; if she married a native husband she would feed faction; if she took a foreigner instead, the realm would be exposed to a kind of bloodless conquest at foreign hands. The celebrations of Mary's wedding in England seemed hearty enough: Pageants, poetry and pyrotechnics greeted the royal couple wherever they went. But the welcome offered to Philip was hedged with many explicit reservations. He would be allowed the title of king but not the power. He was to have no right to the succession nor to the exercise of a regency on Mary's death. The queen's marriage was not to abate her sole sovereignty by one jot. Mary's wifely devotion was recklessly heedless of her own political interests. She did all she could to increase her husband's portion of power at her own expense. If she remained a power-woman it was in despite of her own efforts. Meanwhile, her people's xenophobic distrust of Philip quickly grew into hatred.

Mary's own popularity became, in a sense, a truly religious sacrifice. Having achieved the first desire of her heart — her Spanish marriage — she turned with the same passion and impatience to her second — the restoration of the Catholic faith. Historians dispute to this day the configurations of the confessional map of England at the start of Mary's reign. Probably the indifference to dogma that has been the main feature of English religion since the Reformation was already its preponderant characteristic then. Most people knew little of the doctrinal content of Christianity and cared less. Yet this made the nation as a whole hostile to every kind of zeal — especially when, like Mary's, it was bloodily prosecuted. And the minority of committed Protestants was large enough, staunch enough and active enough, to make the policy of persecution deeply divisive. Mary began her reign with a promise of toleration — or at least a promise that conscience would not be co-erced. But she intended to unpick the threads of the Reformation by rapid stages and towards the end of 1554, when her reign was at its apogee and she had procured parliamentary approval both of reversals in religion and an extension of her husband's responsibilities, she felt strong enough to demand the commencement of persecution. She lit a fence of fire for the containment of heresy. The torch was of her own kindling. It used to be thought that Cardinal Pole, the Pope's legate, was responsible for the persecutions which coincided with his arrival from Rome; in fact, as we now know, his was the milder zeal. It is easy to make the mistake of thinking that the holocaust of heretics was an unfeeling policy too cruel for a woman. But the urgency and passion behind it were typically feminine and typical of Mary. Nor was her intention cruel. A genuine ember of piety glowed amid the flames. Mary hoped to cauterise a national wound and blaze a trail to heaven for her subjects. In the four years that remained of her reign three hundred of them were put to death for the greater good of the rest and the greater glory of God. Yet the effect was precisely the reverse of Mary's intention. No heart was turned towards the Holy and Apostolic faith by the spectacle of her excesses. The burning of heretics served only to enflame Protestantism. Martyrs generated popular mythopœia. Exiles fled to continental seed-beds of heresy in Frankfurt and Geneva where they learned extremist doctrines and effective techniques and from whence they re-emerged after Mary's reign to re-introduce into England a more durable and sharply defined Reformation than ever before.

Mary's career thus conformed to a standard model of the power-woman. She showed the pertinacity, ruthlessness and skill in power-seeking that have enabled a few exceptional women to compete in politics with men. She also displayed the feminine weaknesses and follies that vitiate the work of such women once the main object of their ambition has been achieved. She died amid the ruins of her work. One of the last major new policies she initiated was the renewal of war with France, undertaken largely to please her husband and for the advantage of his foreign interests. The result was the loss of Calais, the last English colony on French soil. Meanwhile, the failure of her religious policies was becoming increasingly apparent, and a national reaction against the humiliations and divisions of her reign was building up. The personal felicity on which she had staked so much was shattered, her

Queen Elizabeth I of England by Marc Shearaerts: From the Woburn Abbey Collection. Sometimes called the "Armada Portrait".

husband having virtually deserted her in the last two years of their marriage. She was left as the genius of Antonis Mor has captured her in her famous portrait: cheerless, pinched, with a touch of pious austerity, her whole being drained to a painful vacuity symbolised by the awful emptiness of her womb. But her reign had one great beneficiary: her sister Elizabeth, to whom she had bequeathed her realm and who had learnt from her example — watchfully and by degrees — practically the whole of her political art.

Yet Elizabeth's had been a hard and precarious apprenticeship. The two sisters had been natural allies but also in other ways natural rivals. In childhood they were flung together by a common fate, for both were rejected by their father and excised from their place in the line of succession to the throne. Both led lonely, isolated, insecure lives. Both were prevented from marrying by the bastardy imputed to them. Both lived under the menace of death that might be inflicted at any moment during the dynastic struggles which always threatened to convulse the realm. At the same time, however, they were aware of the fundamental disharmonies between them. Elizabeth was the daughter of Anne Boleyn — the woman for whom Henry VIII had forsaken Mary's mother. This alone was enough to make Mary resent her. Logically, since Henry had undergone a form of marriage with Anne Boleyn during Katharine of Aragon's lifetime, the two girls could not both be strictly legitimate. And above all, they were separated by that great sixteenth-century sunderer of kin, religion. Though Elizabeth even as a child was enough of a *politique* to admit to any faith that would give her a moment's peace and security amid the fragile hazards of her life, she could not conscientiously bring herself to share her sister's Catholic convictions. Mary's relations with Elizabeth were passionately stormy. Tearful ruptures were followed by equally lachrymose reconciliations. Elizabeth boldly hitched her star to Mary's during the succession crisis that brought Mary to the throne and almost won her sister's love by successfully dissembling Catholicism. But she was adopted as a figurehead by Mary's enemies and in 1554 spent two horrifying months incarcerated in the Tower. Mary believed her guilty of treason; it was but a few weeks then since Jane Grey had paid the penalty of her presumption with her head. Elizabeth can have been in no doubt of the likely imminence of her own execution. She survived by the slenderest of threads. Her sister relented and she was conveyed to the relatively calm internment in Woodstock, the royal hunting lodge near Oxford. Gradually, she made use of the opportunity to convince the queen anew of her religious orthodoxy. It was Mary's dying wish that she should inherit the crown.

Her sister's demise was Elizabeth's unmuzzling. All her life had been spent eluding death by dissimulation and now — though she never lost the trick of concealing her real thoughts — she relished the chance to be mistress of herself. She rejected all Mary's policies. But she applied to her own career as a power-woman the techniques she had imbibed at Mary's feet. Her reign was dominated on the one hand by the determination to avoid Mary's mistakes and on the other to imitate the ruthlessness and resolution that had been her sister's strength.

In her most famous apophthegm, Elizabeth declared that she combined 'the body of a weak and feeble woman' with 'the heart and stomach of a king' and indeed that was her exact image of herself. She ruled by exploiting her own femininity while imitating the masculinity of men. In short, she practised simultaneously the two great alternative technique-systems by which power-women have always ruled. She succeeded to such an extent that she has been claimed to have been a transexual or a hermaphrodite. But successful queens always evoke accusations of transexuality from vain and incredulous men. There is no reason to suppose that she was not in a physical sense thoroughly female. But she had the skill — some would argue that it was typically a woman's skill — to vary her behaviour with a baffling diversity, accentuating now manly, now womanly traits. She was by turns a coquette and a tartar, a statesman and a shrew. In the image she projected through propaganda and through art she was a virgin and goddess and yet also a kingly, sexless icon.

Two fundamental aspects of her policies were determined by the need to withstand the major problems incurred as a result of her sex. She was an exceptional monarch — bewilderingly exceptional — in resisting war and resisting marriage. War, as Mary had found, was an activity in which a woman was at a disadvantage. Marriage, as Mary's example had shown, was a deadly trap for a queen. In pursuing these linked policies of spinsterhood and peace, Elizabeth was able to deploy all the arts and images of womanhood. The marriage question was lively and contentious from the time of her earliest parliaments. The will and advice of almost the entire realm was that she should take a husband as quickly as possible. In most men's eyes the disadvantage of empowering a consort were outweighed by the perils of an insecure succession; at almost no time during the Tudor supremacy had the descent of the throne been predictable, and Englishmen felt they had lived too long with the hazards and fears of such uncertainty.

But Elizabeth was immune to the effects of advice on this matter, more perhaps than on any other. Having seen what befell Mary, she knew better than to take a foreign husband. Having been the focus of the intended putsches of her sister's enemies she was unwilling to elevate any of her subjects, by way of marriage, to a position of potential rivalry with herself. As she told a parliamentary delegation that urged her to marry in 1566, she was sure 'there was not one of them that ever was 'a second person' as I have been, and have tasted of the practices against my sister — who, I would to God were alive again. I had great occasions to hearken to their motions... and I was sought for divers ways.'

Her resolution against marriage was never so forcefully expressed, however, as to make all suitors despair. To keep them dangling on a thread of fine hope was an essential part of Elizabeth's policy and of the political usefulness of queenly maidenhead. She was willing to use coquetterie, and what is now called 'playing hard to get' to influence domestic politicians and foreign princes. The allure of a virgin queen was a challenge which enthralled and ensnared men. Every official portrait painted in her reign emphasised her sexual inaccessibility. She was surrounded by the iconography of chastity. She was Diana, Astraea, Virgo, bedecked with pearls and ermine and perfect spheres, objects of virginal white and umblemished integrity. This very image generated its own appeal. She literally titillated her court. The court physician, Simon Forman, recorded in his diary his dreams of rogering the queen. Her successive favourites — Dudley and Essex — bombarded her beleagured virginity with wooing that was at least verbally bold. But boldness of innuendo was positively encouraged in Elizabeth's entourage, for it suited her purpose, and it was her suitors who were at her mercy, not the other way round. The dream-like quality of Spenser's *Faerie Queen* represents the Elizabeth-centred fantasies of more than a generation of the English élite.

The existence of such a chaste mistress, whose lovers were her subjects, was irresistibly chivalric in an age that sorely felt a want of chivalry. Every Elizabethan aristocrat was a pre-incarnation of Don Quixote. Her accession's anniversary was celebrated each year with anachronistic tourneys, described in fictional guise in Sir Philip Sidney's *Countess of Pembroke's Arcadia* as the festivities of a queen who 'made her people by peace warlike, her courtiers by sports learned, her ladies by love chaste.' Noblemen saturated in the chivalresque put crenellations atop their Renaissance *palazze*. Royal propaganda firmly harnessed this bravado in service of the queen in promoting this annual 'tilting in triumph of Eliza's right'. The knightly masquerade blended into all the other aspects of the royal mythology created around Elizabeth; the return of the Golden Age of peace and prosperity, the virgin-led advent of Arcadian bliss. And the neo-Platonism of the Renaissance found in Elizabeth a numinous emblem of Platonic love. Her admirers were transported into very worship, like Thomas Dekker in *Old Fortunatus:*

> Are you then travelling to the temple of Eliza?
> Even to her temple my feeble limbs are travelling, Some call her Pandora, some Gloriana, some Cynthia, some Belphoebe, some Astraea
> all by several names to express several loves. Yet all those names make
> but one celestial body, as all those loves meet to create but one soul.
> I am of her own country, and we adore her by the name of Eliza.

The extent to which Elizabeth was aroused by the flirtatious conceits that throve around her image must be a matter of doubt. She could hardly have sustained a constant atmosphere of heightened sexual tension in others if she had been very susceptible sexually herself, like Mary Queen of Scots. She had been touched by scandal when she was fifteen. She got involved in an amorous imbroglio with the dashing Admiral Seymour, who wooed her with panache, perhaps hoping to make her fall in love with him and so short-circuit the diplomatic niceties that impeded marriage with so politically desirable a bride. He would enter her bedroom. They would ride off unchaperoned together. He would leap on her bed in sight of her attendants and slap and tickle her under the bedclothes. Others took the affair more seriously than Elizabeth herself. The Admiral lost his head for his presumption. It would hardly be surprising if so horrible a consummation of her love-play, when she was at so impressionable an age, had put Elizabeth off sex for life. Certainly it must have made her wary of a love affair's destructive power. But reasons of state alone are enough to explain her abstinence from romantic pecadilloes once she became queen.

She began her reign by assuring parliament that she meant to live and die a virgin. She rejected or postponed the suits of the King of Spain, the Prince of Sweden, the Archduke of Austria. This reluctance to espouse a foreigner met with general approbation. But marriage to an Englishman was an option at least worth considering, if a suitor could be found whose status was high but whose ambitions containable. Elizabeth's reasons for disliking the prospect have already been made clear, but she was rarely doctrinaire even in her heart's desires, and towards the end of the 1550s, when the pretensions of Mary Queen of Scots to the English throne made settlement of the succession seem imperative, when Elizabeth was still politically inexperienced, and when the advice to marry was assailing her from every side, a possible candidate seemed to be emerging in the person of Robert Dudley, future Earl of Leicester. He enjoyed an unique combination of advantages. His physical charm attracted the queen. His was a companionable presence amid the critical affairs of state that surrounded Elizabeth's efforts to parry internal plots and create a workable religious settlement in England. As son of the Duke of Northumberland, he was heir to great political ambitions and to the leadership of the Protestant magnates. Above all, Dudley's policies seemed to Elizabeth exactly to mirror her own. She trusted his judgement, and felt that business could be safely confided to his hands. He was her acknowledged favourite and was rumoured to be her lover. She had heaped honours and confidences upon him. Only one thing disqualified him from candidacy for the crown matrimonial at this early period when his political and military incompetence had not yet been revealed. He was already married. His wife, Amy Robsart, lived in seclusion at his manor at Cumnor, just outside Oxford. There, as Mr Secretary Cecil and the Spanish ambassador realised, she would be in peril of her life as soon as Dudley felt strong enough to set his cap openly at the queen. Curiously and tragically, when rumours of his murderous intentions were at their height, Amy was found dead at the foot of the stairs at Cumnor, with a broken neck.

The news was terrible. 'Every hair on my head stareth and my ears glow to hear,' declared the English ambassador in Paris. There were few who did not assume that Amy died by murder, and many who believed in the queen's complicity. Yet the overwhelming likelihood is that Elizabeth had never intended to marry Dudley. It was characteristic of her to use amorous language to beguile a political favourite, but it was not long since she had warned parliament of her virginal resolve nor many days since the example of life under Mary had etched wariness of marriage into her heart. If Dudley or some of his friends misread the situation and hoped to disembarrass the favourite of Amy to facilitate his course to a greater prize,

Elizabeth's reaction soon disabused them of their hopes. She would not believe — or at least not accuse — Dudley of murder, but she did freeze him out of her favour, after a momentary display of indifference to the vulgar conviction of his guilt. He remained a great man in the realm, with a powerful affinity and great provincial power, whose co-operation, like that of most of her aristocracy, Elizabeth needed and used. But she never again allowed a presumption of intimacy to cloud his relations with the crown.

The queen remained free to play princely suitors with line if not with net — and this freedom she lavishly indulged. In 1570, however, a diplomatic proposal arose which deserved to be taken seriously. Relations with Spain, which had been the bedrock of early Tudor foreign policy, had long been declining for confessional and commercial reasons. Revolt against Spanish rule in the Netherlands (brewing in the late 1560's and breaking out definitively in 1572) forded upon England a choice between Spanish amity and enmity. In these circumstances, France, England's secular foe, looked more attractive as a potential ally and partner than at any previous time in English history. Indeed, England was on the threshold of a diplomatic revolution that would convert Spain from chief friend to principal enemy and France to at least a sporadic ally, for the best part of more than a hundred years. Two unmarried scions of the French royal house were available at the time in the persons of the Dukes of Anjou and Alençon, brothers of the king. The former was heir presumptive to the throne, and might be a domineering and unpopular influence in England; the latter was twenty years Elizabeth's junior and badly disfigured by smallpox; his prospects of a great inheritance were slender. Thus the two candidates represented hazardous extremes and Elizabeth confined herself to her typical game of dynastic flirtation, seeking and winning a diplomatic alliance without a dynastic link. When Anjou succeeded to the French throne in 1576 Elizabeth's reluctance to commit herself seemed vindicated. Union of the French and English crowns would have caused the forfeiture of England's independence in foreign policy. But the possibility of renewal of the French marriage proposal remained in the wings, as Alençon — who now succeeded his brother as Duke of Anjou — matured and as his political fortunes prospered.

Elizabeth was thirty-eight by the time of the shelving of the French match in 1572 — older than Mary had been at her marriage and too old, perhaps, to be able to guarantee the succession even if she should now marry at last. Her investment in her own cult of virginity was now so heavy that she could not easily discard it. Thus every year that passed made marriage less likely. But in 1578, she judged it propitious to revive the Anjou marriage idea with an earnestness never before manifest in any of her matrimonial dabblings. It is possible that Elizabeth was moved by personal considerations — a feeling, as it were, that now, on the verge of middle age, she faced a last chance to fulfil her destiny as a woman and her obligations to her dynasty. But it is more likely that, as usual, Elizabeth was subordinating her personal will to the exigencies of politics. The fate of the Netherlands — still rent, as they would be for many years, by the confused configurations of their revolt against Spain — was the single most important concern of English policy, for unless the vital stretch of Netherlandish coast opposite England's shores were neutral or friendly, no Englishman could rest secure; and unless the markets of the Low Countries were available to English commerce, the realm would be seriously impoverished. It was not yet suspected even in the Netherlands that an independent Netherlandish state — such as ultimately came into being — could ever exist or survive without a powerful foreign protector and there were parties in the Netherlands that favoured Spain, England, the Holy Roman Empire and France for this role. Spain, provoker of rebellion, was too divisive a choice; the empire too weak and too closely linked dynastically and diplomatically with Spain. Elizabeth was reluctant to commit England directly: her resources would not be sufficient to sustain the defence of the Netherlands against French or Spanish attack and her abhorrence of war was as constant a principle of her policy as her abhorrence of marriage. But she was unwilling to give France a free hand. Marriage with Anjou therefore commended itself as a cheap way of assuring Engish interests. He was the French candidate for the championship and rule of the Netherlands. It would be rash to compete with him but prudent, perhaps, to join him and exploit him.

Thus on this occasion the marriage proposal was kept simmering for nearly four years, while Anjou made two protracted visits to England to press his suit, and was publicly kissed by Elizabeth and called by pet names. But much of this was just Elizabeth's wonted amorous masquerade. Her reputation did not favour a successful consummation. As Anjou's agent wrote in April, 1579, 'I have very good hope, but will say no more till the curtain is drawn, the candle out, and Monsieur in bed.' The early months of wooing were the most propitious. Until January, 1580, Elizabeth's physicians and women were reporting that she had years of childbirth left in her but thereafter such reports cease. The menopause, it seems, was upon her. Her most urgent reason to wed, to 'have a child to inherit and continue the line of Henry VIII,' as she told her Council, was past. She seems to have greeted this fact with only mixed regret. She was now free to pursue the political advantages of wedlock without the formal and physical ties — to procure a 'league', not a marriage, in the diplomatic language of the time. Again her coquettish negotiating techniques were completely successful. When she packed Anjou off to the Netherlands in February, 1582, with a small subsidy, a few men, and many cheap promises, she did a little dance of joy to be rid of him on such politically favourable terms. In the event, his political and military failure in the Netherlands in 1582-83, followed by his death in 1584, obliged Elizabeth to risk direct military intervention in that part of the world herself — an outcome which she had striven to prevent and could hardly have foreseen. Although her comportment during the Anjou wooing — with her continual, baffling changes of mind and mood, her tearful rows with her Council, her flirtatious posturings — looks from a distance like the mercurial mutability of woman at her worst, examined in detail it takes on the appearance of a well calculated political campaign which achieved a surprising degree of short-term triumph.

Ironically, though she had escaped from the Anjou negotiations without marrying, Elizabeth had, at the end of the day, to accept the need to go to war in the Netherlands. In a sense, she had conserved her first great objective — spinsterhood — at the expense of her second — peace. Throughout her reign, avoidance of war was as prominent a theme of her propaganda as avoidance of marriage. Both were snares of a power-woman which she was deeply anxious to elude. Both were disasters of the reign of her sister Mary which she was determined not to repeat. They were coupled in Elizabeth's mind and she pursued them always, as far as possible, together. We see them linked in the famous portrait of Elizabeth by the 'HE' monogrammist, in which Elizabeth appears as the chaste and sublime resolver of the petty conflicts of other goddesses. We see it too in the Astraea portraits, with their direct allusions to the pacific Arcady of the Golden Age, presided by a royal virgin. And we see it in the *Eliza Triumphans* engraving by William Rogers, in which the Queen holds an olive branch. Elizabethan playgoers and poet-tasters were exposed to a barrage of such propaganda in verbal form. The play *Histrio-Matrix* of 1589 contains the representative hymn:

Still breathe our glory, the worlds Empresse,

Religions Gardian, Peaces patronesse!
Now flourish Arts, the Queene of Peace doth raigne;
Vertue triumph, now she doth sway the stemme.

The same impression is communicated by the *Misfortunes of Arthur,* a pageant performed by the students of Gray's Inn in 1588:

That virtuous Virgo born for Britain's bliss,
That peerless branch of Brute, that sweet remain
Of Priam's state, that hope of springing Troy,
Which time to come, and many ages hence
Shall of all wars compound eternal peace.
Let her reduce the golden age again,
Religion ease and wealth of former world.
Yea let that Virgo come and Saturns reign
And years oft ten times told expire in peace.

The first three of these lines allude to the parallel legend of Brutus, son of Priam, who was held to have founded the first kingdom of Britain with fellow-exiles from the Trojan war, as Aeneas was supposed to have founded the state from which Rome descended.

Clearly, then, Elizabeth had a big stake in peace. It is not surprising that she should have toyed with the Anjou marriage in the interests of peace. And when the English involvement in the Netherlands war began in earnest in 1584, she pursued it half-heartedly — niggardly as her detractors said, and never made an effort sufficient for victory. Her eirenism has been mistaken for indecision and has been labelled as typical feminine vacillation. It was feminine, certainly, but inspired by peculiarly feminine political considerations, not by the psycho-sexual irrationality which men sometimes attribute to women. It is worth considering the extent to which Elizabeth disciplined her own sexuality in a political context by comparing her with her contemporary, Mary Queen of Scots. Mary was by no means the mawkish romantic, flighty nymphomaniac or political *ingénue* of some biographers' imaginations. She had many of the necessary qualities of a power-woman — audacity, ruthlessness, ambition and a talent for exploiting men. She almost made a success of queenship in a hostile age and a hostile country. But she lacked Elizabeth's equipment for power. She was more indulgent of her feminine fancies and weaknesses. She was more passionate and emotional — or at least less able to subordinate her passions and emotions to political priorities. She was more easily distracted from staatspolitik by the pursuit of domestic felicity. She deserved to be outwitted by her English rival. Nothing better illustrates the difference between Mary and Elizabeth than their respective dealings with men, whom Elizabeth dominated and to whom Mary was a victim. Mary's early experience with a husband, Francis II of France, who was meek and vapid and with whom she had grown up in unexciting tedium, hardly equipped her for the tough world of predatory males that awaited her in Scotland, her hereditary realm, where she decided to take her chance after her husband's death. She found the Scots already smarting under female regency and ready to accept even a woman's sovereign presence, if she guaranteed the national independence of Scotland and tolerated the Protestant religion. But they also expected her to marry wisely — an object frustrated by Mary's desire to exploit her unwonted freedom to choose a husband, as well as by the dearth of suitable candidates.

Mary was in a dilemma similar to those which Mary Tudor and Elizabeth resolved in their contrasting ways. A foreign match — to the heir of Spain, before his madness incapacitated him, or an English nobleman like Dudley — would be unpopular in Scotland. Alliance with any one house among the faction-riven Scottish nobility would cause discord at home and raise up a rival to her own authority. In the circumstances she might have done best to imitate Elizabeth's masterly inactivity. But even merry widowhood did not suit Mary. In selecting Lord Darnley, son of the effective leader of the Catholic party within the Scots nobility, she made a highly contentious choice of consort. The Protestant nobles were provoked into defiance of the crown. Mary resorted to arms to repress them and secured a victory despite the succour Elizabeth gave the rebels. Her caprice had cost her dearly and in the long run, success, which now induced over-confidence, was to prove more deleterious to her cause than failure. She went ahead with the ill-starred Darnley marriage, which brought her little personal satisfaction and was soon to work out its own political tragedy. She felt encouraged to proceed with a restoration of the Catholic church in Scotland and to launch an assault on the Protestant Kirk whose strength she fatally underestimated. Finally, her marriage aligned her fortunes with those of one noble party: she may have felt more secure thereby than in the lonely eminence she had previously occupied, fending the factions off and playing them against one another. But she lost more through the alienation of new adversaries than she gained by the adherence of new friends.

Marriage brought Mary one great boon. Within a short time she was pregnant. But in every other respect the upshot was disastrous. The worst possible case ensued and Mary was surrounded and outstripped by terrible factional and confessional divisions while having to face a challenge for authority from the husband she had so rashly espoused. In his craving to oust his wife from power, Darnley allied with his own religious enemies. The conspirators murdered Rizzio, the queen's Italian secretary, on whom she was increasingly reliant, and carried out a coup aimed at divesting her of personal rule. In the wake of the murder, however, though the queen was obliged to accept the humiliating tutelage of the Protestant lords, it was Darnley rather than Mary who was excluded from the inner circles of power. Mary re-established a *modus vivendi* with the rest of her enemies but virtually ostracised her consort. In June 1566 the birth of her son strengthened her hand. But in the morally debauched Scottish court, where murder and intrigue bred desperate insecurity, she hardly felt strong. Her estrangement from the husband she loathed and dependence on the murderers of her friend made her nervous, lonely, vindictive, and highly vulnerable to the promise of a strong deliverer.

As a papal ambassador shrewdly wrote of her, 'one cannot expect much from those who are subject to their pleasures.' In the strained atmosphere of late 1566, Mary fled from her political plight into the arms of a lover. The horrors of her life as a power-woman drove her to take refuge in the assurance of her own femininity. It was not her pleasure alone she sought — though it seemed so to the disgusted observers of her conduct — but security, comfort, solace and protection. The man she fell for, the Earl of Bothwell, judged her psychology with a perceptive eye. He realised that what Mary needed above all was a virile refuge, a tower of strength. To judge from hints Mary herself left, he opened his suit by raping her; later he ravished her — carried her off to his castle at Dunbar. By then, Darnley had gone the way of Rizzio — horribly murdered and his corpse blown up with gunpowder. Mary and Bothwell may well have been privy to the plot, but the entire council, including the Protestant lords who were to accuse and punish the earl and the queen, had already virtually countenanced murder as the only sure means to rid the realm of the despised and troublesome consort.

Even Mary's hasty marriage to Bothwell — brazen act of shame though it was, denounced as such in the streets and court alike — might have been

Catherine de Medici, Queen of France, wife of Henry II of France (1519-1589).

less than fatal to the queen's interests had she but carried one party or faction with her through the deed. But only the Catholic cause could provide her with any strong support. And Bothwell, indeed, was the leading Catholic magnate. But in one vital respect his credentials were profoundly flawed: he was already married. And the only means whereby he and Mary could contract a form of marriage together was by a shabby and hurried divorce and a wedding by the Protestant rite. That she should have been prepared to go through this desperate and unprincipled charade shows the depth of Mary's infatuation with her lover. She was not strong enough to resist his demand for a marriage — for though he was a good judge of Mary he was a poor judge of the realm and believed he could be a king indeed in Scotland once he had legal custody of Mary's person. Nor was she strong enough to take decisive advantage of Darnley's murder to blame and destroy the Protestant lords and rule alone with the backing of the Catholic party. She lost her head, in short, in a contemptibly girlish way. The outrage of the realm was cleverly exploited by the Protestant lords, while Mary and Bothwell were abandoned to their fate by their erstwhile Catholic supporters. The sordid dénouement is well known: Bothwell's flight and wretched death in exile; Mary's incarceration: her flight and rescue by Elizabeth, who wished to control this valuable political pawn herself; Mary's restless ambition, which made her a figurehead in her Sassenach prison for discontented English Catholics; her new plans to marry within the English Catholic aristocracy; her hopeless plots to sieze her Scottish throne with Elizabeth's help or unseat Elizabeth with the help of Spain; and at last Elizabeth's decision to cut short conspiracy by cutting off her rival's head. On the eighth of January, 1587, the queen of Scots knelt at the scaffold in her best red knickers, thinking herself a martyr. Even in death her almost theatrical sense of spectacle did not desert her.

Elizabeth was to die very differently. Mary's death was a fitting end to a life of passion and romance. Elizabeth declined coldly into a lonely old age. She never wavered from her rigid pursuit of the primacy of political interests, even when her ageing emotions were most cordially engaged. For thirteen years from 1577 she found some personal consolation for the romantic opportunities sacrificed in her youth to public duty. In that year, Robert Devereux came to court and attracted her eye for his 'goodly person' to which he gradually added evidence of a certain modest ability in politics and war. Elizabeth wallowed — harmlessly enough, as she thought — in his flattery and renewed in his pleasant company something of the flirtatious relish with which she had managed her servants and courtiers when she first came to the throne. But Essex — for she soon ennobled him with the earldom of that name — was too callow in politics to imbibe safely all the heady honours with which the queen regaled him. His ambition was bloated beyond his ability. He aspired to power, perhaps to supreme power, and when in the late 1590s his military prowess seemed to falter in Ireland — the intractable graveyard of so many reputations — he risked all on a desperate gamble. He attempted a putsch with the aim of siezing the old queen's person and ruling himself in her name. When his plot was discovered, he thought the queen's affection would protect him.

Because he always saw her at her most feminine and most vulnerable, he failed to realise that this was a facet of her personality which she kept under inflexible control. He forgot that he was dealing with an imperious queen, not a foolishly besotted old maid — a woman capable of functioning as impersonally as a political abstraction. In February, 1601, he was beheaded for treason. The queen had set her face against clemency — the white face that stares impassively from her protraits was never whiter nor more impassive than in this last act of the ruthlessness of a power-woman, by which she condemned her young playfellow to death and herself to a stricken and regretful loneliness in the last two years of her own life. The conflicts of power and womanhood run so deep that it is almost impossible for a successful power-woman to find personal happiness. The hubris of Mary Queen of Scots was her weakness, that of Elizabeth her strength. She had deployed femininity and affected virility at will to maximise her power. She had coped, as a ruler, with all the handicaps of her sex. But she had failed, as a woman, to cope with the handicaps of rule.

CHAPTER EIGHT

Queen Christina and the Power Woman's Art

In the early autumn of 1650, in the elegant but jerry-built piazza in front of the royal palace in Stockholm, workmen were straining and sweating to complete the erection of a stupendous edifice in time for an imminent coronation. Vast planks of wood were hoisted aright, until they dwarfed the surrounding buildings; great expanses of canvas cloth were stretched over them and stuck down with arcane confections of resin and gum. Then the whole contraption was painted in *trompe l'oeuil* to resemble stone, smothered with mock friezes, inscriptions, cofferings, medallions, Corinthian columns and fluted pilasters, and finally surmounted with twenty-four vast statues, hewn of wood but, again, painted to look like stone. The result was a great triumphal arch of classical inspiration, which brought to this cold northern *burg* something of the wealth and warmth of Rome. It symbolised the policy of the young Queen of Sweden, Christina, who hoped to capture the essence of Mediterranean civilisation and transplant it, with transforming effect, into her distant kingdom. It was erected in honour of her joyful and triumphant entry into her capital city. Its designer, De La Vallée, a Parisian *arbiter elegantiarum,* had been brought hot-foot from Rome with designs based on the Arch of Constantine. No public expense was spared in its erection: the glues alone which held it rather precariously together cost 8,000 Swedish pounds. Its capacious triple-arch would accommodate the most glittering procession Stockholm had ever witnessed. The statues that adorned it stood for the antique virtues revered by the queen: Truth, Religion, Faith, Charity, Concord, Patriotism, Fortitude, Wisdom, Prudence, Justice, Peace, Theology, Philosophy, Love of Virtue, Vigilance, Liberality, Generosity, Honour, Victory, Glory, Good Counsel, Temperance and Abundance.

This auspicious aperture was not built to endure. But it outlasted Christina's reign. Christina tore through Swedish history like a ferocious sirocco, a warm wind from the south, revolutionising Sweden's constitution and culture before suddenly — as it seemed — changing her allegiance, embracing Catholicism and retiring to Rome to savour a civilisation and religion she esteemed more highly than those of her homeland. She left behind her, among some admirers, the reputation of a power-woman *hors de pair,* who suppressed in her political career all the shortcomings of her sex. The inscription on her triumphal arch was fulfilled: 'Divae Christinae Regnandi Artibus supra Sexus et Aetatis Suae Captum Insigni.' But the sudden self-eclipse of her career made her reputation equivocal. Particularly, of course, among her fiercely Protestant countrymen the conviction of her sagacity was not universally shared. But at least they remembered her as one of the most intriguing of women and — above all — the most learned of queens.

For Christina, literacy was an instrument of monarchy and a means of compensating for the incapacities of her sex. When Patin called her 'as lustrous in letters as her father was in arms,' he caught the point of Christina's bookishness exactly. She could not be a warrior-sovereign; despite her claim to proficiency in duelling, there were no edged weapons for her personal use in her armoury. One of the justifications she advanced for her own abdication was that 'the realm would be granted a man and a champion who when war threatened could ride with his people to battle, which a woman could not do'. She never forgot that her father had given his life on the field of Lützen, like of the Gothic *heerkönigen* of old. Therefore, unable to continue that tradition of kingship, she resolved to be a philosopher-king instead. She first acquired her love of books at the hands of her tutor, Bishop Johannes Matthiae, in pursuit of her father's wish that she should have a boyish education. Thus from her childhood her learning symbolised virility. When, in 1646, Cardinal Mazarin was minded to send her some rich presents to assist his diplomacy, he was advised in Paris — already the capital of *haute couture* — to supply small saddle-ponies and perfumed lingerie. But the French ambassador in Stockholm knew better. Send her books, he advised: he knew they were, as she herself said, 'the only things she cared for'. Mazarin's gift was as from one bibliophile to another. Christina eagerly unwrapped the packages with her own hands as soon as they arrived. Later she paid the Cardinal the best of compliments by buying up his library when he was exiled from France.

The contents of her library confirm other evidence of her intellectual proclivities. The only catalogues which survive date from after she left Sweden. Even so, it seems remarkable how little interest Sweden held for her. Just twenty-five titles concerned Swedish subjects, and of these most were chosen because they were addressed or dedicated to the queen. The most comprehensive collection was of standard texts of classical authors. Admiration for classical civilisation is an unbroken thread which binds all Christina's tastes and policies. She also collected some modern humanists — she possessed, for instance, Luis Vives on the education of a Christian princess — but the evidence of the marginalia she scribbled in many of her books shows her gradually veering away from humanism towards theology and devotion. Her library was particularly rich in these subjects; among the fathers, she liked the neo-platonists best: Fr Manderscheyt, the Spanish ambassador's confessor, tells us what a voracious reader of them she was. This interest in Platonic tradition overstepped the bounds of Christian orthodoxy: she pestered Descartes with such questions as whether a Christian could properly believe in the infinity of the cosmos. She dabbled in Pythogorean, Ramist and Hermetist texts. Equally hazardous to orthodoxy, perhaps, was her prodigious collection of the Bible in every possible translation and edition. Interest in Biblical scholarship was something she carried with her from her Protestant into her Catholic phase: she had been a great patroness and promoter of Biblical criticism back home in Sweden, urging her scholars, for instance, to produce a new Polyglot Bible that would demonstrate, to the confusion of the Catholics, the shortcomings of the Vulgate of Jerome. And it is remarkable that although Catholic devotion is well represented among her books — especially that of the Jesuits to whom she owed her reception into the Apostolic Church — her interest in Calvinism never waned. In part, it was hatred of the Lutheran dogmas forced upon her at home that drove her into the arms of Holy Mother Church; Calvinism was as viciously proscribed in Sweden as Catholicism, and therefore had a comparable fascination for her. She sought out Isaac de la Peyrère on her removal from Sweden and so encouraged him to publish his heterodox views that he fell foul of the Inquisition. She read Gerard Vossius, Grotius and even Philippe Duplessis-Mornay. And she admired Saumaise enough to write fulsomely to his widow on his death. All these were outspoken Calvinists; yet Christina, darling of successive pontifs, did not scruple to study them. She remained, even as a Catholic, undogmatic in her religion. The seeds of a syncretist and ecumenical approach, sewn by her Erasmian tutor in her earliest lessons, stayed with her throughout life and accompanied her gradual drift, in maturity and senectitude, towards a resigned and inclusive pietism.

She was almost as much of a glutton for paintings as for books. When she inherited the Swedish throne, there was only one painting in the royal palace. Within the short span of her reign, she had turned it into the greatest gallery in the world. She deliberately delayed negotiations at the close of the Thirty Years' War to give the Swedish army time to capture Prague and send the imperial collection — at that time the world's finest — in crates to Stockholm. Later, when another imperial collection was sold, she wrote to her agent that she *trembled* lest the canvases she coveted should slip through her fingers. The impact of her art gallery transformed Swedish art, which had not yet joined the Renaissance. Her pictorial voracity was more than a political response in an age when art was a necessary adjunct of empire. Christina's passion was fed by the genuine compulsion she felt to surround herself, in her northern fastnesses, with an ambiance of classical and Mediterranean magnificence: this, even more than any military victories or diplomatic recognition would mark Sweden's definitive reception as a great power in the mainstream of European culture. She immersed herself in a sculptured Parnassus. She was also a genuine connoisseur. She knew what she liked and was impelled by a real collector's drive to acquire it. Her choice of paintings takes us to the heart of her taste. She loved best the Italian painters of the high and late Renaissance. It was the voluptuously enfleshed spirituality of Raphael, Tintoretto, Veronese and Titian that most appealed to her. Raphael was her special favourite. Though she was never able to acquire many of his works, she planned and schemed and longed to get them. Of course, these paintings had a specifically devotional appeal to Christina — emblems of her attraction to the resplendent, triumphalist Catholicism of the counter-Reformation. But she also loved them for their luxurious, almost tactile ostentation. She was happy to discard Netherlandish canvases except — of course — for those of Rubens: their austerity, lachrimosity and pungent realism did not appeal, compared with the conspicuous richness and corporeal glories of the Italians.

Christina's own writings reveal as little of her inner enigma as the façade she presented to her baffled contemporaries. For a woman of such widely acknowledged brilliance and such a powerful love of literature, she wrote surprisingly little. It may be that hers was a genius incapable of sustained effort: most of what she did attempt is slight, episodic or unfinished. She never had any professional motive to force on the agonising pace of literary creation. She always remained a dilettante, in both the best and worst senses of the word. On the other hand, her output may have been restricted, like Oscar Wilde's, by the effort and ingenuity of her conversation. She was in her day a famous — or, to some, notorious, talker, who adopted an almost pedagogic style of conversation, common among scholars but shocking to diplomats and courtiers.

She enshrined some of the apophthegms with which her conversation crackled in a literary form that was typical of her era. The idea of publishing collections of maxims had been popularised by La Rochefoucauld. Christina, never one to under-rate her own wit, made two collections of her own — more prolix than those of their French model — in her *Ouvrage de Loisir* and *Sentiments héroiques*. It was a combative style, designed to stimulate controversy, not to fill in time or communicate real feelings. She loved to coin phrases for their sonority rather than their substance, their impact rather than their import. She provoked and teased her interlocutors with outrageous remarks. Best of all she loved paradox. It was all part of her personality — her pleasure in intellectual acrobatics, her determination to bewilder others and conceal herself. But it could lead to misunderstandings. It is obvious, for instance, how her reputation for atheism arose. On one of her journeys she met the *savant* Morisot and asked him what religion he thought she professed. When he, of course, replied, 'Catholic,' she answered, 'You are wrong, monsieur: I follow the religion of the philosophers,' and bade him search for it in the poetry of the epicurean Lucretius, whose philosophy never more than very selectively resembled her own. Even Morisot was dumbstruck by this conversational stuffed eel-skin. Lesser wits may have been deluded by Christina's *ballon d'essai*. Christina sustained this kind of performance in all her talk. Every gambit was a challenge, every *tête-à-tête* a debate.

When she did put pen to paper, it is hard to be sure whether she was being any more frank, even in the few leaves she wrote of her own autobiography, which she intended as a real *cri de coeur,* an exposition of the soul, inspired by St Augustine's *Confessions*. Like Augustine, she repeatedly addresses God; but even in the invoked presence of the Almighty, her recollections are coloured, if not deliberately distorted, by hindsight. Superficially, the autobiography is calculated to present an image of humility: 'My ignorance and my sins are mine,' declares the queen, 'and my virtues and gifts — if any there be — are God's.' Her protestations of wretchedness are not mere affectations. They betray a real insecurity. The same flavour is caught in some of the marginal postillae of her books, where she had no reason to seek to deceive anyone but herself: the self-abasement of her jottings, where she proclaims herself 'nothing' and the surprising claims

Queen Christina of Sweden 1626-1689.

they make — surprising in a queen who knew every privilege and every luxury — of exposure to misery and suffering, are corroborative echoes of the apparent inferiority complex revealed by the autobiography. In another sense, however, Christina's humility is a smoke-screen thrown up by her smouldering pride. The God she invokes so cordially is an image of herself. The pages are a vindication, disguised as a reproach. If she feels real guilt, it seems less for her sins than for her failure to prosecute her ambitions to the summit of worldly glory she craved. Her claim that if God gave her the dominion of the world, 'I should count as nothing all that is not Thee,' is the self-betrayal of a dedicated politician who protests too much. The real lesson of the remark is that not even the dominion of the world was too big an ambition for Christina to contemplate.

In her marginalia and other writings, we can trace some intellectual and spiritual development. Her stoicism and humanism are gradually displaced by Catholic quietism. This is confirmed by external evidence of the progress of her intellectual life, which she began as a freedom-seeking rebel against narrow, doctrinaire Lutheranism, and which she ended as a disciple of Miguel Molinos, whose anti-dogmatic religion of the spirit swept Rome and much of the Catholic world in the late seventeenth century. She also reveals her susceptibility to hero-worship, her adulation for the superman. Alexander the Great was the idol of her life — a phantasm on whom she lavished the admiration never called forth by marriage to a worldly husband. In writing little essays on great men of classical antiquity, she was inhibited by her literary perfectionism from ever getting very far, but her essay on Alexander was the most extravagantly hewn of all. Time and again she returned to it, like a dog to some beloved fetish. She re-wrote, re-moulded, worried it and cherished it, but never finished it because she could never feel that she had done justice to her subject. Alexander retained an altar even in the temple of her Catholicism. She took the name Alexandra at her confirmation, ostensibly in deference to the pope, Alexander VII, but really in honour of the hero. When she arrived at Innsbruck in 1662 for the most solemn occasion of her life, her formal espousal of Catholic verity, the day was celebrated with a pagan extravaganza — Cesti's *Magnanimitá di Alessandro,* written and performed as a gesture to Christina's cult. Alexander, of course, was a figure of almost universal appeal and significance. Christina's admiration for him was peculiar to herself, but she did share one common interpretation of his story as an example of the mutability of life, especially of power. This is that theme of the only poem known to have survived from her pen, 'Io sono il tempo alato', in which she sings

> sol per unico dono
> della mia ferità lasciai perfissi
> per le tenebre e gli abissi.

By the time those lines were written, late in her life, she must have felt that her own story illustrated the same idea.

Christina's self-image emerges only obscurely from her writings. But it is clearly portrayed in the most characteristic art-form of her court — the court-masques, pageants or *ballets de cour* which were acknowledged media for propaganda and political expression in the early seventeenth century and which, in Sweden, reached their apogee in Christina's reign. The queen herself contributed to their devising. When Descartes arrived in Stockholm at her bidding, he found her engrossed in the preparation of a masque that would glorify her in much the same way as the cult of Elizabeth of England had glorified the Faerie Queen. Christina was portrayed in the same terms in all her ballets — as the presiding genius of a renascent classical civilisation, a virgin goddess, eirenic and chaste. Above all, she is seen through the pageants as a tamer of passions — that is, a queen triumphant over the weaknesses and deficiencies of her sex. In the *Diana Victorious,* for instance, of 1649, Christina, apotheosised in one of Elizabeth's favourite roles, subjugates the god of love. It would not be fanciful to see in this a deliberate reversal of the story line of the *Roman de la Rose.* The theme and libretto of another ballet-masque of the same year, *Les Passions victorieuses et vaincues,* are even more explicit:

> Cyrus, Alexandre Pompée,
> Les Césars et les Scipions
> Permirent aisement l'entrée
> De leurs âmes a ces passions
> Et les virent assugeties
> A ces cruelles ennemies
>
> En ce siècle deux grandes Reynes
> De nos esprits et de nos coeurs
> En tout et tousjours Souvereines
> Ne connoissent point de vainqueurs:
> Et nous font voir assugeties
> Ces dangereuses Ennemies.

In the first two of these lines the direct influence of Christina can be detected: Cyrus, Alexander, Caesar and Scipio were the classical heroes to whom she devoted some of her own prose belles-letters. The two great queens of the second of the stanzas are Christina and her mother, who was her guest at this pageant. The import of the verses is clear enough: Christina transcends the limitations of womankind to rival and excel great male rulers in domination of the passions. Hardly more subtle was the ballet Christina made Descartes — much to his own shame — write for her. The *Naissance de la paix* was Descartes' first project on his arrival at Stockholm in 1649. Identifying Christina as an eirenic saviour, it echoed the messianic prophecy of a female world-ruler who would bring universal peace, uttered by Saint-Gabriel in his *Mérite des Dames* of 1640: 'In place of war,' he wrote, 'and all this great carnage, men will rejoice in the sweetness of deep peace throughout all the states of the world.'

As significant for an understanding of Christina's self-image as the particular messages of the various ballets de cour is the general message which the use of the art-form conveys to us about the nature and priorities of Christina's court. They were vibrant spectacles, killingly expensive, breathtaking in their special effects. They were a noisy and colourful celebration of Sweden's homage to the culture of continental Europe. The fashion they followed was Parisian and Mediterranean. They were saturated with classical allusions. The French ballet-master who taught Christina's courtiers how to dance and was — so to speak — the artistic director of her masques, spoke the literal truth when he claimed that he had arrived in 1637 and 'civilised the court'.

Christina had to be a tough baby to survive a December birth in the icy, hyperborean climate of Stockholm. When she first appeared on that cold day in 1626, she was at once mistaken for a boy, if we are to take her own late word for it. It is not impossible: a man-child had been prayed for with the sort of fervour that overshoots hope and creates expectation. Even after the century of monstrous regiment, women rulers were still not readily accepted. The neostoicism of the period, which was to have a profound effect on Christina, at least in the years before her conversion to Catholicism, equated the female with weakness. Justus Lipsius believed women were capable of ruling, but should not do so in defiance of law or custom. The greatest blue stocking of the seventeenth century, Anne-Marie van Schurman, whom Christina admired and cultivated, was caustic about feminism and only favoured female education because she thought women's volatile passions demanded the restraint of academic discipline. Denis de Godefroy, one of the most eloquent jurists to uphold sex equality in the early seventeenth century, defended the 'Salic Law' which excluded women or the female line from succession to the throne of France. Christina herself was contemptuous in her own writings of women's general capacity for rule.

The outlook for a power-woman at the time of Christina's birth was thus at best equivocal. Though her father, Gustavus Adolphus, loved her as a daughter, he feared for her as a queen. He commanded that she be given a boy's education to fit her for kingship. 'May this girl be worth a son to me,' he prayed. Though he died when she was only six, her upbringing was in this respect in conformity with the king's wishes. Christina acquired in infancy a love of boyish pursuits which never left her. Strenuous athleticism, madcap hunting and hard equestrianism were favourite recreations. But the most masculine and most beloved item in her curriculum was study. Christina inherited her father's lively, critical intellect and quickness in learning. She was the sort of child who probed and challenged everything her tutors said. She was fortunate in those tutors, especially in the closest to her, Bishop Johannes Matthiae, who shone as a beacon of enlightenment amid the encircling gloom of the bigoted and doctrinaire Swedish clergy. He was a Christian humanist in the tradition of Erasmus, who struggled for a more syncretic, even ecumenical approach to Christianity than was tolerated in the strictly Lutheran kingdom. He was also a superb scholar and teacher, who won Christina's affection and respect. In him she found a substitute for the father she had lost, even to the extent of calling him father. She was secretive even as a child — and it was a trait she conserved throughout adulthood — but to him she confided more than to any other soul. He imbued her with an unquenchable thirst for erudition. He introduced her to the pleasure of reading, which remained her most absorbing pastime, a retreat, as she put it, into the improving, 'life-giving conversation of the dead'. She rapidly acquired all the ornaments of a princely education, especially in languages, for which she showed a prodigious facility, classics and scripture. When she was thirteen, she was praised by the Chancellor Axel Oxenstierna, who headed the Council of Regency that ruled in her minority, as 'not like unto a woman, but courageous and wise.' The education her father had prescribed for her wrought its intended influence on her. She was a tomboy in her sports and a prince in her studies. The virility of her intellect and of her personality were noticed by almost all her contemporaries and, on her part, it was designedly so: lacking confidence in women's suitability to rule, she accentuated whatever was masculine in her make-up. The same impression of the precocious child as Axel Oxenstierna received was also felt by Sforza Pallavicino, who found in her 'nought of a child except her age, nought of a woman except her sex.' Madam de Motteville's famous aphorism on Christina — 'science are to her what needle and thread are to other women' — was typical of contemporaries' perceptions of the queen and a stout testimony to the success of Johannes Matthiae's teaching. Statesmen were satisfied with this effect, but it encumbered Christina in some ways. Her upbringing alienated her from the traditional satisfactions of womanhood. She was never happy with her own sexuality. Diffidence in her own appearance — for she suffered from a slight deformity in the alignment of her shoulders as a result of an accident in infancy — compounded this and made her casual or uncaring about feminine pre-occupations as coiffure and couture. She performed her morning toilette in a quarter of an hour. For childbirth she never felt anything but distaste, from children never anything but revulsion. Though she could talk endlessly of love and sex, she always felt a physical fear of them.

This is not to say Christina was entirely without feminine traits. Like Elizabeth I she could use coquetterie to advantage. We know from such realistic protraits that survive among the countless commissions designed to flatter her that her looks were not exceptional, and that she suffered a deformity — 'a slight irregularity,' she said — her exhumed remains confirm. But she had a talent for striking men as beautiful — 'lovely as an angel', as Per Brahe typically remarked. Though careless of her appearance, she was capable of feminine vanities at times — in selecting a dress for a special occasion or sampling the wares of the cosmeticians of Paris on her escape from barbarous Sweden. She loved dancing as well as her more mannish recreations. Like Elizabeth, too, she could infuriate and beguile men with her frequent changes of mind — partly to create an aura of mystery and to conceal her real thoughts. As one of her librarians wrote, 'She says one thing one day, another the next so that no one would really know what she has in mind.' Her femininity, in fact, was of the secretive, tempestuous and enigmatic variety that makes a consummate power-woman. She uttered the best epigram on herself when she wrote in anticipation of a political imbroglio, 'I love the storm and fear the calm.'

Outside the hours of study, her childhood was unrelievedly unhappy. She adored her father while he lived, but he was often away on campaign, as befitted one of the greatest soldier-kings of history. Christina wrote him touching little letters in German asking him to come home with presents for her. But, as befits a soldier-king, he died young on a foreign field, fulfilling his own premonition and leaving his daughter as his only heir. Christina's mother was no help. She felt the bereavement even more acutely. She was a neurotic, restive and possessive woman who hated her husband's absences and was prostrated by his death. She returned to Sweden with the embalmed corpse only after two years' delay in her native Germany. She and her little daughter embraced effusively on that occasion, but it was an unique moment, called forth by the unusually charged atmosphere of emotion. Most of the time her mother made Christina feel fearful and rejected. She was probably glad in 1636, when the Senate removed her from maternal tutelage and restored her to the guardianship of her aunt-by-marriage, the Countess Palatine Catherine, who had cared for her during her mother's absence. One source of consolation in her childhood was the affectionate friendship of her cousin, Charles Gustavus — a 'childhood sweetheart', with whom she play-acted a little girl's game of courtship, bidding him never forget her when she was only eleven and promising to cherish his keepsakes. Ironically, Charles Gustavus fell in love with her — probably the only man ever to love her for herself rather than the prospects of power she represented. He wooed her throughout their adolescence.

Unhappily for Charles Gustavus, by the time she came of age Christina had outgrown her fancy for him. She warned him repeatedly that their relations could never again be amorous, but were to be governed by politics. This was essential to her queenly self-respect. If they ever married, she told him, it would be 'for reasons of State entirely, not love, at the instance of our Estates.' The reasons of state which demanded marriage were a matter of engendering an heir. The question of her marriage was one of the most difficult political problems of Christina's reign, because it was inseparable from the two other great tasks she was obliged to try to accomplish: the achievement of peace, and the settlement of Sweden's internal problems of government. Sweden was still adjusting to a sudden and spectacular inruption into the ranks of the great powers. In the late sixteenth and seventeenth centuries the configurations of power in Europe were convulsed by a northward displacement of the continent's economic centre of gravity away from the Mediterranean basin, which hitherto had always been the heartland of European civilisation, to the nations of the Atlantic, Baltic and North Sea. The change was as rapid, volcanic, and decisive as the effects of continental drift. In the fifteenth century, Sweden had been so obscure and its influence so local that not even the papal chancery was quite sure who ruled it. Now those who did not smart under Sweden's hegemony vied for its favour. Swedish merchants traded in Guinea and North America. Swedish armies fought in Prague and Alsace. The economy boomed explosively on the profits of foreign investment and the spoils of successful war. Christina presided over a nouveau-riche nobility who within a single generation's span had moved out of their rustic hovels — single-storeyed and thatch-roofed — into baroque palaces in their newly conjured-up 'bonanza' capital at Stockholm, where they vied to learn French dances and ape their queen's artistic tastes. Never before had such a primitive veneer been grafted so quickly or so improbably onto such a primitive infrastructure. Christina's Sweden shared some of the absurdities and contradictions of Ranavalona's Madagascar or Waugh's Azania.

Like all parvenus, Sweden was despised as barbaric in the south: even the cosmopolitan Christina found her eccentricities condemned as a barbarian's excesses when, late in life, she lived in Rome. And as an example of early modern *Wirtschaftswunder* Sweden badly needed modernisation of its manners and its institutions to accommodate its new wealth and equip it for its unwonted global role. Christina aimed to wrench Sweden out of barbarism and archaism. Her father's armies had conquered much of Europe; now she proposed to launch a conquest in reverse and conquer Sweden for European culture. For a hundred years 'Gothic' had been a term of abuse in the Mediterranean world. But in Sweden the Renaissance had hardly penetrated and Swedish esteem for the Goths was as intense as the rest of Europe's esteem for the Romans. There could be no more striking measure of Sweden's cultural backwardness. The nation's native historians, like Georg Stiernhielm, still revelled in mythical genealogies that linked the Swedes, through the Goths, to Gog and Magog. There could be no more obdurate barbarity than this, which evinced pride in its own barbarism. Christina, whose book-learning had introduced her, as a child, to the splendours of the south, spent her life detesting and defying the Swedishness of Sweden. Gothicism and barbarism had to be stifled and escaped. She began by trying to bring the south to Stockholm — ransacking the rest of Europe for treasures and tastes. When that failed, she deserted Sweden and fled to the south. Like Philby or Burgess in Moscow, she found a spiritual 'home' in Rome.

The modernisation of Swedish institutions was as intractable a problem as the Europeanisation of Swedish culture. There were only two organs of government beside the crown that wielded authority throughout the realm: the Råd or Senate, a magnate council of ancient origin that advised the monarch and functioned as a supreme court of appeal, and the Riksdag or Estates, a representative institution that consented to new laws or taxes and in former times had possessed the privilege of electing and deposing the monarch. The Riksdag conserved a peculiarity which, since its formation in the fourteenth century, had reflected the distinctive feature of Swedish society. The large independent class of peasant yeomen was constituted as a separate estate and elected representatives to its own house: in most parliaments in western Europe, the peasantry was unrepresented. Ironically, the very independence that had won the peasants of Sweden this singular privilege was on the wane by Christina's day. Feudalism, which was disappearing in the west, was actually growing in Sweden, which was gripped by aristocratic revanche, as the nobles encroached on the crown lands and exploited new sources of wealth, to the relative impoverishment of the peasants and the crown. Power always goes whoring after wealth and the nobles presumed to supplant their longstanding policy of co-operation with the crown by an outright arrogation of power to themselves. They extended their jurisdictions with their lands. Some of them — especially among the magnates of the Råd who enjoyed a taste of sovereign authority during Christina's regency, hoped to restore the elective monarchy that had prevailed in previous centuries, until the House of Vasa imposed the principle of hereditary succession in 1544. The fear of oligarchy, or even of republicanism was no idle fancy. Axel Oxenstierna, whom Christina would later accuse of planning a Protectorate like Cromwell's, was believed by the French ambassador Chanut to regret the passing of the old Swedish system. In 1649, Christina roundly declared that the Senate was opposed to her dynasty and wanted an elective monarchy on the Polish model. Of Sweden's other close neighbours, England became a republic in effect in the mid-1640's and committed the horrible sacrilege of regicide in 1649. The northern Netherlands had overthrown the monarchy of the Habsburgs in the late sixteenth century and achieved general recognition as a sovereign republic in 1648.

For Christina, the crucial relationship was with the magnates. They were too powerful to crush, too threatening to appease. She had to harness the support of other estates to frustrate the republican and oligarchic schemes of her adversaries, while retaining enough noble sympathy to ensure effective government. The best way to safeguard the hereditary monarchy was by ensuring the succession. But to provide an heir, it was generally believed, she would have to marry. Christina was thoroughly aware of the pitfalls of marriage to a power-woman. She had read Camden's *Annals of Queen Elizabeth* in her childhood and chose to follow that great queen's example of spinsterhood. Like Elizabeth, she withstood pressure from her Council and the Estates to choose a husband. The French ambassador, Chanut, was characteristically perceptive when he wrote of her disinclination to share power with a husband and her delight in reigning alone. Moreover, to have selected the 'internal' candidate, Charles Gustavus, would have been an encouragement to faction, while a foreigner like Frederick William of

Brandenburg would have embroiled Sweden in the pursuit of alien interests. She once told Chanut that she thought marriage at best 'une violence nécessaire'. She was increasingly inclined to reject it altogether. Throughout 1647 and 1648 she kept Charles Gustavus's hopes alive by responding to all entreaties with professions of a preference for him above all other candidates, while refusing to commit herself definitively. But even at that time she was formulating a bold and brilliant new solution to the matrimonial conundrum. It was a stroke of radical ingenuity worthy of her critical intelligence.

Christina's first task was to secure the sovereign place in the government that was hers by right; she was excluded initially by her immaturity; but some of the magnates hoped that her sex would also be an impediment to her assumption of real power and that the effective regency of the Senate could be indefinitely prolonged. But Christina was bent on the enjoyment of real authority from her earliest years. She later wrote that the thought of the crown consoled her for her father's death. When she assumed the ceremonial functions of a monarch at the age of six she was, in her own recollection, 'such a child that I had no conception either of my happiness or my unhappiness, though I do remember my delight at seeing people at my feet and kissing my hand.' As the French ambassador realised, she meant 'to run this country herself'. She took her first step towards wresting the initiative when she was only ten years old, manipulating the Senate's choice of her guardian to suit her own preferences. From 1643 — two years ahead of the official attainment of her majority, — she insisted on being present at the Senate's deliberations. By the time she came of age, not even Axel Oxenstierna could gainsay her. She retained his services, but she firmly asserted the priority of her own will: the Chancellor was subtly transmuted, by a kind of reverse alchemy, from satrap to servant. 'Now', she proclaimed in 1647, 'the fate of the country rests entirely on my shoulders.'

She intended that her coronation should symbolise her power and represent the incontestability of her sovereignty unmistakably to her people. To Paris she despatched the personable young courtier, Magnus de la Gardie, whom enemies accused of being her lover, to cull the secrets of the latest fashions in splendour and spectacle from the shrine of taste. The result was of a brilliance previously unimagined in Sweden, which had never before experienced a coronation dedicated so single-mindedly to magnificence. When the crowning at last took place in 1650, there were evocations of absolutism in the order of procession which stressed the magnates' subordination to their sovereign. There were imperial echoes — the triumphal arches, the purple-saddled and caparisoned steeds. There were hints of a remoter exoticism in the throng of stately camels. There was conspicuous consumption in the form of ever-flowing fountains of wine — intoxicating in more ways than one in a country where grapes were an outlandish rarity. If court ceremonial remained relaxed, compared with the pomp of Paris or Madrid, it was only because Christina was still hazily informed about southern standards in the elegances of absolutism. When the Spanish ambassador, Don Antonio Pimentel, arrived in Stockholm in 1652, Swedish etiquette was upgraded to the Spanish level. But the coronation and the revolution in etiquette were only reflections of the real authority Christina had largely established by 1649.

Christina's plan was to secure the succession and obviate the need to marry at one stroke. Charles Gustavus was her chosen instrument. By getting him adopted as her heir she could remain unmarried without exposing the realm to a contest for the succession: thus she would gain the advantages of Queen Elizabeth's policy of spinsterhood while avoiding its perils. Charles Gustavus was so devoted to her that there was no danger in elevating him to rivalry with her. She knew her man. Though some of his advisers urged him to attempt a coup he never threatened Christina's crown as long as she wore it. Even after her abdication, when he had gained supreme power, he chivalrously kept open his offer of marriage. But to get him accepted as her successor was no easy matter: it required all Christina's political skill to achieve it. She was confronted by three main sources of opposition: Charles himself, who wanted to marry her, not connive in her plan to prevent their marriage; the Estates, who wanted an heir of her own body and distrusted Charles as a foreigner; and, above all, the Senate, led by Axel Oxenstierna, who wanted to frustrate all plans for an ensured succession in order to divert more power for themselves and re-assert the electoral principle. Christina overcame this formidable array of opposition by applying the old maxim, 'Divide and Rule.' She exploited the tensions between Senate and Estates to cajole the latter and coerce the former. Her first move was to give Charles control of the army, so that he would have sufficient power to assert his rights on her departure. The Senate perceived her drift and disallowed the move, but she took advantage of the continuing state of war on the continent to appoint Charles to a command abroad. Then in January, 1649, when he was safely distant, she revealed her full proposal to the Estates. The words she chose are worth quoting, for they amount to a brilliant exposition of the political manifesto of a power-woman, who knows the disadvantages of female rule and is determined to forestall them:

> It is not what is best for me, nor consideration of my exalted position, nor what is to the advantage of Charles that we must bear in mind. Our supreme law must be *securitas patriae.*

She engaged in debate on the merits of her plan with all the rhetorical skills she had learnt from her classical education, and in the end so far convinced the reluctant Estates as to secure Charles's election as successor. This, however, was only a partial victory. The form of words with which she wished Charles to be designated was 'Hereditary Prince'. 'Election' — which had also intruded into the wording of the proclamation of her own accession — was a term of opprobrium to the House of Vasa. She wanted the Senate to have no loophole through which to re-introduce an elective monarchy after her death.

She did not press the point at once, but renewed her attack in the Riksdag of the following year. Now she pursued her plan not only with rhetorical flair but also with political acumen. She began by launching an attack on the fiscal and judicial privileges of the aristocracy and on the great wealth they had accumulated thanks to Axel Oxenstierna's influence by depredations from the royal demesne. In this she gained the support of the clergy, towns and peasants, who were prepared to oblige her by promoting her succession plans in defiance of the Senate. She also succeeded in sundering the unity of the noble class, winning over individual members of the lower aristocracy, who were jealous or resentful of the Senate. Stockholm was full of anticipations of great mutations in the state. Annalists claimed to observe a ghostly attack upon the city. Poltergeists rattled the wooden buildings from within. Down the narrow, jerry-built streets wailed the shrieks of wraiths. The dead seemed to join the living in intimidating Christina's enemies. The result was a triumph for her case. The Senate surrendered. The hereditary principle was vindicated. Charles's future crown was assured. Any suspicion that Christina would not be true mistress of her realm was dispelled: 'The Queen indeed reigns in person,' wrote Chanut. To Axel Oxenstierna's guarded protests Christina replied with a despot's diktat: 'I am aware that this is an *exemplum sine exemplo,* but I find it justified since what I have done was for no other consideration than love of the fatherland.'

Had Christina some ulterior motive for choosing celibacy, apart from the proper political prudence with which a queen should behold the prospect of marriage? Certainly the virulence of her misogamy seems to call for some explanation. Distaste for sex may have had something to do with it. Even when, late in life, she surrendered her being wholeheartedly to a strongly physical passion for a man, she chose one 'whom piety prevents from becoming my lover' — the ingenious reformer Cardinal Azzolini. Her cousin, Maria Euphrosyne, had her own explanation for Christina's guarded response to overtures from Charles Gustavus: 'a maiden,' she observed, 'often rejects whom she secretly desires.' In 1647, Magnus Gabriel de la Gardie, whose closeness to the queen made some people suspect an intrigue between them, confirmed this diagnosis, and in a generalised form the theory turned up later as a subject for debate in one of Christina's Academies in Rome. On the other hand, some historians have explained Christina's misogamy by claiming that she was a lesbian. Her tomboy-childhood, her early loss of her father, her unhappy relationship with her mother — all are typical elements in a lesbian syndrome. But there is no contemporary evidence to support this speculation. Christina was accused of lesbianism along with every other kind of sexual extravagance by the coarse French pamphleteers who turned their scurrilous talents against her in the 1650's: but they had similar calumnies to fling against all their enemies, and Christina was by no means the only power-woman to attract smut from hack scatologists. She loved whatever was outrageous and liked to shock men by making jokes of these accusations. But to take either the jokes or the slanders which inspired them at face value would be unwise. Her letters to Cardinal Azzolini present us with evidence of normal sexual desires, fraught with only healthy inhibitions. Descartes, the guru of her years in power, warned her that love could be more destructive than hatred; like most gurus, he was only telling her what she already wanted to hear. To music — the Italianate music she always loved because it put her in mind of the south — she set a poem of Petrarch's, *In morte di Laura,* in which Love, destroyer of life, is arraigned in Reason's court. It is not surprising that this poem should have attracted her. It nicely expressed views of her own.

Even as she was exulting in her triumph over the Senate in 1649, Christina was contemplating an even more sensitive constitutional coup: the abjuration of the Lutheran faith, which was a lynchpin of the Swedish state, and the adoption of Catholicism. Although her childhood reading had been censored by the Estates 'lest the Queen be infected with Popish or Calvinistic errors', the seeds of her conversion were implanted by her education. Johannes Mattiae was a sincere and orthodox Lutheran, but the scandal of Christian schism troubled him as it troubled all enlightened and tolerant Christians after the Reformation. Like Erasmus, he favoured the re-establishment of concord between the sundered churches. In particular, he took an interest in ways of reconciling Calvinism and Lutheranism. The catechism he published in 1626 no doubt represents the kind of religious instruction he gave Christina: it is a remarkably broad-minded document, which seeks to avoid bigotry. This was to Christina's taste. Her questioning, critical mind was repelled by the narrow outlook of the preachers to whose arid homiletics she was incessantly exposed. The story she tells in her autobiography, of her revulsion against the uncompromising damnation threatened by a preacher she heard as a child, may not have had for her at the time the spiritual significance she later ascribed to it — she saw it as a kind of signpost on the road to Damascus — but it has some representative significance. Much later, when one of her old court chaplains asked what had turned her from Lutheranism, she replied, 'Your sermons.' She used her own powers of patronage to mitigate the rigours of the Swedish Lutheran establishment. She visited the disputations at Uppsala University, where the syncretists — the party that favoured Protestant ecumenism, put up a bold show of toleration. She promoted syncretists to influential positions in the heirarchy and the University. She particularly relished the chance this gave her to snub the advice of Axel Oxenstierna, one of the most dogmatically unbending of the Lutheran *vielle garde*.

But Laodicean religion did not satisfy her. She began to seek alternative paths to religious consolation in classical and modern philosophy. When Chanut arrived at court, he found a young woman whose interest in religion was profound — particularly in anything to which Swedish censorship deprived her of access — but whose conception of virtue was stoical. She sought an eminence that could only be attained by merit, a freedom that could only come from wisdom. This was laudable, but pre-Christian. It was what Christina called 'her own religion'. Chanut, however, introduced her to Catholic verities of which she had never before had an opportunity to hear. He was one of the few men at court learned enough to converse with her on equal terms and she conceived a lofty esteem for his judgement. At Chanut's invitation, she sent for philosophical enlightenment to the most profound thinker of the age, René Descartes, whose faith in the Catholic Church was unimpaired by the originality of his own intellect. In only a few chats, he laid the foundations of Christina's future faith. 'I have Descartes to thank,' she wrote, 'for the facility with which I overcame many of the difficulties which restrained me from Catholicism.' Unhappily, Descartes proved a martyr to Christina's proselytisation. The burden of rising for philosophy tutorials with the indefatigable Christina at five in the morning in the freezing air of the royal library wrecked his health and consigned him to an early grave within five months of his arrival in Stockholm. But the queen's interest in the Roman faith was now irreversibly aroused and other means of access to instruction were fortunately at hand.

Lars Skytte, Swedish ambassador in Portugal, had been received into the Catholic Church. His friend Francisco Macedo visited Stockholm for Christina's coronation in 1650 and addressed a panegyric to the queen. Macedo's brother, Antonio, arrived in the capital soon afterwards as chaplain to the Portuguese ambassador: his official role was as interpreter, since the open practice of Catholicism was not permitted in Sweden, where the establishment would have looked askance on the presence of a Jesuit. But Antonio was able to use his ambassador's audiences as a cloak for the proselytisation of Christina. She soon convinced him of her anxiety for formal instruction and sent him in the utmost secrecy to Rome with a missive for the General of the Society of Jesus, in which Christina declared

> I should consider myself fortunate if, through some Italian members of your Order, I could receive assurances that you consider me, albeit unknown, worthy of your friendship and further correspondence.

The evangelisation of the mighty was something of a speciality of the Jesuits and the allure of such an illustrious convert was irresistible — a regnant queen, head of a country which had been the standard-bearer of the Protestant cause in the Thirty Years' War, and one of the most esteemed women of her day for learning and brilliance. Two Jesuit 'secret agents', professors of mathematics and theology who could defend themselves in conversation with the Hyperborean Minerva, arrived in Stockholm, disguised as merchants, in March 1652. Christina had by now resolved most of her doubts and was eager to embrace a faith she was convinced was true. The generously tolerant Calvinist scholar, Claude Saumaise, who had been employed at her court, realised her desire to become a Catholic and opened a further line of communication for her with Jesuits in Antwerp. She could

Maria Theresa Empress of Austria 1717-1780.

also rely on the help of the Spanish ambassador — Chanut had been recalled to Paris in June, 1651 — who could assure her of a safe haven in Antwerp when public avowal of her Catholicism should force her to flee Sweden. But to extricate herself from her homeland, to which she was bound by her obligations as sovereign, would require time and care. Christina nourished the perilous secret of her Catholicism, within a small circle of reliable friends, for nearly four years while she made her preparations.

It may be that she would have abdicated even had her change of faith not impelled her. She often admitted to reveries of a 'quiet life'. Her scholarly and speculative tastes could be best indulged apart from the cares of statecraft. Moreover, she had cause to be fearful of her health. Strange fevers assailed her during 1650 and she thought seriously about admitting Charles Gustavus to a share in the duties of government. In March, 1651 — when her Catholic convictions were already growing within her — Chanut hinted to Paris that she might not retain the crown for long. Her preparations for Charles's accession made her own continued occupancy of the throne strictly unnecessary. Even so, it was only the desire to find fulfilment in the open profession of her new faith that drove her to take a decisive step towards the relinquishment of the throne. She hinted as much to her Senate when she later told them that God alone knew her real motive. In August 1651 she asked the Senate and Estates to accept her abdication. But her subjects professed themselves unwilling to forego her 'princely wisdom'. She asked her Jesuits whether she could remain a crypto-catholic and so retain her crown; but this was a course which she did not desire and which they would not permit.

By the time she forced through her second abdication proposal she had laid careful plans to ensure success. After toying with the possibility of remaining on Swedish soil, in a fief hived off for her in the islands of Gotland and Ostland, she resolved to succumb to her heart's desire and go to live in Rome, the capital of her faith and the cynosure of the classical civilisation she had always admired. Not for the first or last time a 'barbarian' monarch would be seduced by the warmth and culture of the Mediterranean, Christina — another 'Gothic' queen — was following in Amalasuntha's footsteps. She had to rely on Charles Gustavus to continue to honour their longstanding friendship and keep up the payments of income from her Swedish estates: in Swedish law, these could have been forfeit when she announced her apostasy from Lutheranism. And her journey, until she should reach the safety of Antwerp, would be fraught with hazard as she passed through Protestant territory. But she abandoned herself to these risks and, having commended herself to God, she travelled in great danger, disguised as a man — thereby incidentally creating an absurd legend that she was a transvestite — and at last, after a stately progress from Antwerp, entered the eternal city on 23rd December, 1655. Bellini rebuilt the Porta del Popolo, through which she passed, for the occasion, adorning it with the inscription: 'Felici Faustoque Ingressui.' In a century of lavish spectacle, it was one of the most marvellous of days. The Pope believed it would adorn his pontificate with fame that would re-echo down the centuries. The Catholic world exulted: the joy in heaven over the sinner that repenteth was on this occasion, apparently, immeasurably enhanced by the convert's great status.

The renunciation of her throne did not mean that Christina ceased to be a power-woman. The arrangements she made at her abdication ensured that she would continue to have the status of a sovereign queen within her own courts and in the precincts of her own palaces. This gave her power — within a restricted sphere — without responsibility and a right of life and death over her subjects which she did not scruple to exercise when she believed one of them betrayed her. She had not renounced the pomp or the instincts of a power-woman. 'I find it less inconvenient to have a subject garrotted than to live in fear of him,' she wrote in vindication of her continued right of capital punishment. She played a political role in Rome. She brooded over conclaves, mediated between disputants and waged in her court wars of etiquette between rival ambassadors. She sent emissaries around Europe in support of papal plans for a crusade. At length, she aspired to return to the arena in which she was so skilled, not only as a sovereign queen but also as the chief executive of a nation. In 1656-7 she schemed for the Neapolitan crown and even achieved the remarkable feat of procuring a treaty from Mazarin promising that France would conquer that kingdom for her in exchange for the reversion after her death. The plan came to nothing. Spain's hold on Naples was too tight to be dislodged. But Christina continued to find consoling prospects elsewhere — bidding improbably for the Swedish regency on Charles Gustavus's death and getting a surprising welcome from the people of southern Sweden when she ventured — daringly but briefly — anew on Swedish soil. Frustrated in that quarter, too, she entered her candidacy for the Polish crown — an old appanage of the Vasas — when the throne fell vacant in 1668. But by that time she had too many failures in her past. Even the bishops — who might have been expected to favour a candidate backed by the pope — laughed her candidature to scorn. Christina turned within herself, to the realm of her own soul, which she had always found most fascinating and loved best. She comforted herself with the pious quietism of Miguel de Molinos, sharing her devotion for that charismatic guru with other ageing ladies of Roman salons. She toyed with her memoirs, entertained scholars, gloated over art and ate her heart out in her hopeless love for Cardinal Azzolini. When she died on 19th April, 1689, she was faded in everything save her girth, which had grown with the unwonted inactivity and over-indulgence of her declining years. Yet even when she was pitiable she remained impressive — one of the outstanding practitioners of a power-woman's art of all time. As she looked back, she saw even her abdication as heroic 'strong, manly and powerful', she said — an act which identified her with Sulla or Charles V. But in reality, it was a self-denying ordinance which deflected her from her destiny. The failure that had followed her since then could hardly mask the bravura of her life: her great days of power, when she out-manoeuvred wily Machiavels like Oxenstierna or Mazarin, won wars and decreed peace. Her conversion had been the undoing of her career as a power-woman but it had been a characteristically bold and radical adventure, which had brought her to the threshold of a greater kingdom, not of this world. She is honoured with an exceptional monument to her memory above her grave in St Peter's Cathedral — an elegant confection of piety and classicism of which she would surely have approved.

CHAPTER NINE

The Age of Catherine the Great

Apart from Christina, no power-woman of the seventeenth century left an exemplary record behind her. Louisa of Portugal, for instance, in a career which was a pathetic echo of Christina's, was forced into a nunnery as an escape from the consequences of a disastrous regency. Marie de Medici, regent for the infant Louis XIII, embroiled France in political difficulties from which only the genius of Richelieu could extract her. Anne of Austria, who performed the same function in the minority of Louis XIV, confided the realm to her Machiavellian lover, Cardinal Mazarin, and helped to precipitate the Fronde rebellions. Despite their poor showings, however, these women had a positive and beneficial effect on the future image of the power-woman. It was an effect they achieved indirectly, by way of their patronage of feminist writings.

From this point of view, it was fortuitous that France experienced so much female influence, for literary and intellectual fashions were set there. France, since the days of Anne of Beaujeu, had an established tradition of female regency. The reign of Francis I, for instance, had begun with the king's mother, Louise of Savoy, as a royal coadjutor who negotiated the *Paix des Dames* of 1529 between France and Spain with the female regent of the Netherlands, Margaret of Austria. Louise was regent of France during her son's Spanish captivity. After her death, the king relied heavily on advice from Margaret of Angoulême. And the second half of the sixteenth century was dominated by Catherine de Medici, who taught the art of kingship to successive monarchs (they were, however, uniformly unsuccessful pupils) and helped to introduce the concept of toleration into the confessionally divided politics of the age of religious wars. In so doing, she helped to create the myth of the power-woman as bringer of peace and resolver of conflict, which formed such a prominent part of the ideological armouries of Elizabeth I and Queen Christina.

French law was unalterably hostile to female sovereigns but these regencies afforded an opportunity to inspire a more generalised propaganda in favour of power-women. In 1559, for instance, almost as soon as

Catherine de Medici achieved her first supremacy, the jurist Baudouin traced the history of sexual discrimination in Roman inheritance law, showing how Justinian's Code had relieved women of their disabilities. French lawyers generally in the late sixteenth century showed an increasing willingness to take a liberal view of women's rights to succession to fiefs. Numerous writers almost simultaneously discovered that wifely subjection to husbands did not necessarily imply the subjection of all women to all men.

But it was under the seventeenth century regents, Marie de Medici and Anne of Austria, that feminism — at least, feminism of a kind — in literature really flourished. This was directly the result of the regents' patronage. In 1652, for instance, Anne invited D'Audiguier du Mazet to shatter in precise prose the defenders of the Salic Law. Out of the work done in the regents' court circles a new stereotype emerged — the *femme forte,* an almost preternatural hybrid of feminine and masculine virtues, of beauty and strength, of meekness and might, of eirenism and prowess. This hypothetical paragon was admirably portrayed in Le Moyne's *Ode à la Femme Forte:*

> La femme forte a ses emplois:
> Sur les devoirs et les lois.
> Ses actions sont concertées.
> Tranquille sans oysiueté
> Active avec sérénité,
> Elle scait les labeurs et les grâces.

Writers dwelt, in the France of the regents, on the heroism and public fame of women in history: no themes could be more pertinent in attempting to establish womens fitness to rule. But it is only rarely that one finds celebration of the *femme forte* allied with a more radical feminism. Many writers asserted female equality, but few advanced arguments for female superiority over men generally other than in jest. It took the pugnacious blue stocking, Suzanne de Nervèze, to claim in 1642 that men should content themselves with the honour of being born of women and leave the rest to their female betters. Indeed, the effect of the literature of the *femme forte* was to convince the erudite world that female rulers, although acceptable, were exceptional — rule-defying prodigies, thrown up only occasionally in the course of history. The attitudes bequeathed by the seventeenth century to the eighteenth are typified by the writings of Francois Poullain de la Barre, who spanned both centuries in the duration of his life and also in the nature of his thought. His four tracts written in defence of the concept of equality of the sexes towards the end of the sixteen-hundreds anticipate the enlightenment of the age of the *philosophes.* He points out that it is wrong to infer from differences between the sexes that men and women are necessarily unequal; he observes that girls learn faster than boys, that they are better at medicine, theology and history, and he claims that more women than men believe in the circulation of the blood. His main argument is perfectly admissible: a sexual basis of classification is less useful in categorising mankind than differences of climate, customs and diet. In the eighteenth century, therefore, European power-women competed with men against a background of widely assumed sexual equality, and the presumption that female rulers would be *femmes fortes,* prodigiously equipped with transexual advantages.

The eighteenth century in Europe was dominated by two power-women whose superficially contrasting characters masked similarity — even in some respects identity — of political techniques: Maria Theresa of Austria and Catherine the Great of Russia. They led lives which counterpointed one another, like Victoria of England and Isabel of Spain in the next century. The one was a distillation of matronly virtue, a devoted wife and concerned mother, cultivating at home a *ménage* blissfully united and uneventful. The other was a virago who throve on domestic conflict, voracious in her sexual appetite, recklessly devoted to sensualism, indifferent to her offspring and inimical to her spouse.

Of the two, only Maria Theresa was born in the purple, yet her upbringing was in many ways less regal than Catherine's. Unlike Russia, the Habsburg dominions to which Maria Theresa was heir presumptive from her birth in 1717, knew no precedents for female rule. Her father so hoped and trustd that a manchild would be sired in due course that he dismissed the chances of Maria Theresa's succeeding and neglected to prepare her for her destiny — neglected, almost, to make any more than formal provisions for her accession to the throne. The constitutional relationship of a Habsburg monarch to his subjects was complex. There were no uniform institutions throughout the Habsburgs' divers and disparate domains. The ruler was count here, duke there, king in another place; in some areas he was an autocrat, in others confined by aristocratic privilege or representative estates. In some realms he was an elective and in others an hereditary head. Two domains were of transcendent importance. The Archduchy of Austria was the heartland of the Habsburgs' *Hausmacht,* comprising a great belt of continuous territory in the wealthy south of the German *Reich*. Possession of this inheritance had made the Habsburgs the most powerful princes in Germany more or less uninterruptedly since the thirteenth century, though they had rarely been able to impose a long-lasting hegemony on their rivals. As well as their Archduchy, the Habsburgs possessed in the east, on the Turkish frontier, the Kingdom of Hungary, which had some historical claim to be an elective monarchy although in practice the house had imposed a dynastic settlement upon it. Austria and Hungary together were the bedrock of Habsburg power. Of less material importance but of enormous numinous significance was the title of Holy Roman Emperor — head, that is to say, of the German Reich, which traced its historical origins, rather tenuously, to ancient Rome. The emperor had been a Habsburg for most of the previous half-millemium but elective procedures had never lapsed. The Habsburgs were heirs to a great congeries besides of possessions and claims in Germany, northern Italy, the Netherlands, Bohemia — and numerous other pretensions which were a *damnosa hereditas,* imbroiling them in endless disputes with France, Spain, Poland and the Ottoman Empire. To some of the house's appanages a woman could clearly succeed as of right. To others, such as, most notably, the imperial dignity, she equally clearly could not. In others, like Austria and Hungary themselves, it might be possible to make special arrangements for a woman to succeed.

The solution devised by Maria Theresa's father reflected the heterogeneous nature of the Habsburg monarchy. In 1723, the Estates of Hungary accepted the principle of female succession to the Hungarian crown. In 1732, the Estates of the Reich adopted as an imperial law a settlement of the succession to the Habsburg lands within the Reich collectively, enabling Maria Theresa to succeed her father in default of brothers. But this law, which came to be known as the Pragmatic Sanction, required ratification in all the Habsburg lands separately. It had also to be accepted by the major princes of the Empire and the foremost monarchs of Europe in order to be assured of success.

The Pragmatic Sanction only envisaged Maria Theresa as Habsburg heir as last resort. Her father fought tenaciously to get the law adopted and accepted not because he hoped or expected that his daughter would succeed but because at the very worst he hoped for a grandson by her and wanted to ensure the throne for this putative infant. He was unwilling to tempt Providence by giving her a princely education. The accomplishments she was taught were wifely and ladylike: comportment, dancing, singing: she was never allowed to indulge a fancy for equestrianism — that was too much the pastime of a tomboy — and only rarely to take part in her favourite sport of shooting. Music was the family hobby and Maria Theresa was instructed soundly enough to accompany the great professional singers of the day. But this was drawing-room talent, devoid of political significance. For the rest she emerged from her schooling at the hands of arid and old-fashioned Jesuits with a passionately felt Catholic faith, a sound competence of Latin and an almost unrelieved ignorance of politics and modern history. She was to regret the deficiency deeply, but her education did not impart enough love of learning for her to attempt to teach herself. She never read for pleasure, and only rarely for instruction.

On the other hand, she did acquire in childhood — perhaps from the pseudo-historical panegyrics prescribed by her tutors — a profound reverence for her ancestors and, therefore, a sense of her own regal dignity. Unlike her father, she never doubted her destiny. Though she lacked any intellectual basis of statecraft she evolved an instinctive queenliness — a way of bearing herself and projecting herself, of exploiting her femininity and emulating men. It was the English ambassador who first noticed that she was 'a princess of the highest spirit ... of a temper formed for rule and ambition' but, because she was excluded in adolescence from political life, it was in the domestic matter of a choice of spouse that her strength of will first made itself felt. Maria Theresa was determined to marry her heart's choice: Francis Stephen was son of the Duke of Lorraine, an old boon companion of her father's. Almost any other suitor would have been a better political match. Francis Stephen had been introduced to the court early as a prospective choice for the princess, when the likelihood of her succeeding her father still seemed remote and the need for a grand husband of lofty international stature was not yet urgent. To the subsequent embarrassment of all concerned, Maria Theresa fell in love with him, literally at first sight, cherished him as a childhood sweetheart and would gainsay him for no rival, however great or useful. Her love was utterly sincere and utterly innocent. In an age when paramours were an accepted part of everyone's social equipment, she never took another lover. The royal husband and wife cultivated a modest domesticity much beneath their station, by their own hearthside in dressing-gowns and bedroom slippers they were 'made for bourgeois marriage', as one Prussian observer said. Throughout their life together, Maria Theresa wrote tender little love-letters in a peculiarly macaronic language of their own, interjecting Italian endearments to 'caro mio viso' from 'la votre sponsia dilectissima' — for Italian was her preferred language for romance as for poetry — into her cryptic, untranslatable French. He was her 'little mouse', she his 'little puppy'. Perhaps the greatest mystery above her love for Francis Stephen, after its exclusivity, is its inexplicability. Like so much female affection, it was unmerited. Francis Stephen had a certain business flair, which enabled him to transform the ancestral penury of his house into a modest fortune, but he lacked strength of character, political sagacity, military skill and general intelligence. When he conducted ambassadorial interviews, Maria Theresa had to listen outside the door and interrupt whenever he was about to commit some gaffe. He was not even faithful to her, as she was to him. The object of her adulation, in short, was a shallow and reckless mountebank.

Partly thanks to her own tenacity, they were married when she was nineteen. It is indicative of how Maria Theresa was underrated that her husband was now admitted to the inner councils of the Habsburg empire, from which she remained excluded. They were given an early foretaste of government by virtue of one of those wheeler-dealing territorial settlements that characterised eighteenth century diplomacy. As part of the price for French recognition of the Pragmatic Sanction, Francis was forced to cede his dynastic inheritance in Lorraine in exchange for the Grand Duchy of Tuscany. Indeed, it was made clear to him that his compliance was a prerequisite of his marriage. 'No renunciation, no Archduchess,' the Austrian statesman, Bartenstein, brusquely told him. After the wedding and after Francis Stephen's brief and inglorious intervention in the war against the Turks, the young couple were packed off for a festive visitation of their new possession. But it was part of Maria Theresa's syndrome of domesticity to dislike travel and detest foreign parts. They were soon back in Vienna, keeping an eye on developments in the more important milieu of the emperor's court. There was no evidence that either of them possessed any political *nous*. By 1741, when her father's death vacated the throne for Maria Theresa, she had proved herself in only one capacity: she had borne two children, and was pregnant with a third — a son, the future Emperor Joseph II, who would be able in due course to re-establish the rhythm of male inheritors of the Habsburg dominions.

Her adoration of her husband, her taste for domestic felicity, her pre-Victorian prudery, are all reminiscent of nineteenth century England. Uniquely for her own time, Maria Theresa was censorious of other people's morals and tyrannical in her efforts to discipline them. In 1747 she established a Chastity Commission — a sexual inquisition empowered to carry out searches, discover actresses in compromising assignations, arrest men and women on presumption of immorality, immure females of loose life in convents and deport those guilty of scandalous behaviour. The Commission had a short life and a merry one. Two companies of players were exiled. The great soprano, Satini, was banished. But public indignation and popular ridicule soon brought the snooping to a close. The Commission was quietly disbanded only six months after its establishment, though some of the investigators were re-employed in Maria Theresa's secret police, which made a speciality of prurience. Throughout her life her court was — sexually — a Serbonian fog, where one incurred imperial displeasure for sexual peccadilloes and general contempt for chastity.

Maria Theresa was impervious to sex, but she was susceptible to sexless gurus: first the Jesuits who had supplied her childhood tutors, then a curious little sage of Portuguese origin called Don Manoel Telles de Menezes e Castro, Count of Tarouca. In some ways, he resembled Queen Victoria's John Browne — a 'natural' wise man, drawn into the royal confidence from outside the conventional elite, chosen instinctively by the Queen alone as a confidant and counsellor detached from the hurly-burly of faction. Tarouca was already verging on middle age when Maria Theresa assumed the crown, after a long career in Austrian service, first in the army, then in the administration of the Austrian Netherlands. The queen soon recognised that the ugly and unprepossessing foreigner had extraordinary powers of insight and exceptional gifts of sagacity and sincerity. First she insisted on daily audiences to discuss not only the affairs of the Netherlands but also the business of the empire generally. Gradually she edged Tarouca into a more personally confidential role. Yet no one was more astonished than he when she made him her lay confessor and conscience 'to show me my faults and make me recognise them ... this being most necessary for a ruler, since there are few or none at all to be found who will do this, commonly refraining out of awe or self-interest.'

Tarouca was undeniably useful. He organised Maria Theresa's horarium — up at eight, seven and a half hour's work a day, time for playing with her children, talking with her mother, hearing Mass and taking leisure (but riding, dancing and cards, which she loved immoderately, were restricted. He introduced order into court life and administrative business. And he was conscientious in admonition, sometimes offending by his frankness the queen who had commanded him to be frank. His greatest talent was for smoothing the rough edges of Maria Theresa's relations with her great servants and counsellors, whom she was inclined to wither with blasts of invective and harrass with tantrums. Tarouca knew all about the management of men. With extraordinary directness he warned Maria Theresa,

> Every human being has some weakness, some streak of pettiness. If one does not tolerate these in others, how can one flatter oneself that others will make allowances in turn? Love and trust will cool.

She could be intolerant in other ways. Her lack of book-learning permeated her against the European enlightenment spread by the French *philosophes*. In an age of increasing religious indifference and toleration, she clung to a crabbed and dogmatic version of Catholicism that held heretics in abhorrence. She waged a fruitless struggle to wean her son from his believe in religious emancipation, conceiving persecution to be an ineluctable duty of a monarch. She felt a similar distaste of the Jews, whom she forbade to enter Vienna and expelled from Bohemia. When obliged to discuss a matter of debt with a Jewish financier, she did so only from behind a screen, so as not to confront an heir of Christ's tormentors face to face. Such fastidious bigotry was ludicrous and anachronistic, but Maria Theresa would not be deflected from it even by the intellectual superiority of her son's forceful arguments.

With such a defective education, and such a cantankerous character, the auguries for her competent management of affairs of state on her accession, before she discovered Tarouca, cannot have been good. Yet when she tremulously greeted her counsellors on the first day of her reign, she immediately struck the keynote of her queenly style, instantly inspiring their devotion by affecting vulnerability, while contriving a simple dignity which commanded loyalty. In her black dress, with her characteristically negligent coiffure, she was irresistibly appealing. She showed from the first that she had a power-woman's instinct for political transexuality. 'I am only a woman,' she once said, 'but I have the heart of a king.' This dichotomy rippled through her reign. In Hungary, she was always called 'king', by the masculine noun. When the Hungarian nobility voted to support her first war against Prussia they intoned the traditional formula, 'Life and blood for our King, Maria Theresa.' She was 'King and Mother' to her Estates and 'Mother of the Camps' to her troops. She developed a mania for the horse-riding that was forbidden to her as a child and made the ladies of the court play at the carousel — a mock-tourney that was also a natural part of the education of a boy. She took a passionate interest in warfare and strategy — 'one sphere which really interests me' — and deeply regretted that her sex excluded her from the field. Her ultimate gesture of virile bravado was to challenge Frederick the Great to single combat. She learned to smother meekness with a ruthless display. The queen who wept privately at the bloodshed of the Turkish war, could also write:

> All my armies, all the Hungarians must perish before I cede anything ... You will say that I am cruel: it is true but I also know very well that I shall make good a hundredfold all hard things I do in this hour ... My heart must be closed against pity.

The ruthlessness was forced, but her genuine despotic streak and stubborn, unremitting determination in pursuit of any course on which she was resolved, served to make it possible.

She was a self-confessed mistress of 'our usual refuge, caresses and tears ... and temper.' She wheedled loyalty out of men. Her appeal is typified in the letter she sent to her loyal general Khevenhüller in 1742 (in the darkest days of her war against Prussia, France and Bavaria) accompanied by a little portrait of herself and her infant son which she bad him display to the troops:

> Dear and faithful Khevenhüller — Here you behold the Queen who knows what it is to be forsaken by the whole world. And here also is the heir to the throne. What do you think will become of this child? To you, as a true and tried servant of the State, your gracious Lady offers this picture of herself, and therewith her entire power and means — everything indeed that her kingdom contains and can supply. You, the hero and trusted vassal, shall dispose of all things as you think fit and as you would render account before God and the world in general. May your achievements be as renowned as those of your master, the great Eugene, who rests in God. Be fully assured that now and always you and your family will never lack the grace and favour and thanks of me and my descendants. A world-wide fame will be yours too.
>
> Fare well and fight well.
>
> Maria Theresa.

Despite these power-woman's gifts her accession was, almost inevitably, a disaster for her empire. The Habsburgs had too many enemies, anxious to take advantage of the queen's sex and inexperience. Governments raced to abjure the Pragmatic Sanction. Princes plotted to oust Maria Theresa from her thrones and challenge her husband in the imperial election. Within her realms aristocracies and estates were awaiting a chance to exact concessions and privileges from a weakened crown. Maria Theresa began bravely. She refused concessions to the Hungarians, insisted on the adoption of her husband as co-ruler in Austria, and proclaimed an amnesty. But beneath the display of confidence she was apprehensive. She was encumbered with an impenetrably complex and inefficient system of government which she did not know how to manage, exploit or reform. Her domain, so impressive from a distance, was riven by particularism which impeded co-operation and hamstrung decision-making. When Frederick the Great precipitated the first and greatest crisis of her reign by invading her province of Silesia within a few weeks of her accession, she was utterly unprepared to meet the onslaught.

Frederick's coup was a brilliant piece of opportunism. In his youth the Prussian king had written a tract against Machiavelli, but in reality he was a thoroughgoing disciple of *staatspolitik*. His invasion was unsupported by any principle of ethics or law. He invited Maria Theresa to accept the *fait accompli* in exchange for his support in the forthcoming imperial election, in which Francis Stephen was opposed by Charles Albert of Bavaria. On all sides, sage heads counselled compromise. The English — her only foreign allies — were anxious for peace with Prussia. The gerontocrats of her council, bequeathed to her by her father, were timorous. Francis Stephen was easily duped by Prussian diplomacy. But Maria Theresa was a genuine anti-Machiavel. She followed now — as she always would — the dictates of her heart and duty. She worshipped principle unalloyed by pragmatism. She also had an instinctive sense of the dangers of appeasement. 'Not only for political reasons,' she claimed.

> but from conscience and honour, I will not consent to part with much in Silesia ... No sooner is one enemy satisfied than another starts up; another and another must be appeased, and all at my expense.

In one sense, her instinct was sound; in another, her resolution was fruitless. In a total of fourteen years' warfare over the fate of Silesia, she was forced to yield to Frederick's military superiority, on terms she could have obtained without fighting a single battle. On the other hand, her wars were probably, from a broader perspective, worth fighting. Silesia — albeit an important province, rich populous, industrialised, full of mineral wealth — was the only territorial sacrifice of her reign. On most other fronts, Habsburg lands were extended. She was successful in securing the election of her husband as Holy Roman Emperor and ensuring the reversion of the empire for her son. In many ways, in view of the decreptitude of Austrian defences and finances, it is remarkable that she salvaged so much from the hazards of war. She was directly responsible for such glory as Austrian arms achieved in the first sruggle to convulse her reign, by inspiring the strategy that took General Khevenhüller into the heart of enemy territory in 1742. Her own diplomatic influence played a part in constructing the great coalition of continental powers that waged war on Prussia in the second major war over Silesia, in which the lost province was very nearly recovered.

In 1765, Maria Theresa's husband died. And her famous beauty, which had held Europe spellbound, was dying. She fell silent for days at her husband's deathbed and retired to her rooms to sew his shroud herself. She donned jewelless mourning which she wore for the rest of her life. 'I hardly know myself now,' she wrote to Tarouca a few weeks after the blow, 'for I have become like a beast with no true soul or power of reason.' To begin with, she felt politically stultified and was at first inclined to abdicate all her power at once into the hands of her son Joseph. But she contented herself with nominating him to the co-regency vacated by Francis Stephen's death. He succeeded to the throne of the Holy Roman Empire, too, by virtue of prior election. Henceforth his craving for real power, his restless ambition and uncompromisingly modern philosphical ideals would plague his mother's old age. In her declining years Maria Theresa was a shadow of her former self. Resigning herself to the loss of Silesia, she became increasingly cynical about politics. She gave up an increasing amount of time to correspondence with her daughters — particularly the unhappy Marie Antoinette who often asked her advice about the course of her miserable marriage to the future Louis XVI of France. The ageing empress dowager became easy prey for exploitative courtiers as, relaxing her own tyranny, she indulged the petty despotisms of subordinates. She continued to tinker with the educational and administrative reforms she had burned in her youth to introduce to her dominions; but what little she attained was to be eclipsed by the thoroughgoing radicalism of her son's reign. Hers was an inglorious decline, bereft of love, save from her daughters, empty of happiness, devoid of success.

The unrestrained ambitions of her son, which forced her into what was virtually a power-struggle with him to try to keep him under control, gnawed at her heart and enfeebled her former vitality. In 1772, in collusion with the empire's foremost counsellor, Prince Kaunitz, Joseph obliged his mother, against her better judgement, to consent to the partition of Poland between Austria, Russia and Prussia. Maria Theresa was stricken in her conscience by this departure from the path of principle. When, in 1776, Joseph insisted on attempting to seize part of Bavaria by force, just as Frederick the Great had once seized her own beloved Silesia, Maria Theresa's grief was unbounded. Joseph's importunate adventure had provoked Prussia to war. Maria Theresa threw herself into furious diplomatic activity to try to frustrate her son's bellicose frenzy. It was a last rallying of her old energy. She threatened to abdicate if he defied her by coming to blows with the Prussians — 'I cannot always be forced to act against my conscience and my convictions,' she declared. In fact, she struggled on for a few more years, in nominal sovereignty, but her heart was no longer in the task of governing. In a world overtaken by the virile staatspolitik of Frederick and Joseph, Maria Theresa was a lone and feeble female voice, praying for peace and self-sacrifice. It was redolent of the most profound nobility of her sex to beg Austria 'to be deemed weak rather than dishonest' and to warn that 'the State's greatness and its strength will count for nothing when we are all called to render our final account'. But the words, though they sounded well, had been stripped of significance by the march of events. When, broken by the ruin of her ideals, she died stoically in the arms of her recalcitrant son on 29th November, 1780, it was as if the last light of a gentler age was going out.

Meanwhile, on the eastern margin of Europe, a power-woman had arisen who yielded nothing to men in the exploitation of the new morality, whether in sex or politics. The woman known to historians as Catherine the Great of Russia was born and baptised Sophia Frederika Augusta of Anhalt-Zerbst on 21st April, 1729, the daughter of middling German princelings who penury and political misfortune had driven into the service of the King of Prussia. It was totally unforeseeable that this obscure little girl should, after a triple metamorphosis — of nationality, religion and name — become ruler in her own right of the vast and semi-barbaric empire that henceforth, as a major power, would tyrannise much of Europe and terrorise the rest. She was an ugly and unloved child, but in adolescence she blossomed into beauty or at least attractiveness sufficient to interest Prince Peter Ulric of Russia when he visited the Prussian court. Peter was captivated by all things Prussian, but that in itself was not enough to fix his choice on Sophia, the court was full of emulous mothers on the *qui vive* for a marriageable prince. In any case, Peter was not yet in any sense a brilliant match. He belonged to a cadet line of the imperial Russian house. He had no direct claim to the succession and he seemed to have few prospects save as a pawn in the continual and bloody domestic intrigues of the Russian court, or perhaps as a practitioner of the military arts which were his all-absorbing passion. But at the end of 1741, a Palace coup brought to the Russian throne a grand-daughter of Peter the Great, the Empress Elisabeth, who had once been engaged to a relative of Sophia's and retained some affection for the clan. Furthermore, Elisabeth, though little more than a figurehead in Russia, enjoyed considerable licence in regulating the affairs of the dynasty: in particular, by a law of Peter the Great's she possessed the right to nominate her successor. She was wholly absorbed in the exercise of her unlimited libido, which no marriage could contain, and had no intention of restricting herself by taking a husband. Her search for a politically innocuous heir led her to the person of Peter Ulric, whom she summoned from Prussia and placed under her own wing with the promise of the imperial crown. Suddenly, Sophia's flirtation with an imperial johnny-come-lately had been transformed into a political dalliance of the greatest delicacy and most dazzling potential.

Frederick the Great of Prussia, with his genius for exploiting every opportunity, saw a new chance to foster a Russia-Prussian alliance. He nurtured the remote prospect of marriage between Peter and Sophia until it became a likelihood and at last a fact. The girl's father was promoted to Field Marshal; flattering portraits of her were despatched to St Petersburg; Prussian diplomats pushed the affair along. Peter was a retarded and sadistic psychopath, without any intelligence or charm, but Sophia wanted to marry him for the sake of the power and grandeur he represented. In 1744, she and her mother went to Russia — on approval, as it were, — at Elisabeth's invitation. In August, 1745, now re-christened Catherine at her Orthodox baptism, she wedded the heir to all the Russias.

This marriage was the first of many political coups of Catherine's. To pull it off, she had to muster considerable political skill, for the Russian empire was faction-ridden and unstable; nor were there wanting opponents of German influence and enemies of Elisabeth's plans. Catherine was still a political ingénue, but the character traits which would make her a skilful politician were already formed when she came to Russia. She was already single-mindedly dedicated to power, at any sacrifice of principle or personal preference: a childhood spent in the presence of Frederick the Great had wrought its influence. She already had a questioning, critical intellect, which had harried her tutors, and an inexhaustible capacity for learning whatever was useful or improving. She was hugely haughty and self-willed: as a small child she had even dared to be impertinent to the King of Prussia. She had also developed a less creditable characteristic which she was later able to turn to political advantage: a coarse and undiscriminating sex drive. Her Memoirs recount in frank detail her childish ecstasy in nights of self-abuse and her relish of her uncle's illicit kisses. Her lust would be repressed for a while in Russia by the vigilance of the Empress Elisabeth but it would later erupt with such unabashed excess that her enemies plausibly accused her of echoing the empress Theodora's notorious yearning for extra orifices.

Meanwhile, angling for imperial marriage, she presented a demure and

Catherine — Empress of Russia 1729-1796. After painting by Lempi.

politically detached facade to her Russian public. She taught herself statescraft by reading Montesquieu — auto-didacticism was the only recreation available to her in St Petersburg — and acquired, through perusal of the *philosophes,* an intellectual agility far excelling that of most members of the under-educated Russian élite. She cleverly courted popularity and stored up credit for the future by imbibing the Russian language and culture with apparent enthusiasm — something her betrothed, who was supposed one day to lead this people, never bothered to do. She cheerfully abandoned the Lutheranism in which she had been brought up for the Orthodoxy which was *de rigueur* in Russia — not, as the people believed, from geneuine devotion but from a cynical indifference to all religion. And although it was hard, especially in political circles, to make friends amid the volatile and opalescent Russians, she began, even before her marriage, to create a basis of future support by currying favour with anyone she deemed to have actual or potential influence.

But even after her marriage she could not achieve political security. The anti-Prussian party was gradually growing in influence in Elisabeth's circle — especially after the empress took one of their number as a lover. Catherine, though happy to trim to any political wind, was unfortunately tainted by association with the Prussophile husband. She had come, within a few years of marriage, to hate his moodiness, cruelty and stupidity, luridly over-written in her memoirs, and had been frustrated by his impotence — not only sexually but also from fulfilling her role of bearing children to continue the imperial line, by his impotence. Even after this was corrected by circumcision — a favourite nostrum of eighteenth century surgeons for this particular complaint — his embraces brought her no satisfaction. In 1752, she began to take lovers and was surprised shortly afterwards to find her *vie amoureuse* countenanced by the empress, who seems to have preferred even an heir tainted by bastardy to no heir at all. Catherine's lovers also represented an opportunity to extend and balance her circle of political support outside the range of the influence of her husband. Peter was already an embarrassment. She realised he would one day be a rival. Luckily, she bore a son in 1754. This fortuitous fertility exonerated her in the empress's eyes for all the shortcomings imputed by her foes and she managed to survive the eclipse of the Purssian party in 1759-61. Then fate intervened again to plunge her fortunes once more into the crucible. Worn out with debauchery, Elisabeth died on Christmas Day, 1761. Catherine was empress — but only, as yet, as consort to a husband she viewed with envy, enmity and personal loathing.

This was a predicament in which Catherine could show that she had the mettle of a power-woman. They were dangerous days for her. While she had to conceal the fact that she was pregnant by her latest lover, Gregory Orlov, her husband was open with his threats to repudiate her and substitute his own mistress on the empress's throne. Catherine was incarcerated in her apartments, unable to intervene in the radical — and to some extent random — transformation of Russia on which Peter now impulsively embarked. Had his insanity not been notorious and his reign short, Peter might by luck rather than judgement, have won the reputation of an energetic and enlightened Tsar. His brazen dabblings in Lutheranism and attempt to despoil the Orthodox Church might have been mistaken for reforming zeal; his indulgence of heretics might have been mistaken for toleration; his humiliations of the priesthood might have been perceived as healthy erastianism. In reality, all were evidence of his indifference to whatever was distinctively Russian and heartfelt by his people. Catherine, by contrast, as the French ambassador noticed, was

> assiduous in rendering to the deceased Empress the accustomed duties, which in the Greek faith are many and full of superstition — no doubt she secretly mocks them, but the clergy and people believe her to be very much moved by them and are grateful to her for it. She observes — with an assiduity surprising to those who know her well — the feast-days, fasts, days of abstinence, all things which the Emperor treats lightly but which certainly matter in this country. She is not the woman either to forget or forgive the threat that the Emperor made when he was Grand Duke, namely that he would have her shaved and locked up, as Peter the Great did to his first wife. All that, together with the daily humiliation she suffers mut be fermenting in her brain and only waiting for the right opportunity to burst out.

The ambassador was right. Catherine was scheming to launch a coup which would displace her husband and secure supreme power for herself. All Peter's interventions in government aided her by provoking more Russians into hostility towards the throne. He offended the army by trying to reform it on Prussian lines. He ignored popular feeling in insisting on hurling Russian troops against Denmark in prosecution of an ancestral feud of his own which had no relevance to Russian interests. Even his celebrated emancipation of the nobility from the service imposed upon it by Peter the Great only had the effect of limiting noble service, rather than abolishing it and whetted rather than appeased aristocratic appetites. Yet Peter perversely expected from his people a gratitude which he had not bothered to court. As the English ambassador observed, Peter fell into a 'fatal indolence' after the flurry of activity in which he began his reign. Only in his personal cult of his demigod, Frederick the Great, and his abject devotion to Prussia did he give of himself unstinctingly. He abandoned the independence of Russian foreign policy, promising Frederick, whose portrait he carried everywhere to gloat over reverentially whenever he had the chance, that the armies of Russia would be at Prussia's beck and call. He peremptorily abandoned the Austrian alliance that had almost brought the Prussians to their knees. He thereby turned victory into national humiliation.

Meanwhile, even as Peter alienated support, Catherine accumulated it. She had obtained considerable sums of money from the English ambassador, whom she had captivated. Her inspired choice of lovers had brought her the devotion of the Orlov clan, whose tentacles stretched far and wide in the army and who could secure the support of key regiments for a coup. She was able to mobilise the self-interest of the priests, the patriotism of the army, the opportunism of the aristocracy and the xenophobia of the mob. Her manifesto declared:

> Our Orthodox Church is being menaced by the adoption of foreign rites; our military prestige, raised so high by our victorious army, is being degraded by the conclusion of a dishonourable peace. All the respected traditions of our fatherland are being trampled underfoot. So we, being conscious that it is the honest desire of all our loyal subjects and having God and justice on our side, have ascended the throne as Catherine II, autocrat of all the Russias.

It was a coup-within-a-coup, for many of Catherine's supporters had expected her to install her son as legitimate Tsar and exercise a regency on his behalf. But Catherine pre-empted all power for herself. She was unsentimental about her children. She had never had much to do with her sons: one was a bastard, farmed out to a wet-nurse, the other, as imperial heir, had been snatched from Catherine at birth and brought up by

Elisabeth. She would no more hand over power to him than to any other stranger. Though her self-proclamation had no shred of legality, dynastic instability was so much a part of the Russian scene that no one was shocked. Nor did Catherine's sex seem an insuperable obstacle. After Elisabeth and her predecessor, Anna of Courland, Catherine was the third empress to be elevated to sovereignty, supported only by pretensions of dubious legality, in the course of the century. The novelty which Catherine brought to the Russian concept of a power-woman was not her investiture with sovereignty, but the manner in which she was to exercise it.

She began as she meant to go on, riding in person to perform her *putsch* at the head of her troops, dressed in male attire, borrowed for the occasion from a young lieutenant, riding astride in the fashion the Empress Elisabeth had always tried to forbid her. The hapless emperor was bewildered, arrested and shortly afterwards unceremoniously put to death — almost certainly with Catherine's connivance despite her avowals of innocence. There could be no surer hallmark of a power-woman than to dispossess one's child and murder one's husband to get a crown. Catherine was making it plain that she had transcended all the usual sensibilities of her sex. The impact on her contemporaries was thunderous. In a memorandum written early in the new reign, the minister Panin welcomed 'the age of Catherine the Great, surpassing in excellence that of all your predecessors on the Russian throne.' The name has stuck and so to some extent has the judgement.

Catherine was that rare thing among power-women — a woman who knew not only how to get power but also what to do with it. Whereas the previous Empresses had been cyphers controlled by their counsellors, Catherine rejected any suggestion of conciliar government. She had sought power for its own sake, not for the ancillary vanities that had given Elisabeth so much pleasure. She would rule alone, absolutely. 'The Russian empire is so large,' she declared, 'that apart from the Autocratic Sovereign every other form of government is harmful to it. From the first she adopted a bold course. The treaty with Prussia, which had been one of the pretexts for which Tsar Peter had been unseated, was quietly ratified: Catherine realised that the momentum of war had been lost and that it would cost too much to recreate it now. She was aware of the needs for a period of peace and retrenchment. Thus Frederick the Great could congratulate himself on having made a wise investment so many years before, when he went to such great trouble to insinuate Catherine into the bosom of the Russian ruling house. But the attachment of Frederick and Catherine was based on common interest, not sentiment. Russia and Prussia needed one another's co-operation in dealing with their mutual neighbour, Poland. Thanks to her understanding with Frederick, Catherine was able first to intrude her former lover, Stanislaus Poniatowski onto the Polish throne and then to profit from the partitions which began by disfiguring Poland and ended by annihilating her.

In domestic affairs, Catherine showed the same radical determination as in foreign policy. All her actions were an unique blend of tyranny and enlightenment. She began by putting the last remaining representative of the former imperial line to death: it was a crime which shocked not only her own subjects but also the whole of Europe. Yet she was soon proclaiming a reform of Russian legislation in the spirit of Montesquieu's Laws. This was not just hypocritical vapourising: Catherine was a genuine intellectual who enjoyed her erudite interchanges of correspondence with Voltaire and Grimm. Voltaire conferred upon her the inheritance of Queen Christina's former title, 'Pallas of the North'. But her commitment to the ideals of the Enlightenment was never more than a sincere intellectual commitment. She left Russia in the timeless grip of primitive tyranny — indeed, she tightened that grip and invested all her considerable reforming energy in improving the efficiency of autocracy, rationalising provincial government and extending the reach of the terrible power of the crown. Only in one respect did she mitigate the rigours of life for most of her subjects, by moderating the militarism and bellicosity of the ruling elite. She was no pacifist, but wars were less frequent and less burdensome in her reign than has regularly been the case in Russian history. It is probably fair to say that she eased the nobility's lot: but the benefits were not passed on to the masses. The peasants who rose in their thousands against her rule — especially in the bloody insurrection of the Cossack Pugachev in 1773 — gave their own verdict on the merits of Catherine's husbandry of her subjects.

Her most fruitful legacy lay not in any material achievement so much as in her championship of Russian culture and the Russian sense of identity. Since the enforced Europeanisation of Peter the Great, Russia had been dominated by influences from the west. This worship of whatever was foreign was prosecuted to absurdity by Peter III, who never cared for Russia or even began to understand the Russians: he would have been happier to remain a German or become a Dane; he never saw the possibilities of Russian greatness or viewed his imperial crown as more than a means to pursuing narrower ends within his own chosen Teutohic world. Catherine overthrew him on a wave of xenophobic sentiment. As she admitted to her lover, 'everything was achieved on the basis of hatred of the foreigner.' Thereafter, she devoted herself to the reconquest of Russia by genuinely Russian culture. And she extended its historic bounds, 'russifying' whole provinces where Russian influence had hardly penetrated before except in a purely military and political sense. She is said to have told the surgeons who bled her during an illness to extract all that was foreign from her veins and leave all that was Russian. But she was deluding herself: she had in reality not a drop of Russian blood. She was a foreign émigré who had to struggle to suppress her own German accent. Yet she was converted to love of Russia with all the ardour of a neophyte. Though she toyed with the *philosophes,* her important patronage was reserved for Russian writers. It was Catherine's court that formed the seed-point from which sprang the, great Russian literary flowering of the nineteenth century. It was from the respect for Russian culture which she inculcated in the intelligentsia, that Russian self-confidence and even aggression emerged with overpowering force after her reign. If Catherine's love-life was complex and kaleidoscopic, it was because she never felt much emotional attachment for her numerous lovers — unless for the great friend and counsellor of her mature years, Potemkin. Her real passion was reserved for her love affair with Russia. If she succeeded where Peter III failed it was because, unlike his, her heart was in it.

The matronly Maria Theresa and the concupiscent Catherine cut contrasting figures. But as power-women they evinced fundamental similarities. Both ruled in the tradition established by the celebrants of the *femme forte* in the time of Christina and Anne of Austria. Both were willing to ape men when occasion demanded. Both took pains to cultivate an image of ruthlessness to compensate for their sex. Yet both were also mistresses of genuinely matriarchal techniques, who could use coquetterie — applied, of course, according to their markedly differing standards — and feminine wiles to entrance or suborn men. Both achieved a highly creditable longevity in an unstable age. There was an impressive solidity — an enduring, almost monumental quality about their long reigns. They accustomed men to the idea of female sovereignty and dispelled the rather flighty, ephemeral impression left by the evanescent and unsuccessful power-women of the previous century. Inspired by Maria Theresa's example, Father Caffiaux argued in the middle of the eighteenth century that women were better equipped for government than men. By the end of the age of Catherine the Great, there was a good deal of evidence at hand to support his view.

CHAPTER TEN

Victoria and Isabel

The nineteenth century was divided from its neighbours by the troughs and trenches of war. The period between the Napoleonic and First World Wars in Europe presents features of a distinctive civilisation, which was created in the crucible of conflict of 1792-1815, and unmade in the cataclysm of 1914-1918. The prevailing mood of nineteenth-century Europe was romantic, sentimental, enthusiastic, numinous, nostalgic, chaotic and self-critical whereas that of the eighteenth had been rational, passionless, detached, precise, complacent, ordered and self-assertive. The change that overtook Beethoven's music or Goya's paintings during the Napoleonic wars was symptomatic of the transformation of an entire culture.

An observer addicted to dualist categorisations might be tempted to assert that eighteenth-century civilisation was 'masculine' and that of the nineteenth-century 'feminine'. Certainly some of the collective features of the nineteenth-century resemble the common stereotype of womankind — unreasoning, impassioned, wilful, sentimental. But the new mood did not necessarily favour power-women. Though possessed of certain enduring and singular characteristics, nineteenth-century civilisation was not static: it was changed in the course of its unfolding by technological innovations greater and more intensive than any to which society had ever before been exposed. From the power-woman's perspective, the two most important changes were the rise of feminism as the term is understood today and of representative forms of government — constitutional at first and increasingly, as time went on, democratic. Of these developments, feminism favoured the power-woman but democracy did not.

Like most of the ideologies of the nineteenth century, feminism had late eighteenth-century roots. The doctrine that women together constituted a class of society, historically oppressed and deserving of emancipation, was a product of late eighteenth-century pre-occupations with the rights of man or 'of man and the citizen'. It was first expressed, in language we can recognise as authentically that of a tradition unbroken to our own day, by Olympe de Gouges and Mary Wollstonecraft. The background of these women's thought was revealed in the very titles of their major feminist essays, both published in the revolutionary *annus mirabilis* of 1792 — the *Déclaration des droits de la femme et de la citoyenne* of Olympe de Gouges and the *Vindication of the Rights of Women* by Mary Wollstonecraft. They shared personal similarities, too, as women whose unhappy lives had been full of the frustrations that breed revolutionary sentiments. Olympe de Gouges was really named Marie de Gouze, a butcher's daughter, who struggled to acceptability in Parisian society through courtesanship and talent as a writer. Her change of name was intended to obscure the dull provincialism of her origins and feed a mysterious legend that she was the bastard daughter of some great man. Mary Wollstonecraft was the offspring of decayed gentility, but her struggle was just as grim and her dissatisfaction with life just as deep. Her drunken, spendthrift father dissipated the money intended for Mary and her sisters. She was forced into a series of undignified occupations as paid companion, school-keeper and governess. The unhappiness of her favourite sister's marriage compounded her own. Though never driven to the brazen courtesanship that sustained Olympe de Gouges for a while, she led an irregular amorous life, partly because her radical principles made her despise marriage and partly because her sister's dreadful experience deterred her. After conceiving a hopeless passion for one radical *littérateur,* she became mistress of another. But Gilbert Imlay's brutal and faithless love almost drove her to suicide. In 1797 she was forced back onto more conventional lines, marrying the advanced thinker William Godwin, who influenced Wordsworth: they both professed belief in free love, but this belief seems to have been compromised by the fact that Mary was carrying Godwin's child. He treated her with tenderness: life with him was a form of rescue from the misery of her previous attachment. But Mary died giving birth to their child, cheated of the long-deferred hope of happiness. If Mary found radicalism impractical, Olympe, for other reasons, found it difficult to sustain. In the face of the bloody excesses of the Revolution, she published a defence of the hapless King Louis XVI: within a few months, she was guillotined as a faint-heart, if not a traitress, thus giving an ironical twist to her own feminist slogan, 'Women may mount the scaffold: they should also be able to ascend to the bench.' Her enemies said her execution was a punishment for the lugubrious plays she wrote for the *Comédie française.* But as polemicists, both these feminist writers were brilliantly original. The novelty of their feminism lay in their frank rejection of the entire previous tradition of female championship, which relied on refracting women's faults through a prism of praise. Now, instead of being eulogised as perfect distillations of virtue, women were vindicated for what they were: human patchworks of virtues and vices — more vicious and less virtuous for being oppressed. 'Les femmes ont fait plus de mal que de bien,' admitted Olympe. Their capacity for evil and immorality was, claimed Mary, the result of their exploitation and subjection to misery. The realism of the vision of these writers was as shocking to contemporaries as their 'liberated' styles of life.

Now this feminism was all very well; taken to its logical conclusion it provided a plausible justification for admitting women, on the same terms as men, to the highest councils of nations and the loftiest pinnacles of authority. In practice, however, the doctrine proved less productive of female rulers than the old *femme forte* tradition. In calling for the emancipation of the generality of women, the modern feminism overlooked the cause of the exceptional individuals of singular prowess and ambition, whom the earlier tradition, in neglecting women as a class, had precisely singled out. Moreover, at roughly the same period of history, the advance of constitutionalism and democracy was nearly fatal to power-women. The accidents of dynastic history had thrown up nearly all the earlier examples of female rulers; the apparatus of absolutism had empowered them with the authority to defy or dominate emulous men. Elective and constitutional systems deprived them of these opportunities. Elections forced them to submit to — or rather, deterred them from seeking — the votes of unfairly prejudiced males. Constitutions compelled them to share authority with members of a resentful sex.

As a result, there were few power-women in nineteenth century Europe. Only in remote corners of the world did women wield power as autocratically as a Catherine the Great or as independently as a Maria Theresa. One has to look as far afield as the Madagascar of Queen Ranavalona or the Paraguay of Elisa Lynch to find really conspicuous cases of female absolutism. Both these women were adventuresses operating in far-flung frontiers to which European civilisation was only just beginning to penetrate. But that is the sum of the similarities between them. Elisa was beautiful, sylph-like, accomplished in every form of refinement. Ranavalona was a monstrous woman in the strict sense of the word — monstrously coarse, monstrously obese, monstrously libidinous, monstrously blood-thirsty. On her husband's death she was elevated to the throne of her island realm by a faction of tribal warriors of the Hova clan who wanted a figurehead to guarantee their hold on the country, which acquisition of modern guns had but lately given them. Because female chieftaincy was unknown, Ranavalona was given a series of 'guardians' — actually official lovers — to act as chief ministers. But so brilliantly did she manipulate the system, and so perfectly did she appropriate the superstitions of divine chieftaincy which cowed her subjects, that she was soon able to add to the guardians at will, both in her bed and in her counsels. She ruled as she pleased, with an increasingly corrupt and maniacal bloodlust. Western influence was suppressed, except in technology and court fashions: the savage Malagasy aristocracy indulged in its orgies and bloodsports, attired in strident parodies of Parisian *couture;* the Queen guzzled her gargantuan banquets tearing at the food with her fingers while immaculate gold cutlery lay idly at the side of her plate. Her massacres depopulated the island. They were executed with cruelty surpassing their efficiency. Nobles who dared to profess Christianity — thereby forsaking the worship of Ranavalona's ancestors — were burned alive. Children born on 'unlucky' days were slaughtered, for the queen was a prey to the hag-ridden anxieties that afflict most tyrants and which were exacerbated in her case by a superstitious dread of certain numbers. In 1857, the blackest year of her reign, the executions were almost daily in the capital: hundreds of victims died in a terrible hecatomb at a public bloodletting that March. On one occasion, a Christian wise man from up-country told the queen that all God's children were equal in his eyes. Did that mean the queen was the equal of a slave? The Holy Man and all his followers paid for his affirmative reply by immersion in a rice-pit into which boiling water was poured before it was sealed over with earth.

For all her refinement, Elisa Lynch proved equally destructive to her adopted people. Her Irish forbears were proud but impecunious and when her family sought refuge from famine in France, Elisa resorted to traditional female escapes from penury — first marriage to a French officer, then, when that proved vexatious and unglamorous — to high-class whoredom in the Parisian demi-monde. In Francisco Solano López, son of the dictator of Paraguay, she thought she had found the rich protector she craved. But in return, she gave him more than love. She became his counsellor and his good and evil conscience, feeding the Napoleonic fantasies which obsessed him, helping him, when they returned to Paraguay together and he siezed the dictatorship on his father's death, to turn the country into a strong and modern nation. Asunción was already an old and dignified capital, but it was rundown and seedy with a hicktown air. Elisa brought the glitter and sophistication of Paris to this precarious frontier, creating something of the atmosphere of a Parisian salon around the grand piano she imported specially to be the first in Paraguay, in the presidential palace which she furnished with impeccable taste. But her advice to her lover was politically disastrous. She had no sense of the art of the possible. Though she conceived a fierce patriotism for Paraguay, and taught herself Spanish and Guaraní, she never really understood the needs or limitations of the country. She bore an impassioned hatred — sprung from the most purely feminine envy and spite — for the neighbouring states of Argentina and Brazil, whose sophisticated European civilisation out-dazzled the show she put on in Paraguay and whose social élite snubbed her because of the irregularity of her union with López. Despite the poverty and backwardness of his country, the dictator created the finest army in South America, adapting what he had learned from Prussian methods during his visit to Europe. Elisa encouraged him to use it to teach his neighbours a lesson and win for Paraguay the notice and respect of the world. López, whose *folie de grandeur* was of megalomaniac proportions, needed little encouragement. But his decision to defy his three gigantic neighbours — Brazil, Argentina and Uruguay — was not the mad act it is sometimes taken for. Rather, it was a calculated risk. He counted on plausible but in the event unfulfilled hopes of internal political changes in Uruguay and Argentina. The prize — the hegemony of the entire continent — seemed worth the risk. López had so far militarised and inspired their people that they were willing to die for him in their thousands: their enmity for the soft sophisticates of the Atlantic coast was almost as intense as Elisa's, and they knew that Brazil and Argentina both aimed to annex Paraguay. The people would be fighting for their own independence as well as López's glory. The military feat, should he accomplish it, would be no greater than Frederick the Great's in the Seven Years' War or Napoleon's against the coalitions.

In the event, Paraguayan valour and discipline prolonged the unequal struggle for seven years. While López was engrossed in hopeless military manoeuvres, Elisa served as *ersatz* dictator of Paraguay. She stimulated morale, terrorised opposition, looted the treasury, kept the economy going despite a demographic cataclysm, fought a cholera epidemic and raised troops. When the supply of manhood was exhausted, she raised a regiment of women and led them into battle herself: like the *berserks* of the Vikings, their very appearance drove their enemies to flight. But wars could not be won by such desperate expedients, and when all the forts and towns had fallen to the invaders, and all the armies had been beaten in the field. López and Elisa withdrew to carry on the fight in the mountains and the jungles. As defeat drove López deeper into madness and the armies of the allies closed in, Elisa stood by her lover and maintained the indomitable spirit of Paraguayan resistance. When López and her eldest son by him fell at the defiant last stand of Cerro Corá, she scooped a shallow grave for them with her own hands, before surrendering her own person, with the ruins of her country, to the Brazilian forces. She retired to an honourable but impoverished exile. Even more of Paraguay was sacrificed in Elisa's war than had been lost in Madagascar in Ranavalona's massacres. But at least honour — which to Paraguayans meant more than wealth or blood — had been salvaged from the debacle, and the victors of the conflict recognised the necessity of tolerating Paraguayan independence.

These obscure outposts were romantic and exotic. But they were barely lapped by the mainstream of history that flowed from Europe. In that continent, which exerted over most of the rest of the world an overwhelming influence backed by an overpowering hegemony, the nineteenth century was dominated by a pair of queens who presented contrasts similar to those between Catherine the Great and Maria Theresa. Victoria of Great Britain and Isabel II of Spain were not power-women in the same sense as their predecessors. They were not chief executives of the governments of their respective peoples. Both presided over constitutional systems which limited monarchical authority and diffused power among ministers and representative institutions. These were inescapable constraints of the time. But both were nominal sovereigns and both contrived an enormous degree of tutelary eminence over their nations, of active vigilance over events. Both confronted the constitutional developments of their day in a spirit of conservatism tempered by compromise, endeavouring to keep what they could of power — or at least of dignity and influence — without retarding progress. Both, when they died, left female authority with a diminished role but, on balance, an enhanced reputation.

Victoria was the Maria Theresa of the nineteenth century and Isabel its Catherine. The former was a good wife and mother and exemplar of bourgeois morality, the latter a self-willed and libidinous vixen, whose only ethic was selfishness and whose only pleasure was sex. The contrasting circumstances of their childhoods, the divergent courses of their paths to their thrones, help to explain their differences of 'style'. Victoria was a child of sacrifice. Her father, the Duke of Kent, had given up his mistress and his carefree exile from society to contract a respectable marriage and sire an heir to the throne. Although this same form of discipline was enforced on all the royal dukes of England during the reign of George III, the fertility of the Hanoverian dynasty was almost exhausted and Victoria was the only surviving heir whom their concerted efforts produced. But the singularity of her destiny only gradually emerged, as hopes waned that other children would be born and survive in a senior line. Only from 1821, when Victoria was two years old, did public expectation begin to fix on her as a future queen. And only from the age of five was she subjected to a disciplined regimen, under the tough guidance of that gifted governess, Fräulein (later Baroness) Lehzen. This was the beginning of her preparation for queenship, her consecration to a sense of duty that would always, throughout her life, pin down her personal passions and limit her whims. Her upbringing was completed by guidance from her uncle Leopold, King of the Belgians: presiding over one of the new constitutional monarchies formed in the wake of Napoleon's wars, Leopold was well placed to offer sage advice on the personal conduct and political activity proper to such a monarch as Victoria would be.

Finally, her visits to another uncle, George IV of England, gave her that awe of the office of monarch that she would thenceforth always expect and generally exact from others. Politically insensitive, personally debauched and unrealistically reactionary, George brought the British monarchy to the depths of public indifference or distaste. Victoria was perhaps the only one of his subjects who loved him. But even in his obesity he retained a dignity which favourably impressed her when she was a little girl. Whenever he took her 'little paw', gave her his portrait to wear with pride in a brooch on her breast, or took her on his barge while the band played her favourite tune — 'God save the King' — she learnt a lot about the theory and practice of royalty.

Isabel, by contrast, learnt nothing. She was given no sort of suitable preparation in childhood for her future role. Indulgence and spoiling made her graceless and ill mannered, petulant and egoistic. Where Victoria was brought up in security and serenity, Isabel was an infant queen in a time of civil war. She was born on 10th October, 1830, to spite her uncle, Don Carlos, the heir presumptive to the throne. Her father, Ferdinand VII, and Don Carlos had vied with one another to devise the most reactionary, isolated and unenlightened future for Spain, but despite the comparability of their views, they had never got on and Ferdinand had longed, through four infertile marriages, for an heir to displace his brother and continue the succession in his own line. Don Carlos, however, was unwilling to be so easily displaced. Although the ancient laws of Castile (and perhaps of Aragon, too) had sanctioned female succession, King Philip V, when he had formally combined the crowns early in the previous century, had decreed that thenceforth in united Spain only heirs male should have the crown. Ferdinand felt that what one king instigated another could revoke, but it was also part of ancient Spanish tradition that the laws of succession were 'fundamental' — that is, not able to be made and unmade by the monarch. Don Carlos's case was weak, but it was arguable. He refused to recognise Isabel as heir and rallied all that was obscurantist and reactionary in the country to his banner. The church — fearful of liberalism and freemasonry — supported him; so did the Basques and Navarrese — jealous of their historic privileges which a modern, centralist government might sweep aside. And all over Spain there were quixotic, *hobéreau* noblemen and romantic bandits who resented the rule of the progressive Madrid intelligentsia and were anxious to perpetuate or reconstruct their local influence. More insidiously, Don Carlos appealed to profoundly Spanish sentiments. When he declined Ferdinand's invitation to swear allegiance to Isabel, he professed personal willingness impeded only by his 'conscience and honour'. There were many Spaniards who read the juridical claims on both sides of the succession question as genuinely favouring Don Carlos, and who were willing to lay down their lives for him as legitimate king. There are still many Carlists in Spain. Thousands of them died in successive Carlist wars, of which, considered from one perspective, the Spanish Civil War was the last. Franco himself acknowledged that he would not have beaten his enemies without the aid of the Carlist regiments that swelled his legions. Ferdinand believed that his daughter's birth 'crowned the ardent hopes of our beloved vassals who have sighed for a direct heir to the crown.' In fact, the sighs and the sobbing were only about to start.

Isabel's first political memories were of the great oath-taking ceremony of 1833, at which Ferdinand hoped to secure her position by exacting promises of allegiance from all who were influential in the realm. The princess was frightened by the crowd and distressed by the discomfort and slobberings of the tedious hand-kissing ritual. Consistently with her pampered upbringing, she was pacified with sugar-plums. It was a hollow show. Ferdinand was dead before the year's end. There had been no time to prepare the ground thoroughly. Worse still, Ferdinand had been deluded into making a death-bed recantation of his decree in Isabel's favour. On his short-lived recovery, he had re-instated his former position, but his haverings had undermined public confidence in his dispositions and impaired Isabel's prospects. By accusing his opponents of extorting the infamous recantation from him in bad faith he exacerbated tensions and helped to provoke civil war.

The child-queen, hastily and shakily elevated to the throne at the age of three, was politically all-important but personally neglected. She had no real friend. Her mother was installed as regent — a feckless and spineless creature who had been willing to give Isabel's rights away to Don Carlos. The regent preferred rather to imperil the throne by secret and strictly illegal dalliance with her morganatic husband than to attend conscientiously to affairs of state. Isabel had an aunt who was a tough character and who had stood up for her before — but the political factions who hoped to control the queen manoeuvred her out of the way. When political in-fighting forced her mother into exile, Isabel was saddled with the tutelage of a guardian she detested, who tried to interfere with such friendships as she had been driven by loneliness to make among her personal servants. Uniquely privileged as a child, Isabel was also at the same time seriously deprived. Against this unpropitious background she was growing up to be vain and capricious. When she was five and her mother was the victim of a *putsch.* she asked disingenuously, 'Mama, why don't you get out your cannon?' She and the regent were dependent, in the face of possible Carlist *revanche,* on liberal and constitutionalist support. But Isabel's political education — such as it was — was tied to outmoded ideas of absolutism. Her mother was afflicted with political myopia. When some N.C.O.s arrested her during the pronunciamiento of 1835, she told them. 'Do you know what liberty means? It means obeying the law and showing respect for those above you.' There was little hope for Isabel's schooling. In fact, she was ineducable. She ignored or insulted her tutors; she was backward in all her lessons, slow at and impatient of reading and abominable at French, which, despite its political importance, she never mastered — not even in her maturity when she lived in exile in France. She liked only to play with little dogs, make a mess at table and indulge her whims. Like Victoria, she was ugly, but unlike Victoria she never outgrew her ugliness. Her self-indulgence made her run to fat in adolescence. A skin infection gave her a permanently scaly and scabrous look.

Politically, her realm was the prey of coarse and bloodthirsty warlords.

Queen Victoria of England at her first Council in 1837 (1819-1901).

The Carlist war devastated a country which her father's mismanagement had already impoverished. The long and inconclusive struggle of absolutism and constitutionalism had left Spain without any institutions that commanded general respect. Only the army functioned. But the army was itself divided, each unit following its own emulous generals. The forces had been purged of Carlists, but to strengthen the government's hand in the war, large numbers of radical liberals had been rehabilitated: their allegiance was less to Isabel and her mother than to the principles of constitutional government; many of them were rabidly anti-clerical and even republican. They harried and terrorised moderate royalists as much as the Carlists. Their quarrels — like the Carlist campaigns — were conducted with characteristically Spanish extremes of blood and fire. The royal household was terrorised by turns, as one pronunciamiento succeeded another and the regent and queen were subjected successively to intimidation, humiliation, kidnap or exile. Gradually, two parties crystallised within the army and the urban militia forces on which Isabel also drew for support: the *exaltados,* who wanted to destroy every form of tyranny that had thrived under the ancient regime, whether royal, seigneurial, or ecclesiastical, and substitute full-blown democracy; and the *moderados,* who were concerned only to contain Carlism and introduce minimal constitutional guarantees of liberty. They alternated in power for most of Isabel's reign.

Meanwhile, in the midst of a secure, uneventful and inexperienced adolescence, Victoria ascended her throne in 1837 at the age of nineteen: or rather, one of her thrones, for such was the tenacity of scruples against female rulers in less progressive parts of Europe, even in the nineteenth century, that she had to forego the Hanoverian succession, so long united with that of England and Scotland, in favour of a distant line of male relations.

The assurance, composure and dignity with which Victoria bore herself at her first interview with her privy councillors and ministers impressed all beholders. Melbourne was admiring, Creevey incredulous. But to come to terms with Victoria's desire to retain a place in government — to be constantly informed, frequently briefed, unfailingly supplied with despatches, notified in advance of decisions and granted the illusion, at least, of preserving her perogative over government appointments — was a step with which some statesman of the day were reluctant to comply. For all uncle Leopold's tuition, for all her grave and earnest sincerity, for all her unseen but adamant determination, it was hard for some onlookers to see more than a slim, dark waif — touchingly pretty, poignantly innocent, but politically inconsequential. She could inspire all who served her with feelings of gallantry, but few with feelings of fear. She could cajole obedience but not command it.

This shortfall in her power was not Victoria's fault. Five years before her accession, the Great Reform Act had enshrined the principle of representative government in England. Parliament was now elected by such a broad segment of the country — 'the great mass,' as Lord Grey proclaimed, 'of all that was important in the country' — that its status as a sovereign organ could not be gainsaid. The exclusion or diminution of the power of the crown in favour of government by ministers responsible to parliament — which had been the great goal of eighteenth century Whiggery — was thereby secured. The pretext on which George III had been able to summon and dismiss ministers according to his own taste was now for ever removed. Ministries could be returned as Melbourne said 'smack against the crown'. The approbation of parliament, and therefore of the electorate, was now much more important in the making and maintaining of a government than the favour of the monarch. Victoria could do little other than accept this — albeit tearfully, in the case of the first change of ministry to overtake her in the very first general election of her reign. With her first prime minister, Lord Melbourne, she established a profound understanding. He spotted her sensibilities and pandered to them. Long years of study had given him a certain skill in the pedant's art which was useful in communicating with a moderately intelligent nineteen-year old. He realised the queen wanted to feel a part of the process of government, even if her role was in effect largely inert. He was able to explain clearly, narrate concisely and present deferentially decisions to which Victoria felt privy and party. He made a great play of consulting and confiding. Victoria depended on him so utterly that she was panic-striken to see him turned out of office. Her grief was compounded by the fact that her social world, her playmates and her friends, the people she knew and the houses she frequented, all belonged to the same circle of the Whig aristocracy from which Melbourne came and of which he was political leader. Thus when the Conservatives under Sir Robert Peel were returned to power as a result of the general election of 1837, Victoria felt abandoned in *terra incognita,* fearful and alone.

Her behaviour in this crisis was foolish, but it was the folly of inexperience, not incapacity. She defied the incoming ministry by refusing to change the ladies of her household, insisting on retaining all those of Whig sympathies. This was unconstitutional intransigence. It rendered the government's task unnecessarily more difficult and unfairly curtailed the new prime minister's patronage. Victoria defended her position so resolutely that Sir Robert Peel resigned and allowed her to re-instate her beloved Melbourne. The conservative leader was almost relieved to be disembarrassed of a subservience to Victoria which he found hard to sustain. He sweated in her presence; he fidgeted; he traced nervous little arcs on the carpet with his toe. He was the antithesis of Melbourne's suave self-possession. But he was also an adroit politician who got Victoria's measure as a result of this incident and would not allow himself to be easily out-manœuvred by her again. The 'bedchamber crisis' — as the business of the household ladies was nicknamed — had not been deliberately engineered by a guileful monarch intent on manipulating her ministers: it was a product of Victoria's political ingenuousness. She genuinely did not understand the political form: if she had she would not have cavilled at her duty to observe constitutional propriety regardless of personal feelings. When Melbourne lost the next election outright, she sent for Peel with a fairly good grace; he, for his part, managed his relations with her well, learning from Melbourne's example and soon winning her confidence and affection. Victoria, who had represented him as little less than an ogre in the correspondence of his first ministry, had so far grown up and extended the reach of her judgement by his second, as to observe his loyalty and esteem for her with an unprejudiced eye and graciously concede the purity, even — she acknowledged — the chivalry of his intentions.

This change, which enabled her to get on more or less with all the ministers who served her during her long reign — those she adored, like Disraeli or Salisbury, those she detested, like Palmerston or Gladstone — was not entirely of her own making, nor entirely that of Melbourne or Peel. Even as she was losing Lord Melbourne to political enfeeblement and creeping old age, she was acquiring another confidential adviser whose influence over her was more insidious and whose dominance more complete. This guru, who was nothing less than the political master-mind of the next twenty years of her life, was her husband, Albert of Saxe-Coburg-Gotha. Like Maria Theresa, Victoria married for love; like her, she sustained love throughout her married life; like her, she devoted herself to an agreeable mongamy unruffled by fashionable scandal; like her, she cultivated domesticity, warming her sentiments at the hearthside of nuptial bliss. And like Maria Theresa, she idealised her husband and her married love. The difference between the two marriages lay in the husbands. Francis Stephen was a reed of straw, Albert a tower of strength. Francis was inert, Albert active. Francis accepted philosophically the tutelage of his more brilliant wife. Albert resolutely carved a great political role for himself and sculpted his wife with the same chisel. He was Victoria's Pygmalion and her political maturity was his handiwork.

Albert wooed and won his bride in four days. Victoria had admired him when they first met through the match-making efforts of Uncle Leopold. But she then retreated into coyness and a professed unwillingness to marry. That initial susceptibility, however, was eventually to get the better of her. When he arrived for a second visit in October, 1839, she was captivated by his physical beauty and proposed to him — it would have been an unconscionable presumption to raise such a matter with a Queen regnant — in a gush of girlish arousal. Was his acceptance determined by motives as tender as the queen's? We shall never know. Part of Albert's strength was his reticence. Victoria's emotions were decanted like strong wine into her letters and diaries, which are full of egocentric gush and tell-tale underlinings. Albert's remained bottled up. The probability is that, for him, the betrothal was an act of duty and self-sacrifice — the very virtues which Albert and Victoria came to personify for the people of the nation they headed. He had been a misogynist even as a boy. If he was faithful to his wife it was only because women did not particularly attract him. He manifested typical traits of repressed homosexuality. His marriage was not chosen by himself but decreed by his dynasty. It was undertaken at the behest — even, at the orders — of Uncle Leopold and the Dowager Duchess of Coburg. Albert embraced his wife with specious enthusiasm and — probably — profound resignation.

The potential political significance of the marriage was probably overestimated in Albert's circle. Constitutionalism had already begun to mature on the continent but had not yet attained the cloying ripeness of which the fruits of power savoured in England. A crown matrimonial appeared not only as a glittering social prize but also a means to power. At the very least it would be — and, as events proved, was indeed — a means of influencing British policy abroad in favour of the north German powers, whose constellation was grouped around the rising star of Prussia. Foreign policy, a traditional area of royal prerogative in England, remained a sphere of royal responsibility because it was only through a brother- or sister-monarch that the crowned politicians of continental Europe could be addressed on equal terms. It is not surprising that the fiercest quarrels between the mature Victoria and English statesmen were connected with foreign policy. It is a tribute to Albert's skill as an agent of his continental allegiances that almost all Victoria's most heartfelt interventions were made on behalf of Prussian interests. Even — perhaps especially — after Albert's death when England's national interest proclaimed otherwise, as in the Prusso-Danish war of 1864, which gave Prussia a menancing base for anti-British ambitions in Kiel, or the Austro-Prussian war of 1866, in which Prussia laid the foundations of a German state that would be England's worst enemy for the next eighty years, or in the Franco-Prussian war of 1870, which established German hegemony in Europe, Victoria's voice was on the Prussian side. Only when Prussia failed to rally to England's side in the Crimean War of 1854-56 did Victoria upbraid her 'dearest brother' of Prussia with proper insistence. But this was a case in which Albert's views were in line with those of the Foreign Office.

There were a thousand other proofs of Albert's ascendancy within the royal ménage. While Victoria found fulfilment in her love for him, he — with an appetite for power and action unassuaged by domesticity — searched restlessly to occupy his dynamic and devouring genius. Their initial power-struggle was brief and resulted in Victoria's total surrender. She realised, on the eve of her marriage, that Albert's overpowering personality might encroach on the queenly role she was enjoying so much. She feared his opposition and his domination. She warned him that the English would not tolerate the intrusion of a foreign prince in national affairs. But as she succumbed to his mastery, and as the birth of their children emphasised her physical submission to him and sense of dependence upon him, she consoled herself for the loss of her power-woman's role by convincing herself of her total conformity with him. Like her image of an angelic, superhuman, almost perfect Albert, this was a myth of her own creation. But it served her purpose. It comforted Victoria in the classic dilemma of the power-woman in love. It enabled her to represent to herself her abrogation of political duty as obedience to a personal duty, which morality sanctified and the high calling of wife and mother demanded.

Meanwhile, in Spain, for Isabel, too, marriage had become the most vital question confronting her. She began to take an interest in it in her early teens, but is doubtful whether her curiosity was politically inspired. Her mother's eclipse had brought the dictatorial *moderado* general Espartero to power between 1841 and 1843. Having risen from the ranks, he was snobbishly susceptible to royal glamour and had fawned toadyingly on the girl queen. This only increased her vanity and indolence. She began asking for a husband capriciously — as before she had asked for toys and dogs. The prospect of marriage was an amusing novelty. To the rest of Europe, it was a deadly serious business, which almost provoked a war between the great powers, who saw the crown matrimonial of Spain as a major factor in the balance of power. This diplomatic dimension took out of Isabel's hands a decision she would have loved to make for herself. At sixteen, she was compelled to marry a scrawny and unappealing whimp chosen by the Quai d'Orsai — Francisco de Asís, Duke of Cadiz, whose only merit was that he would perpetuate in the dynasty (in the unlikely event that he would prove capable of begetting an heir) the name of Bourbon.

This disappointment turned Isabel into a power-woman; the effect of Francisco on her was exactly the opposite of Albert's on Victoria. Victoria was induced to yield power by her marriage. Isabel was prompted to take it. All her life she had had her childish desires fulfilled; now that her supreme wish was thwarted by politicians she decided to secure her future wants by entering the political arena herself. It was almost an instinctive reaction — the petulance of a naive absolutist whose enforced experience of constitutional monarchy had taught her nothing about limitations of her role. Yet her sheer determination to have her way would make her a surprisingly effective politician. Two incidents had already introduced her to the possibilities. In 1843, the warring generals, unable to agree on a choice of regent, had proclaimed her coming of age. This sudden accretion of queenly dignity re-inforced her self-importance and made her aware that the warlords needed her. Shortly afterwards, she was involved in a curious way in the downfall of her first prime minister, Olózaga, who induced her to sign an order dissolving the Cortes (the parliamentary institution): his enemies then used Isabel's testimony to procure his disgrace. One again, Isabel discovered what it was to taste power. The political game became an enticing adventure; and she loved adventures, riding out at night alone, deliberately drawing fire from palace guards by flying incognito through the gates, laughing at these reckless sorties and soon — in a sense, most dangerously of all — relishing the hazards of a series of secret love affairs.

Isabel has been almost universally condemned by historians for political incompetence and for the surrender of political advantage to personal sensuality. On both counts, she has been done grave injustice. Her hectic sexual career was deliberately undertaken to spite and humiliate her husband, who had the presumption to believe that the title of king empowered him to rival her for power. To begin with, her lovers were well chosen, like those of Catherine the Great. Her first lover, Francisco Serrano, was the best general in Spain; using his talents, she could defy her enemies: ironically, the confidence she showed in him was justified later when he turned his talents against her. It was only towards the end of her reign, when, coarsened by immorality and fattened by years of sybaritism, she was so physically unattractive that she had to pluck her lovers from the demi-monde. This was more from necessity than poverty of taste. As for the allegations of political incompetence, Isabel's record speaks for itself. In a period of chronic civil war, incessant instability and recurrent *coups d'état*, in a country riven with revolutionaries, radicals and reactionaries all irreconcilably rending each others' forces to shreds, Isabel survived. She occupied the throne for thirty-five years during more than sixty changes of government, two assassination attempts, half a dozen distinct revolutions and as many military dictatorships. She maintained a shaky hold on popularity throughout. And though she was always prepared to compromise her political influence in order to remain in the game, she never utterly forsook it.

For most of the 1840s, though she enjoyed tinkering with the distribution of ministerial portfolios, Isabel did not feel any need to make large-scale political interventions. The dictator Narvaez ran the country more or less to her own taste. But in 1848 a surge of revolutionary feeling swept Europe: Spain was spared the worst excesses, but it became increasingly apparent to Isabel that she must take an active personal role in order to defend the things she held most dear: her crown, which the republicans wished to abolish; the church which the anti-clericals wished to crush, and her mother, whom almost everybody wished to consign anew to the exile from which she had but lately returned. Her finest hour came when she had to confront a full-blooded revolution in 1854. By appealing to the residual popularity she still commanded from ordinary people, and by brilliantly imitating the rhetoric of the liberals, she survived — miraculously, as it seemed to many observers — secure upon her throne. In the Cortes that assembled in the wake of the revolution, only twenty-three members voted for a republic. Despite her professed conversion to liberalism, Isabel meant to re-assert her power. She played off against one another the generals who had master-minded the revolt, winning over the rising General O'Donnell and ousting the ageing Espartero, whom the revolution had briefly elevated to his old dictatiorial eminence. Her counter-coup in 1856 was a great feat of daring. She encouraged her troops in person in the pitched battle before the royal palace. O'Donnell was duly raised to nominal power, but in reality he was her chattel. She sacked him as soon as his usefulness was exhausted and brought back her old war-horse Narvaez. And all these gestures of royal prerogative were meekly accepted by the politicians and soldiers.

But now she went too far. In 1857, she gave birth to an heir to the throne — though his paternity, in view of Isabel's private life, was naturally dubious. This had a subtle effect on the chemistry of power. It was a new source of desperation to republicans and Carlists, a new source of confidence to Isabel. Fearful that Narvaez would establish an enduring power-base of his own, she now dismissed him, too, and astonished Spain by intruding an extreme radical into the premiership. To Isabel's fury, the Cortes voted her choice out of office. Although the queen had succeeded in amply demonstrating her own capacity to make and unmake ministers, the elected representatives of the people had now responded in kind. The queen felt obliged to turn back to O'Donnell. He was too canny to rely again on

Isabel's favour, but created a parliamentary power-base, known as the Liberal Union. In co-operation and relative amity, he and Isabel managed one of the most stable and useful régimes to prevail in Spain during the nineteenth century. But after the unprecedentedly long period of five years, they fell out over foreign and ecclesiastical policy. Isabel returned to her old king-making ways, but by now the soldiers and statesman were growing impatient of her rule. Far from being the political failure condemned by historians, she had been all too successful for her own good. She had alienated most parties and men of power by her mercurial transfers of political favour. Still, even as late as 1866, when Prim, one of the generals she had scorned most humiliatingly, tried to launch a radical rebellion, all the old guard — O'Donnell, Narvaez and Serrano — rallied round to defend her. It was her last victory. The momentum that would oust her was building up irreversibly. The factions were coagulating. She lacked the resources to reward and reconcile the generals to whom she was beholden. She behaved as if there were enough ministries and offices to go round, provided they went round fast enough; in fact, however, her power had been wielded too capriciously and had contributed to de-stabilisation of the political scene. There would be greater security for everyone in politics without her. When the next army revolt broke out in 1868, her former lover, Serrano, was at the head of the rebel troops. Isabel, who had survived so many revolutions, was tempted to try defiance again, but forsaking valour for discretion she chose self-imposed exile in France.

From comfortable retirement in Paris, she observed her homeland with mingled awe, regret and satisfaction: her own deposition, the internal bickerings of the revolutionary victors, the chaos of their attempt at a constitutional monarchy with a trumped-up foreign candidate, the brief and bleak experiment with a Republic, the continuing tradition of military coups which at last, in 1874, brought her son back to the throne she had vacated. She had abdicated her rights in his favour in 1870, declaring herself eased of a great burden. She chose never again to reside in Spain, but her reign took on something of an afterglow in popular minds. Her absence made hearts grow fonder of her and when she paid a visit to her former subjects in 1877, gratifying cries of 'Viva la reina!' recalled the old days when popular favour had helped her outface so many revolts. When Serrano was appointed ambassador in Paris, the former lovers and enemies took up again, in the mellowness of their old age, a friendship which seemed to symbolise the vicissitudes of partisan strife in Spain. By the time of her death in 1904, the former *enfant terrible* had become Europe's *grand dame*.

The years of Isabel's great triumphs and tragedies in the 1860s had been fateful for Victoria, too. When Albert was dead and Victoria emerged from the swathes of grief in which she wrapped herself, his posthumous influence lingered. The Prince Consort reached out from the grave to direct foreign policy along pro-German lines; indeed, he did so in an almost literal sense, since Victoria was convinced that she could establish contact with him through spiritual media. But Albert's passing, which left Victoria feeling enfeebled, really strengthened his widow to resume her career as a woman of power. It was like the passing of an eclipse. Other changes re-inforced Victoria's hand. The sheer length of her reign gave her invaluable experience of public affairs and a stature as statesman comparable with that of any politician of the day. Older men of longer memories — especially those who had dominated the early years of her reign — were dying or declining. And the life of sequestered mourning she imposed on herself in dedication to Albert's memory freed her from time-consuming public engagements to concentrate wholeheartedly on work.

The virtues of work — so much preached and so little practised by the Victorian upper classes — were an area in which Victoria provided an unstinting but unseen example. In the privacy of her closet she pondered every ministerial minute, every ambassadorial despatch, every column-inch of Hansard, every letter and leader in the press. She led an arachnoid existence, gathering paperwork into her corner like flies into a web, methodically ingesting the copious material and weaving traps for unfavoured ministers. Above all, she wrote letters. Aided only by a single secretary, she bombarded her correspondents unremittingly until they gave in, like a British gunboat cannonading distant natives into submission. There has never been a more prolific epistolarian in history. The deference due to her rank meant that her letters must be answered: this alone was enough to secure rapid surrender from most recipients of her voluminous missives. Only Gladstone was prolix enough and industrious enough to beat Victoria at this game.

The letters were the carriers of her personal influence, which grew even as her constitutional perogative shrank. The constitution continued its progressive march. Much to her chagrin, the queen found herself increasingly presiding over a democracy, which she neither liked nor understood. Indeed, she warned Gladstone that she would 'never be Sovereign of a democratic monarchy' — yet that is precisely what she became. The change was so gradual she failed to notice it. Democracy stole up on her unawares. She thought at the end of her life that she had succeeded in preserving her perogative intact, but nothing could have been further from the truth. Her power of dissolving parliament had never been resorted to. It was now forfeit: it had become accepted constitutional convention that dissolution was impossible without ministerial advice. She had lost most of her discretion over ministerial appointments: though she could still effectively veto individual promotions in the 1890s, she was, from early in her reign, at the electorate's mercy in choosing governments. As she complained on one occasion when the detested Gladstone triumphed at the polls, she found it

> a defect in our famed constitution to have to part with an admirable government for no question of any importance or any particular reason, merely on account of the number of votes.

Still, the political importance of the crown survived the erosion of the prerogative. Bagehot pointed out that the monarch retained the right to be consulted, the right to encourage, and the right to warn, and that, wisely wielded, these should be enough to satisfy royal ambitions. Gladstone admirably summarised the position in 1875:

> Although the admirable arrangements of the constitution have now completely shielded the Sovereign from personal responsibility, they have left ample scope for the exercise of a direct and personal responsbility in the whole work of government. The amount of that influence must vary greatly, according to character, to capacity, to experience in affairs, to tact in the application of a pressure which is never to be carried to extremes, to patience in keeping up the continuity of a multitudinous supervision ... The Sovereign, as compared with her Ministers, has ... the advantages of long experience, wide survey, elevated position and entire disconnection from the bias of party ... There is not a doubt that the aggregate of direct influence normally exercised by the Sovereign upon the counsels and proceedings of her Ministers is considerable in amount, tends to permanence and solidity of action and confers much benefit on the country, without in the smallest

degree relieving the advisers of the Crown from their undivided responsibility.

Frank Hardie, who quoted these words as an epigraph to his study of *The Political Influence of the British Monarchy,* has pertinently likened Victoria to a lofty sinecurist with the right to gather information from any quarter, read any State Paper, meet any person, express any opinion and command universal deference. Equipped with these advantages one could easily exert influence of a personal kind over a wide sphere.

To the rights of consultation, exhortation and admonition acknowledged by Bagehot, Victoria could add opportunities to wield power by exploiting and occasionally overstepping the licence allowed her by the constitution. Mediations, intrigues and threats were all means which she could and did use to make dramatic political interventions. Intrigues were dangerously extra-constitutional and she employed them sparingly. But she did not scruple, for instance, to consult opposition leaders on matters of state which were strictly the proper province of the government. She had done so at the outset of her reign, using Melbourne as an 'alternative' prime minister during the first premiership of Peel. That, she acknowledged later, was a misguided act, motivated by partisanship such as she subsequently claimed to eschew. Nonetheless, she played much the same trick on several later occasions, especially during the ministries of Gladstone, when she continued to seek advice from the more congenial Conservatives. Sometimes, she contrived wider plots against her own ministers. For instance, after Gladstone had offended her by the tardiness with which he supplied relief for Gordon in Khartoum, the queen wrote to Lady Wolseley, whose husband commanded the belated relief expedition, urging that General Wolseley should attempt to co-erce the government by publicly threatening to resign. In a similar incident in 1886, Victoria invited the Duchess of Roxburghe to publicise opposition to the government's Irish policy: she realised that she was being scandalously conspiratorial for she begged the Duchess to keep her role secret and to burn or lock up her letter.

Her role as a mediator was nearly always fruitful in forming coalitions or achieving parliamentary compromises that defused crises. It was a role the monarchy would retain well into the twentieth century, when George V helped to bring the National Government of 1931 into being. The most conspicuous case of Victoria's reign concerned the introduction of universal suffrage in 1884. No issue of principle was at stake: all parties were agreed on — or at least resigned to — this decisive extension of democracy; but the clash of parties embittered the debate and the measure was threatened by a procedural dispute which, it was thought, masked a dishonourable squabble for party advantage. Victoria, from her non-partisan eminence, was able to make a stately descent into the political arena to re-establish peace and concord with a compromise largely of her own devising. But though she could manipulate compromise when she so chose, it was as likely to be in defence of an unshakeable prejudice that she would seek to influence politics by sheer obstinacy. She had the threat of abdication at her disposal: abdication was a formidable bee's sting since, according to Gladstone, 'the position of a minister who forced it on would be untenable'. At times Victoria used the threat lavishly. At others, without mentioning abdication, she simply refused to comply with measures which she deemed to be inconsistent with her honour or conscience, her sense of duty or her coronation oath. These were pleas which had served reactionary causes in earlier reigns: George III and George IV had used them to delay parliamentary reform and Catholic emancipation. Victoria's exploitation of them was consistent with this tradition. She set her face immutably against Irish Home Rule, ecclesiastical disestablishment, reform of the House of Lords and — ironically enough for such a privileged woman — what she called 'the mad, wicked folly of women's rights.'

Victoria and Isabel both lived to witness the beginnings of a new century, which would be distinguished by victories everywhere for democracy and female emancipation: these prospects would have brought satisfaction to neither woman. But they could both take pleasure in the parts they had played in assisting the transmission of personal monarchy, in their respective countries, into the democratic age. They represented an expiring species. In the new century, dynastic accident would no longer create opportunities for power-women to arise. Nor would symbolic sovereignty confer upon figurehead monarchs opportunities to influence politics as these queens had done. But their techniques, and all the accumulated wisdom of the power-women of previous centuries, would still be useful to the new breed of female chief executives of government who would achieve power in the democratic age.

CHAPTER ELEVEN

The Female Demagogues

In the twentieth century, democracy has determined the character of the political structures in which power-women have risen. But it has made surprisingly little direct contribution to their rise. Of the women who have made most impact on modern politics, Mrs Bandaranaike, Mrs Gandhi and Isabelita Perón were all brought to power by quasi-dynastic succession, notwithstanding the formally democratic ideologies of the countries they ruled. And Margaret Thatcher and Golda Meir were appointed to chief executive positions which were not directly elective. But all these women had to muster and maintain mass followings. They had the common problem of establishing female techniques of demagogy.

The opponents of female suffrage feared — and some of its militant supporters hoped — that votes for women would make politics sexually divisive. There would be women's parties and cohesive female political allegiances which would swing elections. When the suffrage was extended to women for the first time in Britain after the First World War, the age qualification for women was fixed higher than for men to prevent their superior numbers swamping the polls. But like most expectations of the results of votes for women, this fear proved false. Christabel Pankhurst was the only 'Women's Party' candidate to approach success; after her defeat, the idea of a distinctively female party subsided. Female voters have never shown solidarity. Almond and Verba in *The Civic Culture* advanced conclusions based on opinion polls which few political scientists would dispute:

> Wherever the consequences of women's suffrage have been studied, it would appear that women differ from men in their political behaviour only in being somewhat more frequently apathetic, parochial, conservative, and sensitive to the personality, emotional and esthetic aspects of life and electoral campaigns.

Nor has female suffrage directly increased the power-women's constituency. Most surveys show that women are less likely than men to support a fellow-woman as a candidate for high office. And though the democratic age has thrown up occasional prodigious power-women, they have continued to be as exceptional as in former ages. Denied the support of their fellow-women, whose political conceptions on the whole have remained tenaciously patriarchal, they have established no alternative route to the top but have risen accidentally, or on the shoulders of their menfolk. At every level of political activity — as well as in 'top jobs' in other fields — the numbers of female participants remain small, despite enormous advances towards equality of opportunity. To the feminists' annoyance, the attractions of traditional domestic roles and ingrained feminine self-effacement, continue to inhibit women from breaking into new arenas. At the topmost level — that of chief executives of states — the constraints are greatest.

This background makes the achievements of the twentieth-century power-women all the more remarkable. One should perhaps exclude Isabelita Perón, the cabaret dancer thrust reluctantly into nominal headship of the Argentine state to keep the phantom of her dead husband before the people's eyes: incompetent puppet of the Perónist politicians, she perhaps hardly deserves to be called a power-woman at all. The greatest achievement has, beyond a peradventure, been Mrs Gandhi's, not only because the state she has ruled is the biggest of those which have been subjected to female dominion, nor chiefly because the power she has exercised within India has been so great, but because Indian society is one of the most hostile to power-women the world has ever seen. All the social assumptions of Hinduism relegate women to a minor domestic role. Women who step outside those limits daw suspicion and contempt. Feminine paramountcy is almost inconceivable. The conventions which embody these constraints have two roots, both of tremendous antiquity. The law-codes of the Brahmanical legists imposed subservience on women 2,500 years ago. The religious convictions on which they are based are even older: women are the dross of their castes. Womanhood is a form of divine punishment, visited in re-incarnation for sins committed in a former life. Women must live under tight male tutelage, or they will pollute their families by channelling evil spirits into the home, committing the socially ruinous sin of adultery or associating with a lower caste. In some villages even today, an enquirer will be told that no birth has taken place if the baby is a girl. The ideal of Hindu womanhood is the legendary heroine Sita, whose submission to her husband was such that she walked into flames at his command and endured exile, though innocent, for rumoured impropriety.

The status of women in Hinduism is vividly illustrated by two palm-leaf manuscripts of the seventeenth and eighteenth centuries in the British Museum, the *Bhagavata purana* and the *Radhakrsna keli katha*. The wife milks the cows and cooks her husband's meal: later, she will eat what he has left over or rejected, alone. Afer he has fed, she massages his feet and tends the children, before joining him again for a bout of sexual acrobatics such as Hindus have always highly esteemed. The avenues of escape from this kind of life — if escape be wanted — were traditionally temple-service, which involved sexual atheletics even more prodigious than those demanded in the home, or prostitution. In traditional art, prostitutes — especially those high up in the complex Indian hierarchy of the profession — are shown receiving the supplications of men as well as serving them. A power-woman is therefore suspiciously like a prostitute — or else like a goddess

Traditional values still determine most Indian women's self-image and, therefore, their images of fellow-women. Indira Gandhi, of course, was brought up in familiarity with alternative conceptions. Her family came from Kashmir, where attitudes to women have always been enlightened by Indian standards. Historically, Mrs Gandhi's father observed, 'women had greater rights in Kashmir than in other parts of India.' womenfolk had often been able to dominate households by stealth, while according their husbands the god-like reverence which Hindu convention demanded. Some of them had become sovereign queens in the days of Kashmiri statehood. But it was not chiefly Kashmiri tradition that inspired Indira Gandhi to seek power. It was the western models she got from her education in Geneva and Oxford and from her highly westernised, albeit intensely nationalistic, home background.

Her father was Jawaharlal Nehru, the rich, anglicised Congress politician, the practical and urban counterpart to Mahatma Gandhi's fanatical and idealistic austerity. Indira's connexion with the Mahatma was close in terms of the friendship and political alliance between the two families; but their affinity was remote. Indira's husband, Feroze Gandhi, was only very distantly related. As a Parsi outsider, he was of small account in the nationalist movement. The marriage was a romantic wartime match: the courtship had been conducted very largely in Europe, free from the influence of traditional Indian match-making; and although parental countenance and a traditional ceremony hallowed the union and made it distinctively Indian,

Indira never adopted the conventional Indian wife's role towards her husband. Her childhood had included absolutely no preparation for the wifely role of a good Hindu woman. The nationalist struggle — save for the educational intervals abroad — had dominated it. She had taken part in rallies and demonstrations; she had witnessed violent strikes and riots and bloodshed. In her father's enlightened household she had taken part in the discussion — and sometimes the planning — of these things on equal terms with men. After her marriage the nationalist struggle went on. It remained her first priority. And her role was much more active than her husband's, for he virtually gave up political activism. The post-war period, which brought India to independence and Nehru to power, also saw a distancing between Indira and Feroze. She bore his children, but became increasingly absorbed in helping her father with his work. Nehru, for his part, never liked Feroze and never cordially approved his daughter's choice. The couple separated and remained on friendly terms. When Feroze died suddenly in 1960, Indira was at his bedside, holding his hand.

By then, however, he represented a phase of her life that was well in the past. Her capacity to love was monopolised by her children and her father. Her passion was devoted to politics. Mistress of her father's household, she could observe and, to some extent, manage the entire Indian political world. She was Nehru's *éminence grise*. She performed for him the sort of role Nur Jahan played for the emperor Jahangir — secretary, sidekick, administrator, counsellor, confidante. But because her part was not institutionally defined, few people knew about it. It was a domestic role, within a 'court' that was itself an organ of power. The only hint the world got of Mrs Gandhi's influence was her unobtrusive presence at her father's elbow, everywhere he went. The only formal position she occupied before his death was a purely ceremonial one — the Presidency of the Congress Party, an honorific office whose incumbent was supposed to be uninvolved in everyday politics. Between 1960 and 1965 she had no important official position at all. But the unseen 'fires' which she has claimed to feel burning within her were smouldering. Her ambitions were taking shape amid the gossip about the succession to her ageing father. Above all, she was watchful. 'I was in politics all the time,' she has said of this period, 'I was on the Congress working committees and other committees. I watched it all ... I watched them all.'

She was not, however, a serious contender for the top job when Nehru's death vacated it in 1964. But the ministerial instability which endured for a year gave her a chance to move into the centre of an arena which she had so far only gingerly skirted. The colourless, compromise Prime Minister, Lal Bahadur Shastri, gave her a cabinet post in order to associate her father's memory with his régime. Shastri had almost succeeded in establishing himself as more than a mere stop-gap when his sudden death threw the premiership back into the ring after little more than a year. It was just the right moment for Mrs Gandhi. Her competence had been proved but her success had not been spectacular. She had acquired friends without making enemies. She was seen as able enough for the job, but not so gifted as to be dangerous. She excited little admiration, but less envy. Above all, she was Jawaharlal's daughter. Already, Nehru's time was taking on a golden hue in men's recollection. And in a country where democracy was a newcomer, and the doctrine of re-incarnation gave families a peculiar unity and heredity a special significance, the dynastic descent of power still fascinated people. To the masses, Mrs Gandhi's unique position — as a female politician known to the people, appearing on platforms, addressing and compelling great crowds, taking an active role that was no longer in any sense domestic, as it had been when her husband and father had been alive — gave her a goddess-like mien. Whether she was a benign goddess, like Ganesa or Arjuna, or a destructive force, like the terrible tiger-riding Durga or the bloodthirsty Kali, remained to be seen. But her double dose of divine right was irresistible. At the least, she was seen as resembling one of the legendary queens of old India. Peasants frequently used the world for 'empress' in referring to her. From the point of view of the political establishment, who had to choose Shastri's successor, Mrs Gandhi's virtues, though uncoloured by superstition and largely negative, were equally clear. She would, it was thought, be manipulable and unassertive. She would be infinitely preferable to her rival candidate, Morarji Desai, an obsessive and incorruptible fanatic, who had been through the times of trouble with Gandhi and expected impossible extremes of service, devotion, ascetism and selflessness from his fellow-politicians. Mrs Gandhi got in by means of those age-old factors, popular gullibility and élite cupidity.

In the event, it was the professional politicians rather than the people at large who had their expectations dashed. Mrs Gandhi was not manipulable. She dispensed with the services of the old guard Congress Party set-up and created new channels of government of her own. To the people, if she was any sort of goddess, she was both sorts at once, both nutritive and destructive. She nurtured the masses with social and economic reforms that were often far in advance of popular wishes or popular understanding. She nurtured her own family — paying back the Nehru dynasty that had brought her power, fostering the numinous dynastic idea to which she owed so much. And at the same time she was an avenging, destroying Durga, riding a tiger than devoured enemies and crushed institutions which opposed her or which she considered outdated.

Her policies were a mixture of the populist and the paternalist. The nationalisation of the banks, the humiliation and dispossession of the hereditary princes, for instance, were the foundation of her popularity. Compulsory family planning and slum clearance — both policies with which her son, Sanjay, was ominously associated — were an intolerable imposition on the individual rights and dignity of millions of ordinary people and fed popular discontent with her rule. Paternalism tends to shade into other more onerous and oppressive forms of authoritarianism and Mrs Gandhi, whose style as a power-woman was to affect masculine toughness and ruthlessness, did much to invite the accusations of dictatorial methods and ambitions which were soon levelled at her. In 1969 she showed formidable *sang-froid* in unsentimentally splitting the Congress party and sacking the elder statesman of India, Morarji Desai: Congress was the creation of her father and of Gandhi; its integrity was almost as inviolable as that of India's sacred cows. So unthinkable was an India without Congress that most of the parties which have succeeded it or split from it have included 'Congress' in their names. Desai had a venerability which verged on sanctity as a result of his old comradeship with Gandhi. More than a deplorable sacrifice, he made a dangerous enemy. The same shameless authoritarianism was shown by Mrs Gandhi in attempting to muzzle the press — of which she has a fear and loathing akin to Tony Benn's — through a law of 1970 giving the state a fifty per cent interest in all publications. And the same radical, ruthless determination was shown during the Bangladeshi crisis of the following year, when she sharply re-routed the traditional direction of India foreign policy by signing a Friendship Treaty with Russia and then marching into Bangladesh to impose a solution on terms favoured by India. At the conclusion of the fighting she took advantage of the patriotic mood of the country by hesitating to relax the state of emergency proclaimed to facilitate the war; indeed, she compounded it later by adding a state of internal emergency with little apparent justification. When she deferred elections to preserve her parliamentary majority, she appeared to be making a naked bid for dictatorship.

If Mrs Gandhi was a tough politician, she was also an arbitrary one, from her earliest days of power, and it is arguable that there was something feminine about that arbitrariness. She is candid about acting intuitively: she had a 'feeling' that the Bangladeshi revolution would succeed, a 'feeling' that elections were needed in 1977. She also often claims instinctively to 'know' that a thing is right. This is a well known characteristic of female psychology. Men are regularly infuriated by this female debating technique, which puts a point beyond rational discussion by an appeal to a mysterious and esoteric form knowledge which, because it is unidentifiable, is undeniable. Equally feminine and more easily exploited for ill was her indulgence of the corrupt excesses of her son, Sanjay, while he lived. Motherliness — as the Empress Wu might have named her — is a terrible weakness in a power-woman, which probably caused her defeat in the 1977 elections and threatened permanently to deprive her of power.

Of course, her attitude to power was not solely the product of her hormone balance. In a sense, she has acted arbitrarily because she has been unconstrained by principles: this in itself is arguably more characteristic of women than of men, but in Mrs Gandhi's case it is a result of her upbringing. Her free thinking, westernised family gave her no burning allegiance to any creed save nationalism; and nationalism was a burnt-out case by the time Mrs Gandhi came to power. This left, as it were, an ideological vacuum in her heart. She has been free to respond pragmatically or capriciously to problems as they arise. This effect has been increased by her isolation. Like rulers all over the world, and like all people of substance in India, she has become surrounded with courtiers, who refine information into flattery and refract news so that its more noxious beams escape her. Apart from her vaunted intuitions, she has little awareness of the people's real mood, particularly as she distrusts the media. Her insulation against information was fatal in the 1977 elections, when she genuinely believed she would win. It contributes to the obsessions with persecution and betrayal to which she is prey — which in turn have tended to feed her reputation for ruthlessness.

In 1977, she blundered rashly out of office. She was not a real dictator: the fact that she was prepared to appeal to the verdict of the electorate and yield even when that verdict was adverse shows her genuine acceptance of democracy. But she behaved dictatorially enough to drive all her enemies into coalition. The allegations of electoral malpractice which began the crisis that toppled her were merely a pretext: she was guilty only of technical

Indira Ghandi, Prime Minister of India and Margaret Thatcher pictured together in London where they held talks. Mrs. Ghandi's visit to Britain coincided with the start of the Festival of India which ended on November 14th 1982.

infringements of the code, such as generally passed unheeded, but she erred in thinking she could bludgeon disquiet by extending the emergency and arresting her foes. In a country as large as India, with so many devolved sources of authority in the complex provincial network, there is no workable compromise between democracy and totalitarianism. By taking dictatorial half-measures, Mrs Gandhi merely stimulated discontent. By threatening her enemies, she stampeded them into action. The Janata coalition which opposed her in the 1977 elections was the only alliance broad enough to defeat her. For a moment the defeat looked comprehensive, definitive. Mrs Gandhi lost her own parliamentary seat — which had been a family fief since Independence — and was expelled from her own party. The new government made persecution of her a prime policy objective.

But adversity called forth her best abilities. Many power-women in history have seized authority. But very few have managed to return from the wilderness to re-capture it after defeat. Mrs Gandhi, after reacting stoically to the election result — she was the only member of her household who ate a hearty dinner that night — painstakingly reconstructed her electoral power-base by tirelessly touring the provinces, no longer a destructive Durga athwart the rabid tiger of radicalism, but a benign goddess — 'the only one who can help us', as peasant women said, re-inforcing the support she had retained in south India, reconstituting the support she had lost in the north. Again she dramatically split the Congress Party, forming a schismatic fragment of her own which rapidly outgrew the official rump. But the decisive factor in her favour was not of her own making. The Janata coalition collapsed under its own corpulence. Riven into warring factions whose only common purpose had been detestation of Mrs Gandhi, it possessed neither the coherence to formulate policy nor the ability to carry it out. Janata was a broad-beamed vessel, but it lacked ballast. It capsized and was at once revealed as the work of shoddy shipwrights, as it splintered and sundered. Mrs Gandhi was returned to power with the biggest parliamentary majority in Indian history. Her fourth term of office has excited relatively little unrest.

Until this sudden reversal in her fortunes, Mrs Gandhi's career had parallelled to an astonishing degree that of her Sri Lankan neighbour, Sirimavo Bandaranaike, the world's first woman prime minister. So closely did the course of their lives resemble each other that it is hard to resist the impression that mutual influence must have contributed. Both women rose to political prominence as the heirs of great political dynasties. Both picked their way — sometimes carefully, sometimes clumsily — through the cultural and confessional divisions by which their countries were riven. Both adopted strategies of exploiting — as well as or rather than healing — those divisions. Both drove their enemies into powerful coalitions by raising the threat of dictatorship. Both hoped to survive electorally by pursuing radically populist policies. Both failed and both were decisively turned out of office by electoral defeat. The crucial difference was that whereas Mrs Gandhi led a united party and was faced by a divided coalition, Mrs Bandaranaike was a precarious coalition leader, faced by a cohesive alternative government. Thus Mrs Gandhi has returned in triumph, while her Sri Lankan counterpart has remained in the wilderness.

Sri Lanka provided in many ways a much more receptive environment to female political success than India. Although large Hindu and Muslim minorities were opposed to the idea of a power-woman, the majority Sinhalese Buddhist culture was remarkably fair to women, who enjoyed considerable freedom under customary law and had occasionally exerted power in pre-colonial times. Indeed, it was Victorian perceptions of womanhood, brought in by the British, rather than any traditional hostility, which inhibited women from taking part in the politics of the colonial era. The introduction of universal suffrage in 1931 and of free education for all in 1945 created conditions in which women could compete for power; but few chose to do so. Since independence in 1947, only 15 women have taken seats in parliament and only 34 have been elected to local government posts. Although women constitute between a quarter and a third of the membership of most political parties, in the last election only eleven out of 168 seats were contested by women. The women of Sri Lanka, despite their opportunities, have tended to prefer domesticity to leadership.

Mrs Bandaranaike's tastes might have inclined her in the same direction had marriage to a man whose obsessive passion was politics not politicised her own life. She dates the inception of her social awareness back to the great malaria epidemic of 1934-35, when she engaged in voluntary work, but her political initiation really came with her marriage in 1940, when she was twenty-four years old, to S.W.R.D. (Solomon) Bandaranaike. The Banadaranaike clan had been prominent in politics and administration throughout the period of British rule. Naturally part of the élite, they had been formally ennobled by the British. Solomon, like Jawaharlal Nehur, was British-educated, westernised and free-thinking. But he was also a political opportunist with an eye to the main chance: he espoused socialism in order to give his political ambitions popular support; Buddhism in order to appeal to the majority religious culture — just as his ancestors had accepted Christianity to impress the British; and linguistic nationalism in order to generate fervour among the Sinhalese-speaking majority who resented the inflow of Tamil-speaking Indian immigrants.

In the early days of independence, policies of national unity carried greater appeal than the divisive politics advocated by Bandaranaike. At first, he worked within the ruling coalition. His widow has claimed that it was at her suggestion that he broke from the government and made a successful bid for power in his own right in the general election of 1956. Meanwhile Mrs Bandaranaike built up a power-base of her own. She began in the Lanka Mahila Samiti organisation — the women's movement. It is rare for a power-woman to appeal directly to a female constituency (though Margaret Thatcher managed it in the British elections of 1979); it would have been impossible for Mrs Gandhi, for instance, to do so in India. But the relatively emancipated role of women in Sri Lanka made it possible for Mrs Banadaranaike to acquire a network of partisans of her own, engaged in social projects throughout the country and especially in the electorally crucial rural areas. She also took a prominent part in electioneering for her husband's party. Though she had no known role in policy-making, she was as experienced as anyone in the country at handling the building-bricks of politics by the time her husband became prime minister. As she has herself pointed out, 'I was known as S.W.R.D.'s wife but I was also very well known in my own right. Where a previous Prime Minister's wife may not have been able to step into her husband's shoes as I did when the call came from the people, the fact remained I had gathered my own experiences in public life through several years, and in several ways.'

Although 'S.W.R.D.' was louder in threatening to homogenise national culture by force than he was active in persecuting minorities, his government was unacceptable to the large and numerous ethnic, linguistic and religious minorities of Sri Lanka. His assassination in 1959 was an episode in a continuous history of racial and religious violence. Close association with the martyr's mantle and tight control of the party machine made Sirimavo the natural leader of her dead husband's followers. There had to be a brief interregnum: Mrs Banadaranaike was too shrewd to forfeit support by too hasty a bid for the fallen crown. A few months' decent withdrawal into purdah brought her to the eve of the 1960 General Election. 'I am not seeking power for myself,' she disingenuously announced, 'but have come forward to help the S.L.F.P. candidates so that the Party can continue the policy of my late husband.' The professional party leaders hoped to keep her out of the top job and so maximise their own power, but the indecisive result of the election left them with no option but to give Sirimavo the presidency of the S.L.F.P. Her appeal to the electorate on behalf of her murdered husband proved to be nicely calculated: under her leadership her party swept to victory in the second election of the year, in July.

The promise of continuity with her husband's policies had been her making. Fidelity to that promise would prove to be her undoing. In a country as divided as Sri Lanka divisiveness can only work as a short-term expedient. She outraged the religious minorities by showing gross favour to Buddhist educational institutions. Her plans to enforce the mass emigraton of Tamil-speakers alarmed all moderate forces and all who hoped for and believed in national unity. Because in the normal pattern of Sri Lankan politics the allegiance of the Sinhalese majority is divided between two parties, it is imprudent to alienate minority support with the reckless abandon Mrs Banadarnaike displayed. But her defeat in the 1964 general election was not so catastrophic as to weaken her hold on her own party. And leftist disenchantment with the pragmatism of the new government gave her a further opportunity to create a successful coalition in time for the 1970 elections.

Her six years out of office seemed only to have increased her yearning for untrammelled power. Nor had the experiences of her first spell of power taught her anything about the advisability of moderation and reconciliation. In an outrageous burlesque of Mrs Gandhi's methods in India she embarked on an orgy of nepotism and arbitrary power. Virulent 'counter-insurgency' measures, the shackling of the presss, the immoderate indulgence of her dubious son, Anura, interference with the integrity of the courts and the extension of the term of parliament at a time of electoral unpopularity — all these were acts of defiance of democracy which neither the other parties nor the electorate at large could tolerate. Mrs Bandaranaike's 'solution' of the ethnic question in 1974, when she reached agreement with Mrs Gandhi on the selective repatriation of Tamil-speakers to India, only excited further disquiet among the minority and increased the demand of Tamil separatists not merely for federalism but for their own independent state. The general election of 1977 was the most decisive in Sri Lanka's history. Mrs Bandaranaike's party was left with only eight seats. The only great Sinhalese party, the U.N.P., polled over 50% of the vote and provided 139 out of 166 members of the new assembly.

Mrs Gandhi and Mrs Bandaranaike have been thoroughly representative power-women in blending masculine and feminine traits with variable success. For an unmistakably and uncompromisingly feminine type of twentieth-century power-woman, we have to look to the example of Golda Meir, Prime Minister of the State of Israel from 1969 to 1974. This is not to say she exploited her femininity with the sexiness of a Cleopatra or the coquetterie of an Elizabeth I; she was never a physically attractive woman and she attained power only at the age of seventy-one. But she was a mistress of matriarchal techniques. They came not from within herself but from the Jewish tradition in which she was brought up. Golda Meir was Jewish Momma writ large, who ran the state as Jewish mothers all over the world run their matriarchal households.

Her need to mother her country was a result of frustrated maternal ambitions at home. She was born in Kiev in 1898. Anti-semitism was inescapable and her Jewish identity was defined for her, from outside herself and even, in part, from outside her family circle, by the hatred and contempt of others. The insecurity of life was summed up by her sister's panic-stricken reactions to Golda's childish threats to expose her Zionism to the neighbourhood policeman. With the 1905 revolution bursting bloodily about their ears, the family fled to join their father, who had preceded them to America and found a job in Milwaukee. It had taken Golda's father three years to built up a base from which they could start a new life. But Milwaukee genuinely represented deliverance. An exodus from bondage to a promised land. But opportunities in America set up tensions in the home: the same experience was endured by many immigrant families, who had to struggle to maintain their traditional culture in an environment that was no longer hostile (as it had been in Russia where their identity and values flourished in adversity) but simply indifferent.

Golda and her sister fell out with their parents because they wanted to have careers and take part in socialist politics — not work in the family shop and get married as soon as possible. Domestic felicity has been lost by the family, even as material sufficiency and confessional freedom were attained. Golda learned socialist Zionism from her sister. Later, when the tensions in the home eased and the First World War was on, Zionism became a uniting force in the family, with her mother offering lodging to Jewish boys on their way to volunteer to fight with the British against the Turks for the liberation of Palestine. It was by campaigning for a Jewish homeland at rudimentary hustings, which she set up outside the local synagogue, that Golda began active political life. The Balfour Declaration in November 1917 gave her the courage to marry Morris Meyerson, a sweetheart of long standing and prepare to decamp for the putative 'Jewish National Home'.

It was not until 1921 that the young couple were able to make the journey and by then the outlook in Palestine was neither romantic nor alluring. Violence had broken out between the indigenous Arabs and the immigrant Jews who seemed to threaten to displace them. That violence was to dominate Golda Meyerson's life in Israel and continues to dominate the life of the state she helped to found. As soon as they could the Meyersons joined the kibbutz of Merhavia. Militant feminism was rife here — even more so than in egalitarian America. But a form of ideological extremism more insidious than this began to corrode Golda's personal happiness. The children of the kibbutz were brought up communally. Golda longed for a baby but the herd-rearing methods that were essential to the primitive communism of the kibbutz revolted her husband. Only when the deterioration of his health forced them to leave the kibbutz in any case, could they begin to think about raising a family.

A rift in the marriage had begun. It would gradually widen. Not even a move to Jerusalem and the birth of a son and daughter assuaged Golda's hankering for the kibbutz. But even though it caused the breakdown of her marriage — beginning the alienation of her children's affections in the process — the departure from the kibbutz had positive consequences, too, for it freed Golda to take part in political work on a national scale with the Women's Labour Council. This brought her into direct contact with all the leading politicians of the Jewish community in Palestine. She became a spokesman for the Labour Council and its umbrella organization, the *Histradut,* which, through its work of laying the economic foundations of a Jewish state, constituted the kernel of the Jewish nationalist movement in Palestine. She had a part in the collective decisions of the Jewish leadership, both to give active help to Britain against Hitler, despite the Jews' differences with the British government over British policy in Palestine, and then, when the war was over, to fight the British for attempting to stop Jewish immigration and frustrating the prospects of a Zionist state. When the State of Israel was proclaimed on 14th May, 1948, Golda Meyerson was the only woman on the rostrum. She was immediately sent on a public relations mission to the United States: this represented exclusion from office at home but also a chance to establish herself in a vital role, for it was from Zionists in America that the funds to lay the infrastructure of the new state would have to be raised. Despite Israel's professed willingness to accord equal rights to Arab citizens and 'contribute to the advancement of the entire Middle East', the neighbouring Arab states had responded immediately to the inception of the new state with a war that would be long, bloody and expensive.

The other external area of vital concern to Israel was the Soviet Union. According to Mrs Meir's memoirs, without arms from the eastern block, Israel would have been unable to withstand the initial Arab onslaught and create a basis for victory in the latter half of the year. Already before her departure for her whistle-stop tour of the States, Golda had been nominated as ambassador to Moscow. She was there for less than a year. Russian policy was swinging back to anti-semitism and hostility to Israel; Russia was becoming an area of marginal utility to the State of Israel and Golda was better employed elsewhere as foreign fund-raiser extraordinary. This roving life crippled her efforts to be a good Jewish mother. Her husband was a fragment of a past life: she was raising money in America when he died in 1951. Her children grew apart from her. But her way of life brought political rewards. Having been prominent in the Histradut and then served as an ambassador in key arenas, she was ideally equipped to occupy successively the posts of Minister of Labour and Foreign Minister when she rose to Cabinet Office in 1956 — now called 'Mrs Meir' as a result of Prime Minister Ben-Gurion's insistence on the adoption of Hebrew names. It was gratifying to Golda to be so near the centre of the stage during the critical years of Israel's national drama, but her role was largely decorative. To begin with, she was the cabinet's token woman; increasingly, as time went on, the female elder statesman. Her achievements as foreign minister in projecting Israel's case before the world were creditable, but unspectacular. She was uncertain whether the fruits of office had been worth the personal sacrifices she and her family had made.

By 1965 she decided that, having missed out on Jewish motherhood, it would be 'better to be a full-time grandmother than a part-time minister'. So she turned down the largely cosmetic role of deputy prime minister and began a self-proclaimed retirement. It was never a complete retirement: in the dark days around the 1967 war she resumed her roving, fund-raising activities. These were years of terrible danger for Israel, but as the young state confronted those dangers successfully, feelings of strength — even of complacency after the smashing victories over the Arabs achieved in the Six Day War — began to erode national unity. In-fighting among the political élite began to poke through the thin paper-skin of unity created by crisis. when the long-serving Prime Minister Levi Eshkol suddenly died in February, 1969, a compromise candidate for the premiership was desperately needed to forestall a power-struggle between emulous politicians. It was in these circumstances that Golda Meir was plucked from retirement by the ruling party caucus to lead the nation. She was appointed *faute de mieux*. She was nobody's first choice. She was not directly elected — nor could she have been, to judge from the opinion polls at the time. Nor did she expect or seek the job. It was genuinely a greatness thrust upon her: probably a woman whose self-image was so thoroughly feminine and who had no wish to ape or emulate men could never have achieved supreme power in any other way. As she wrote, 'I became prime minister because that was how it was, in the same way that my milkman became an officer in command of an outpost on Mount Hermon. Neither of us had any relish for the job, but we both did it as well as we could.'

The analogy with her warrior-milkman is a reminder that the nature of the crisis which brought Golda Meir to power concerned defence. It was to prove an inappropriate context for her emphatically feminine style of leadership. To begin with, however, Golda loved being premier. She relished the chance to be mother to a whole nation: it was a role which combined the two themes of her life: political dedication and truncated motherhood. Although her fame and popularity were small at the time of her unexpected elevation, the atavistic mother-love of the Jewish people soon won her a place in Israeli hearts. But Golda, like so many of her people, was a victim of the complacency that attends the afterglow of victory. The real priority of her years of power, as can be seen with hindsight, was the unsuspended struggle against the Arabs. But Golda, like a good mother, was more concerned with social and economic problems. She put the material prosperity of Israelis first. The errors of judgement which her government made in the months before the Yom Kippur War of 1973 are now facts of history. Like Margaret Thatcher during the prelude to the Falklands crisis of 1982, the prime minister was an uncritical recipient of the advice of soldiers and diplomats about matters which fell naturally outside a woman's distinctive sphere of interests. Female inexpertise in war, which had handicapped so many power-women of the remote past, has continued to limit women's effectiveness as ultimate decision-makers even in modern states. In her memoirs, Golda Meir has claimed that she, of all her cabinet, was most apprehensive of the chances of a recrudescence of war, but that she was fatally re-assured by her subordinates. In fact, she had just decided to forbid the pre-emptive strike demanded by service chiefs when, on the most solemn Jewish festival in the calendar, which made rapid mobilisation impossible, the Egyptian army launched its brilliant attack across the Suez Canal and flung the politics of the Middle East back into the crucible of war.

At the end of the day, the honours of the war lay with Israel. But Arab — especially Egyptian — morale had been so far restored that the balance of power seemed to have shifted decisively against Israel. It was impossible to see, at first, that the statesmanship of Egypt's President Anwar Sadat would turn the consequences of the war into the basis of potential peace and stability in the region. For Golda Meir's career — anyway drawing to its close now that she was entering advanced old age — the results of the war were as fatal as if Israel had been defeated outright. She lingered in office, with reduced support in parliament after the elections of December, 1973, for the sake of appearances, while the curtain was run down. The power she had built up — the following in the country, the stature among her ministers — had been dispelled in the trauma of the war and the blame that had accrued to her for its uncertain course and outcome. In the last months of her government she was reduced again to the stop-gap, compromise-premier status with which she had begun five years before. She tinkered unhappily with coalition-making while younger and more professional politicans worked out a settlement of the succession among themselves. By June, when a clear successor had emerged in the person of Yitzhak Rabin, Golda Meir was ready — indeed anxious — to return to retirement.

A distinctive approach to the problems of being a power-woman — neither the virago style of Mrs Gandhi and Mrs Bandaranaike nor the motherly image of Mrs Meir — is offered by the British Prime Minister Margaret Thatcher. Her public image is characterised by the tough, virile terminology she attracts. By the Soviet News Agency's felicitous corruption of a name coined for her by Marje Proops of the *Daily Mirror,* she is ubiquitously known as the 'Iron Lady'. Something of the same sense of unyielding strength is conveyed by the French soubriquet 'Madame Non'. Jokes from the time of her great challenge for the Tory leadership about Mrs Thatcher being 'the only man in the shadow cabinet,' 'the only Tory man enough to fight' have continued to dominate the way most people think of her. Indeed, she seems to have become de-sexed as time has gone on. In the early days of her rise to power her sex was a very important constituent of her identity as a politician. It was as the 'token woman' of Tory cabinets that she got her first big chance. Womanhood was a handicap when she made her bid for the party leadership, firstly because the choice of a female ran contrary to party tradition and expectation — she herself had declared only a few months before that she did not expect to see a woman leader in her time — and partly because her opponents were able to pour scorn on the stereotype of the hatted middle-class suburban lady whom she was said to typify. On the other hand, it is generally thought from the evidence of opinion polls that it helped to be a woman in the 1979 General Election: the main issue in that election was inflation and many voters, especially housewives, are said to have thought her sex better equipped Mrs Thatcher to understand what high prices meant in the context of family budgeting. Certainly her simple but active home life — in which she always found time in the intervals of politicking to be with her husband and children, cook and go shopping — was made a target of publicity by P.R.O. men eager for votes and newshounds keen on human interest. Finally, her sex was relevant to another, enduring part of her early image: her perfect grooming, discreet dress, immaculate hair and *soigné* make-up, which evoked the womanly ideal of 'always looking one's best' and seemed to prove that femininity and political competence were compatible. Gradually, however, the old, feminine Mrs Thatcher has been displaced by a new, sexless or even rather masculine Mrs Thatcher, who is 'hard' or 'tough' according to one's politics, unmoved by womanly compassion — so her enemies say — for Argentine war-victims or British unemployed, uncompromising with trade unionists, intimidating towards the Russians, contemptuous of the appeasers of the nation's enemies, ruthless with political opponents.

It is ironical that her public image should embrace such marked contradictions, for Margaret Thatcher has always been a straightforward and uncomplicated woman — straightforward and uncomplicated in her values, straightforward and uncomplicated in her beliefs, straightforward and uncomplicated in her loyalties, straightforward and uncomplicated in her work. The roots of her adherence to honesty and sincerity were laid in childhood. She comes from a household of 'salt-of-the-earth types' whom the sophisticated intellectual élite of metropolitan society know only from the scenes of *This Happy Breed* or *Cavalcade,* but who genuinely exist in their millions in provincial England. Margaret was born to Alfred and Beatrice Ethel Roberts in Grantham on 13th October, 1925, above the grocer's shop which served her parents for a vocation and a living. They were strict Methodists of the old school, cheerful and dutiful, hymn-singing, chapel-going, Sunday-observing. They adhered rigidly to the gospel of work. They filled their home with Victorian furniture and Victorian values. Book-learning was the only idol tolerated in their rigorously monotheistic world. They prospered through thrift and accumulated the rewards of virtue: friendship from their fellow chapel-goers; gratitude from the poor they helped; respect from the neighbours whom their apparently boundless energy, zeal and moral high-seriousness impressed. In the small-town community in which he lived, Alfred Roberts was a personage who shone by his very excellence. He partook of local politics without party affiliation and rose to be Mayor. Margaret learnt from his example to value duty, integrity, independence and hard work. She was an intelligent girl, but what put her near the top of the local school and won her a place at Oxford was sheer superiority of effort rather than exceptional talent. She liked debating at school but only became directly interested in politics at Oxford. Though her father was no party man, she felt drawn to the Conservatives because she identified conservatism with her own home-absorbed creed: she has devoted a good deal of her career to keeping the Tory party aligned with the values and interests of small-businessmen, independent-minded individualists, socially mobile families and hard-grafters.

A provincial ingénue like Margaret was naturally conspicuous in Oxford, even during the war when the usual way of life of the University's *jeunesse dorée* was turned upside down. Moreover, not many girls read chemistry: Margaret was hoping to turn the subject to later use as a patent lawyer. The Conservative Association in the University adopted her enthusiastically: in view of her sex and modest origins, this acceptance was vital for her future career. She was already an activist — in the sense of going canvassing and organising meetings — when Churchill's rejection by the electorate in 1945 shocked her into entering politics wholeheartedly. Assiduous attendance at party conferences brought her adoption as a candidate in an impossible seat: 'Would you accept a woman?' said the agent. The idea was rejected out of hand by the selection committee but they were persuaded to take a look at Margaret. Her sincerity and enthusiasm were irresistible.

It was while fighting the huge socialist majority in Dartford that she met Denis Thatcher. He was one of the local Tory aficionados — not keen on a political career himself but anxious to do his bit locally for the cause. The young candidate found in him a man who shared her values and who was ready to give her his support while she pursued politics and built up a career at the bar. They announced their engagement on the eve of polling day in the October, 1951, General Election.

The need to gain legal qualifications and acquire a practice, together with the pressing demands of the young family she soon began to raise, naturally interrupted Margaret's politics. It was in her efforts to get established as a lawyer that she first encountered sexual prejudice: on the whole, her path has been so unimpeded by discrimination that she has never felt the need to get excited about feminism. It was probably unwise of her to switch her interests as a lawyer from patents to tax: the tax bar is clubbish and old-fashioned and she found it difficult to get on. Having tasted both politics and the law, she found politics the preferable career: there were more opportunities in it — and what was more, the opportunities were better attuned to her own heart's desires, to duty on a grand scale, to the advancement of her values. Her record as a candidate in Dartford had — it is generally acknowledged — been outstanding. But it still took a long time to get a safe seat. Meanwhile, Margaret Thatcher could make the most of being female. This was a rare advantage for a power-woman: most of them in history never got the chance to taste the satisfactions of nuptial and domestic felicity. But Mrs Thatcher had a fair run at home-making. She had her devoted and infinitely helpful husband; her twins; and the happy hearthside to which she rushed home every evening after work without pausing for a drink with the lads.

When at last the chance of a safe seat in Finchley, a London constituency, catapulted her into parliament in the Tory landslide of 1959, her bliss was complete. Home life, the parliamentary round and work within the constitutency could all be combined without unmanageable demands on her time. Legal practice could be gratefully given up. As the ablest and best qualified of the handful of Conservative women members of the new parliament she was bound to achieve cabinet office quickly as the 'token woman' whose inclusion was by now *de rigueur.* The portfolios she held in successive Tory governments until 1974 were women's work — education, social services — not the sort of thing of which future prime ministers are made. Prior to the premiership, she never held any of the traditional great offices of state.

Yet during Margaret Thatcher's ministerial years, while she discharged her duties competently but inconspicuously, with her usual devotion to hard work, changes were overtaking the political system, particularly within the Tory party, which would ultimately help her to supreme power. The method of selecting the Conservative party leader was gradually modified, and the field was gradually opening up. Traditionally, the leader was chosen by the Queen when the party was in office, and 'emerged' from a 'charmed circle' of aristocrats and party managers when the Tories were in opposition. In 1963, when Harold Macmillan resigned, the cry went up for 'a man of the people'. But the leader who emerged was the fourteenth Earl of Home. When Home reformed the procedure and introduced direct election of the leader by Conservative M.P.s, a dramatic change ensued: Edward Heath took office, the first grammar school boy to lead the party, the first leader without an already established place in society.

Tinkering with the leadership selection process had brought instability to the top. After Heath had lost three general elections out of four by October 1974 — leading the party to two successive defeats on platforms of his own devising in which most Tories only half-believed — clamour accumulated for further changes. Ironically, Heath only submitted to the demand for frequent leadership elections because he was sure he would win and silence his critics. His conviction was not based on his record. He was aware that his electoral strategies had been vulnerable. He had chosen to fight the two general elections of 1974 on mutually contradictory platforms — first calling for a clear mandate for 'firm government', then, after an unsuccessful attempt to bodge a coalition with the Liberal Party, for a 'government of national unity'. He continued to adhere to the principle of support for an incomes policy as a means of coping with inflation and industrial stagnation: but this had already proved the ruin of successive governments, including his own, and presented the electorate with no real Tory alternative to the policies of other parties. Yet though he realised his strategy was at fault, Heath believed he was right in the basic issues of principle and that his policies would be vindicated in the coming months and years. More important, in convincing him to throw his hat into the ring in a new leadership contest, was his certainty that there would be no credible challenger.

One potential leader had the popularity and support a challenger required. But Willie Whitelaw had been too closely identified with the Heath régime to mount an attack on his leader now. Of Heath's ideological opponents, Sir Keith Joseph lacked the ambition to be prime minister, though he was on the *qui vive* for a candidate to support. Enoch Powell had already left the party in disgust: in any case, age disqualified him and his trenchant views on immigration put him *hors la loi* in a society that had adopted multi-racial shibboleths. Edward Du Cann preferred the inconspicuous power he wielded from the back-benches to the brash and hazardous glory of party leadership. In short, Heath's opponents were reduced to casting around for a candidate with an urgency born of desperation.

In these circumstances, Margaret Thatcher, ever dutiful, offered herself as a sacrifice for the anti-Heath cause. She did not doubt that it would be a sacrifice. Neither she nor her sponsor, Sir Keith Joseph, believed at first that she could win. This was not only because of the difficulty of overcoming sexual prejudice, but also because of the lack of relevant experience, the domination of the party machine by Heath-men, the concerted hostility of the press and the suburban, bourgeois image with which Mrs Thatcher was stigmatised. The mood of the party was for 'teaching Heath a lesson' rather than unseating him — Tory M.P.s wanted to demonstrate their disquiet with his continued pursuit of the incomes policy chimea and their dissent

Golda Meir, photographed in 1950 at the Israeli Embassy in London, where as Israel's Minister of Labour and Social Security she held a press conference.

from the electoral strategies which had produced defeat. Above all, as the most perceptive backbenchers knew, the parliamentary party was sick of Heath's style of leadership. He was dictatorial, aloof, rebarbative, swift to chide and slow to bless. He was intolerant of views other than his own. Some old Tories feard that traditional conservatism would be silenced and excised from what had hitherto been a broad church with common values but widely differing views. In fact, as events proved, most pundits and participants underestimated the strength of these personal dissatisfactions with Heath. Only two backbenchers of exceptional acumen, ability and experience — Angus Maude and Airey Neave — knew the party well enough to realise that Margaret Thatcher could win.

When she stepped into the arena she got an immediate boost from the sheer relief most M.P.s felt that Heath was actually going to face a challenge of some kind. Her credentials as a candidate of the right-wing opponents of incomes policies and Heathian radicalism were unimpeachable. But to win, she had to capture the votes of at least some of those who, while accepting Heath's policies, detested his style. Here, her comforting image as a traditional Tory lady was more a help than a hindrance. But it is probably a fact that many of the M.P.s who voted for her on that fateful day in 1975 did not positively want her to win. She won the poll as the result of luck, supplemented by the brilliant electoral management of Airey Neave. Heath's team, alienating support by their usual aggressive posture, made the cardinal error of treating the leadership contest like a parliamentary election, in which each side tries to generate support by claiming a momentum in its favour. It was perfectly true that in some respects there was a pre-election momentum in Heath's favour: most soundings of constituency parties, of peers, of the old charmed circle and of the shadow cabinet (where Keith Joseph was Mrs Thatcher's only supporter) showed clear majorities for Heath. But in view of the desire of many electors to teach Heath a lesson, it was imprudent to make too much of this. Heath-men's confident predictions of landslide victory on the first ballot only fed fears they were intended to allay and drove votes into the Thatcher camp. Some of Heath's canvassers ingenuously allowed themselves to be misled by phoney promises of support. Airey Neave, by contrast, planned his pre-election announcements perfectly, underplaying the extent of his candidate's committed support and thereby encouraging the waverers. On the day, intending abstainers voted *en bloc* for Mrs Thatcher. Contrary to every prediction in the lobbies and the media, she got an absolute majority on the first ballot. Many M.P.s almost reeled with shock when they realised what they had done. But it was too late to go back on a decision they had in effect taken unwittingly. It would have been impossible in the second ballot to deny Mrs Thatcher the fruits of her victory.

She thus won the leadership almost without any of the stuggling and scheming that has attended the rise of most power-women. The premiership came to her in a similar way: her own tremendous efforts to cultivate electoral appeal attracted little support, to judge from the opinion polls. But the relentless oscillations of the electorate's allegiance brought a reaction in the 'seventies against every form of radicalism and a return to the traditional values which under her leadership the Tories re-asserted with vigour. By attracting the anti-inflationary female vote, and by pointing out that economy should be run like a household budget, as every woman knew, she cleverly exploited her sex; but for the rest, she made little contribution to her own victory. Once in power, though she continued to apply household principles to budgetary management, she soon lost the female voters. She willingly put on the armour of the Iron Lady. She affected — and some commentators suspected that it was little more than affectation —

unyielding steadfastness in prosecuting her policies in the economic field, whatever the short-term cost in hardship to the unemployed, decline in the public services and stringency in traditional industries. This image of relentlessness was electorally unfortunate, until the Falklands crisis of 1982 called forth just the resolute qualities which Mrs Thatcher had in abundance.

Misreading the apparent indifference of successive British governments to those remote islands and their handful of inhabitants, and aware of the eagerness with which Britain sought to disembarrass herself of responsibility for them, the Argentine government rashly risked an invasion: their hope was to provide their under-employed soldiery with glory and paper over the deep mutual hostilities of the various sections of the Argentine people. But the slow, relentless wrath of the British was aroused. Mrs Thatcher was in her element. A British amphibious force was despatched over eight thousand miles at enormous cost in cash, lives and *matériel,* to vindicate British honour and restore British land and subjects to British rule. The world was astonished that a British government should possess the courage to take such risks and undergo such costs to redress a *fait accompli* that could quickly have been shrugged off by a more pliable and practical régime. There was no doubt that it was Mrs Thatcher's personal policy. She had become that rare thing — a power-woman who throve in war. The total victory of the British forces seemed to justify her resolve. In some ways, it evoked, on a bigger screen and scale, the Tory leadership crisis in which she had shown similar courage, taken similar risks — albeit on that occasion with only her personal career and reputation rather than with the lives of thousands of servicemen and the good name of the entire nation — and achieved a similarly happy issue. Enoch Powell, with characteristic shrewdness, had realised that the crisis would be a decisive test of Mrs Thatcher's reputation for unremitting purpose. At the start of the crisis, he predicted that it would show 'of what *mettle* the Iron Lady was made.' At its conclusion, he announced that a 'ferrous substance' had been subjected to 'analysis' and demonstrated 'strong and tensile qualities, suitable for all national purposes.' 'The Falklands factor', as the psephological pundits called it, transformed Mrs Thatcher's electoral popularity. At the time of writing, it is unclear whether this effect will endure or whether the prime minister's determination to prosecute her economic policies as relentlessly as her strategy in the Falklands will lead to comparably successful results.

CONCLUSION

If Mrs Thatcher does make a success of it, she will be able with some justice to claim to be the first successful power-woman in history. Many have failed in their personal lives; many have failed in their political goals; some have failed in both. Judgements about historical 'failures', it might be objected, are always facile and subjective. But a brief retrospect over the power-women who fill the pages of this book will reveal how many of them left their states in ruins, how many of them abdicated or were deposed, how many of them led wretched lives at home, and how many of them seemed to exhaust all their guile and skill in the winning of power and were awed by its responsibilities.

After their femininity and their power, failure was the great feature the power-women possessed in common. The most important problem they present for analysis, after that of their paucity, is therefore that of their apparent inexpertise.

Arguably, it is in the reasons for their paucity that the roots of their failures lie. There is an extraordinary paradox at the heart of the history of women rulers in men's worlds: although there has never, as far as we know, been a human society which has normally been ruled by women, there has never been a state, however hostile to the power-women idea, which has not succumbed at some time or times to female dominance. Not the mysoginism of ancient Hellas, not the anti-feminism of Confucian China, not the hostility of Hinduism in India could, as we have seen, stop the rise of an occasional woman ruler. It is worthy of notice that this is equally true of the cultural system popularly held to be the most dismissive of women's civil liberties, Islam.

Although since the middle ages the power-woman has generally been a western or western-inspired phenomenon, women gained effective supremacy, and even nominal sovereignty, in, for example, the Fatimid Caliphate of the late eleventh and early twelfth centuries, Muslim India in the thirteenth and seventeenth centuries and the Ottoman Empire during a long period of frequent regencies in the late sixteenth and seventeenth centuries. Their modes of ascent were familiar: regencies for young or absent sons, dominance over *fainéant* husbands, representation of the descended virtue of great male ancestors. Their methods were familiar, too: the exploitation of their sexuality, the adoption and manipulation of surrogate males, the affectation of masculinity. Their examples show how, whatever the cultural context, that power-woman's weapons have been remarkably unchanging throughout history. They also serve to suggest that power-women thrive as well in unlikely as in likely contexts. Like Marx trying to predict the mise-en-scène of early proletarian revolutions, feminists have been astonished, for instance, to find that the first female rulers of democratic states have occurred not in an obvious locale like America, where women are pushy and aggressive, husbands hen-pecked and the ideological environment propitious, but in Asiatic fastnesses of male prejudice and pride.

But in all these contexts, and others where the emergence of power-women was less surprising, the power-women were as meteoric in their rarity as in their rise. Gynecocracies exist only in myths, where their function is usually to depict woman-rule as dangerous or disastrous, or in the maunderings of old-fashioned anthropologists, or in the partisan dreams of extreme feminists. The idea that matriarchy prevailed in the remote past of most societies, which found eloquent apologists in the late nineteenth and early twentieth centuries, is now discredited and in ruins, much as some feminist writers would love to believe it. Apart from the ambiguities of ancient myth and the inconclusive vestiges of matrilineal descent systems in some cultures, no evidence has ever been found to support the matriarchal thesis. The inference that mothers, having the natural guardianship of children, are natural guardians of the state, is attractive but, in itself, unconvincing. The plain fact that no matriarchy has ever been found among the whole vast myriad of human societies known to historians and anthropologists has obliged scientific opinion to acknowledge that patriarchy is the normal — indeed, as far as is known the only — basis of power-distribution between the sexes in actual states. In all the areas where we have traced the rise of power-women, the prevailing assumptions have been patriarchal. The women have always seemed odd in their adopted roles. Sometimes they had to flout the law or ancient custom to get to the top. Sometimes they had to break the mould of conceptual, notional and terminological prejudices which militated against the very idea of female rulers. In every case, their triumphs were, at least, contrary to convention and expectation.

In partial consequence, the power-woman's task has invariably been harder than that of her male counterpart. In these circumstances, her failures are no dishonour to her sex. Furthermore, the expectations with which she has generally been surrounded have forced her to compete with men on sexually alien terrain: most societies, that is to say, have demanded masculine behaviour, mentalities and priorities even of their female rulers. Many, as we have seen, treat their power-women as honorary males, calling them by masculine names and titles. Faced with such tenacious and ubiquitious insistence from their subjects, most power-women have bent with the wind. They have almost all aped men in some degree; they have often claimed to resemble men — to have a male spirit or a male 'heart and stomach'; they have generally affected the aggression and ruthlessness which are conventionally thought to be characteristic of men rather than women. Many of them have dramatically — and generally wretchedly — foregone the typical feminine satisfactions of a loving relationship with one's husband and children in order to serve the state; others have found the demands of a woman's sexual, reproductive and nutritive roles incompatible with political priorities and have foundered on the rocks of the dilemma. Few power-women have de-sexed themselves completely: too many have found the manipulation of their own sexual allure to be politically productive; few have been able to dispense with intuitive responses to politics; others have been nepotists or have tended to 'mother' their states; none can really be said to have mastered the vital male preserve of war. But generally, it is probably fair to say that the most successful power-women have been the most mannish. The most abject failures have been those who have too easily been deflected from the single-minded pursuit of political goals by sexual infatuation or mother-love. Again, these shortcomings are neither surprising nor a matter for blame. For obvious reasons, women have rarely had a chance to be educated for rule. Most power-women came upon their opportunities by chance or stealth, without the years of preparation that have gone into the making of male rulers. It is arguable that in terms of sheer competence — could competence be easily isolated from other factors and quantified satisfactorily — women rulers have excelled men. Even imperfect success in adverse circumstances constitutes a remarkable achievement. They have failed only against unreasonable expectations foisted on them by societies which have pre-judged female rulers and adopted norms and goals set, ultimately, by men for men's sake.

We have yet to see a genuine matriarch. Though Golda Meir came close to providing one, we have yet to see an example of a woman ruler who transcends affected masculinity to rule by unashamedly female means, who projects onto the screen and scale of the state the techniques by which women all over the world rule their own hearthsides. Is it possible that a large and complex society could ever be ruled by love and by the fostering of emotional dependency and by super-rational, intuitive decision-making? In short, will a power-woman ever arise to fulfil the prophecies made in the propaganda of Elizabeth I or Queen Christina? If such a prodigy seems impossible, it is because distinctively feminine behaviour and feminine mentality — if they exist at all — are inimical to politics. Genuinely female priorities have always been more detailed, more personal and more individual than the manipulation of masses — which is the politician's business — allows for. It is part of the profound wisdom of women to realise that there are no political solutions to the problems of human suffering and unhappiness: only in the gentle and tender arts of loving and caring for those close to one can such solutions be found. These are *raisons du cœur* which extreme feminists would deny; but most women seem to recognise their commonsense: that is why they tend to exasperate opinion pollsters and eschew political participation even in emancipated democracies. Of course, women may yet be politicised by hitherto unseen or half-glimpsed social and economic changes and even, perhaps, by further biological evolution. But, as far as the past is concerned, it is, perhaps, in their rarity and their haplessness and their little success that the power-women have been most representative of their sex.

SELECTIVE BIBLIOGRAPHICAL ESSAY
GENERAL

The most sensitive and exhaustive study of feminine identity remains S. de Beauvoir, *The Second Sex* (1953). For matriarchy see the massive and now sadly antiquated but still impressive compendium by R. Briffault, *The Mothers* (1927). An entertaining recent attempt at vindication of the matriarchal thesis by a feminist is E. Morgan's *The Descent of Women* (1972). See also A. Montague, *Natural Superiority of Women* (1952); J. Duché, *Le premier sexe* (1972); P. Spacks, *The Female Imagination* (1975).

Women's studies have spawned innumerable works on the place of women in society: one most valuable collection is M.Z. Rosaldo and L. Lamphere, *Woman, Culture and Society* (1974), which is perhaps the best introduction to the entire subject. Important Feminist critics of the stereotype of submissive womanhood are J. B. Rohrbaugh, *Women: Psychology's Puzzle* (1981) and E. Badinter, *The Myth of Motherhood* (1981).

CHAPTER I

On women in antiquity: M. R. Lefkowitz and M. B. Fault, *Women's Life in Greece and Rome* (1981); M. R. Lefkowitz, *Heroines and Hysterics* (London, 1981); D. Schaps, *Economic Rights of Women in Ancient Greece* (1975); H. Lloyd-Jones, *Females of the Species; Semonides on Women* (1975); J. P. V. Balsdon, *Roman Women* (1962) and S. B. Pomeroy, *Goddesses, Whores, Wives and Slaves* (1975).

On Cleopatra: J. Lindsay, *Cleopatra* (1971); H. Volkmann, *Cleopatra* (1958); O. Von Wertheimer, *Kleopatra* (1951).

CHAPTER II

In general, P. Brown, *Religion and Society in the Age of St Augustine* (1972); J. Bury, *History of the Later Roman Empire* (1889); A. H. M. Jones, *The Later Roman Empire* (1973) provides the broad background. On Placidia, V. A. Sirago, *Galla Placidia* (1961) and S. I. Oost, *Galla Placidia Augusta* (1968). On Amalasuntha, T. H. Hodgkin, *Italy and her Invaders,* iii (1885).

CHAPTER III

The best study of Wu Chao is by C. P. Fitzgerald, *The Empress Wu* (1968) but see also L. Lanciotti, *La donna nella China* (1980), which also includes an important essay by Kazua Enoki, 'Confucian Women in Theory and Reality'. A general collection from Stanford is M. Wolfe and R. Withe,

Women in Chinese Society (1975). See also N. Swann Lee, *Pan Chao: Foremost Woman Scholar of China* (1932).

CHAPTER IV

E. Patbagean includes some sensitive work on women in *Structure sociale, famille, chrétienté à Byzance* (1981) C. Diehl, *Byzantine Portraits* (1927) discusses various women, including Irene, on whom see also the contribution by S. Runciman to D. Baker, *Medieval Women* (1978). There are some invaluable pages in C. Mango, *Byzantium* (1980). See also G. Buckler, *Anna Comnena* (1929); A. Bridge, *Theodora* (1978).

CHAPTER V

D. Baker, *Medieval Women* (1978); E. Power, *Medieval Women* (1975); G. Duby, *Medieval Marriage* (1978); R. Pernoud, *La Femme au tempts des cathédrales* (1981) and S. M. Stuard, *Women in Medieval Society* (1976) are all invaluable for this chapter. See also C. S. Lewis, *The Allegory of Love* (1936) and J. Huizinga, *The Waning of the Middle Ages* (1962). Few power-women of the middle ages have attracted good biographies but there are studies of *Blanche of Castile* and *Eleanor of Aquitaine* (who has attracted a vast amoung of indifferent lierture) by R. Pernoud (1975 and 1967 respectively). Ou Eleanor see also W. W. Kidler, *Eleanor of Aquitaine patron and politician* 1976).

CHAPTER VI

M. Angenot, *Les champions des femmes* (1977) covers feminist apologists in French literature from c. 1400 to c. 1800. P. Mayer, 'Plaidoyer en faveur des femmes', *Romania,* vi (1877) and R. Kelso, *Doctrine for the Lady of the Renaissance* (1956) are further guides to relevant texts. On Isabella, the most authoritative study is T. de Azcona, *Isabel la católica* (1964). See also F. Fernández-Armesto, *Ferdinand and Isabella* (1975), from whom I take the translations of quoted poetry and J. Hillgarth, *The Spanish Kingdoms,* ii (1978).

CHAPTER VII

I. Maclean, *The Renaissance Notion of Woman* (1980) is indispensable for the background and for a bibliographical guide. Among innumerable blooks on the principal characters, D. Loades, *The Reign of Mary Tudor* (1979), A. Fraser, *Mary Queen of Scots* (1969) and P. Johnson, *Elizabeth I* (1974) are perhaps the best. See also J. E. Neale, *Queen Elizabeth I* (1979); A. Plowden, *Marriage with my Kingdom* (1977); F. Yates, *Astraea* (1975); R. Strong, *The Cult of Elizabeth* (1977), G. de Boom, *Eléanor d'Autriche* (1943), V. Da Bled, *La société francaise du XVIe au XXe siècle,* iii (1904).

CHAPTERS VIII and IX

I. Maclean, *Woman Triumphant* (1977) is essential reading. On Christina, G. Masson, *Queen Christina* (1968), C. Weibull, *Christina of Sweden* (n.d.) and the magnificent National museum exhibition catalogue, *Queen Christina of Sweden* (1966). There are some outstanding contributions in the collection edited by M. von Platen, *Queen Christina of Sweden* (1966).

Among many works on Maria Theresa, C. A. Macartney, *Maria Theresa and the House of Austria* (1969); R. Pick, *Empress Maria Theresa* (1966) and E. Crankshaw, *Maria Theresa* (1969) offer useful introductions. The definitive study of Catherine is I. de Madariaga, *Russia in the Age of Catherine the Great* (1981) but see also H. Troyat, *Catherine the Great* (1979) as the most vivid of innumerable biographies.

CHAPTER X

There are studies of Olympe de Gouges (L. Lacour, *Trois femmes de la révolution,* 1900) and of *The Life and Death of Mary Wollstonecraft* by C. Tomalin (1974). Victoria has inspired some excellent biographies — especially those of L. Strachy, *Queen Victoria* (1921) and E. Longford, *Victoria R. I.* (1969). See also J. A. R. Marriott, *Queen Victoria and Her Ministers* (London, 1933), A. Cecil, *Queen Victoria and her Prime Ministers* (1953) and F. Hardie, *The Political Influence of Queen Victoria* (1938) and *The Political Influence of the British Monarchy* (1970). On Isabel, M. T. Puga, *El matrimonio de Isabel II* (1964) and R. Olivar Bertrad, *Así cayó Isabel II* (1955). There is no study of Ranavalona but her reign can be pieced together from the missionary recollections of W. Ellis. See also M. Brown, *Madagascar Rediscovered* (1978). On Eliza Lynch, H. Pitaud, *Madama Lynch* (1900).

CHAPTER XI

R. Adam, *A Woman's Place* (1975) provides useful background against which to study Mrs Thatcher as do J. Jaquette, *Women in Politics* (1974) and M. Stacy and M. Price, *Women, Power and Politics* (1981); the authoritative account of her rise is P. Cosgrave, *Margaret Thatcher* (1978). Some useful material is in P. Murray, *Margaret Thatcher* (1980). The best book on *Mrs*

Gandhi is by D. Moraes (1980); for the background, A. Gaur, *Women in India* (1980). For Mrs Bandaranaike, the hagiography by M. Seneviratne, *Sirimavo Bandaranaike* (1975) and the essay by S. R. Dubey in S. R. Chakravarti et al., *Turmoil and Political Change in South Asia* (1978). For the background, T. Fernando and R. N. Kennedy, *Modern Sri Lanka* (1979). For Mrs Meir, the best introduction is her autobiography, *My Life* (1975).

To pursue the idea on Islam mentioned in the Conclusion, see L. Beck and N. Keddie, *Women in the Muslim World* (1978) and W. Walther, *Women in Islam* (1982).